Teaching Literacy
IN THE
VISIBLE LEARNING
CLASSROOM

6–12
CLASSROOM
COMPANION
to *Visible Learning*
for Literacy

Teaching Literacy
IN THE
VISIBLE LEARNING
CLASSROOM

DOUGLAS FISHER
NANCY FREY
JOHN HATTIE
MARISOL THAYRE

https://resources.corwin.com/vl-literacy6-12

CL CORWIN
LITERACY

FOR INFORMATION:

Corwin

A SAGE Company

2455 Teller Road

Thousand Oaks, California 91320

(800) 233-9936

www.corwin.com

SAGE Publications Ltd.

1 Oliver's Yard

55 City Road

London EC1Y 1SP

United Kingdom

SAGE Publications India Pvt. Ltd.

B 1/I 1 Mohan Cooperative Industrial Area

Mathura Road, New Delhi 110 044

India

SAGE Publications Asia-Pacific Pte. Ltd.

3 Church Street

#10–04 Samsung Hub

Singapore 049483

Publisher and Senior Program Director:
    Lisa Luedeke

Editorial Development Manager: Julie Nemer

Editorial Assistant: Nicole Shade

Production Editor: Melanie Birdsall

Copy Editor: Cate Huisman

Typesetter: Hurix Systems Pvt. Ltd.

Proofreader: Theresa Kay

Indexer: Karen Wiley

Cover Designer: Rose Storey

Marketing Manager: Rebecca Eaton

Printed in the United States of America

ISBN 978-1-5063-3237-6

This book is printed on acid-free paper.

SUSTAINABLE FORESTRY INITIATIVE

Certified Chain of Custody
Promoting Sustainable Forestry
www.sfiprogram.org
SFI-01268

SFI label applies to text stock

18 19 20 21 10 9 8 7 6 5 4 3

CONTENTS

Chapter 5. Student-Led Dialogic Learning   97

Chapter 6. Independent Learning   125

Chapter 7. Tools to Use in Determining Literacy Impact 155

Visit the companion website at
https://resources.corwin.com/vl-literacy6-12
to access videos and downloadable resources.

LIST OF VIDEOS

Note From the Publisher: The authors have provided video and web content throughout the book that is available to you through QR codes. To read a QR code, you must have a smartphone or tablet with a camera. We recommend that you download a QR code reader app that is made specifically for your phone or tablet brand.

Videos may also be accessed at
https://resources.corwin.com/vl-literacy6-12

ACKNOWLEDGMENTS

The ideas in this book come from a wide range of researchers and teachers who have individually and collectively helped us refine our ideas. We appreciate all of the interactions we have had with literacy experts around the world. Having said that, we are indebted to two individuals who have significantly shaped the ideas in this book.

Kristen Anderson is Senior Director of Global Consulting and Evaluation at Corwin. Her knowledge of visible learning and her commitment to high-quality learning for all students is unparalleled. She has been a significant source of support for our work and has greatly assisted us with the translation of complex ideas into classroom practice. Kristen also facilitated the original meeting between the three of us, which resulted in the Visible Literacy Learning initiative. Beyond her knowledge of visible learning, Kristen is a brilliant presenter of ideas and a deeply caring colleague. We are honored to have her leading our work. She is a wonderful friend and advocate.

Lisa Luedeke is another ally and friend from Corwin who has shaped the Visible Literacy Learning experience, from books to professional learning. As an author herself, she understands the power of the written word. She is an amazing thinker who has an uncanny ability to forecast teachers' needs. She has skillfully guided our thinking, asking critical questions that have allowed us to integrate our ideas. She is passionate and committed, and we are lucky to have her support for our efforts.

PUBLISHER'S ACKNOWLEDGMENTS

Corwin gratefully acknowledges the contributions of the following reviewers:

Leslie Blauman
Author, Consultant, and Teacher
Cherry Creek School District
Centennial, CO

Michael Rafferty
Director of Teaching and Learning
Region 14 Schools
Woodbury, CT

Melanie Spence
K–12 Curriculum Coordinator, Assistant Principal
Sloan-Hendrix School District
Imboden, AR

INTRODUCTION

We'd like to introduce you to the Danish philosopher Søren Kierkegaard, the father of existentialist philosophy, who wrote

> If we wish to succeed in helping someone to reach a particular goal we must first find out where he is now and start from there.
>
> If we cannot do this, we merely delude ourselves into believing that we can help others.
>
> Before we can help someone, we must know more than he does, but most of all, we must understand what he understands. If we cannot do that, our knowing more will not help.
>
> If we nonetheless wish to show how much we know, it is only because we are vain and arrogant, and our true goal is to be admired, not to help others.
>
> All genuine helpfulness starts with humility before those we wish to help, so we must understand that helping is not a wish to dominate but a wish to serve.
>
> If we cannot do this, neither can we help anyone.

Kierkegaard died in 1855, long before *Visible Learning* or *Visible Learning for Literacy* had been conceptualized, much less published. But look at how much he understood about the work teachers do every day. Here are some key takeaways from this philosopher:

- There has to be a goal.

- Attaining that goal requires an understanding of current performance.

- Teachers have to know stuff, but even more important, they need to understand what their learners understand.

- If we just try to show how much we know (rather that impact students' learning), we do so to be admired rather than to be helpful.

- Teachers should strive to serve others and ensure that goals (learning) are reached

These are among the key points from *Visible Learning* (Hattie, 2009) that guide the lessons described in this book. There is no one way to teach, or one best instructional strategy that works in all situations for all students, but there is compelling evidence for tools that can help students reach their goals. In this book, we use the effect size information that John Hattie has collected over many years to make the case that some things are more likely to be effective than others. Before delving into the lessons themselves, we will explore the ways in which John created his effect size lists.

For readers unfamiliar with visible learning, we'd like to take a moment to explain. The visible learning database is composed of over 1,200 meta-analyses of studies that include over 70,000 studies and 300 million students. That's big data when it comes to education. In fact, some have argued that it is the largest educational research database amassed to date. To make sense of so much data, John focused his work on meta-analyses.

A meta-analysis is a statistical tool for combining findings from different studies with the goal of identifying patterns that can inform practice. In other words, it is a study of studies. The tool that is used to aggregate the information is an effect size, represented by *d*. An effect size is the magnitude, or size, of a given effect. Effect size information helps readers understand the impact in more measurable terms.

For example, imagine a study in which teaching students to write while having them chew gum resulted in statistically significant findings ($p < 0.01$, for example). People might buy stock in gum companies, and a new teaching fad would be born. But then suppose, upon deeper reading, you learned that the gum-chewing students had a 0.03 month gain in reading ability over the control group, an effect size pretty close to zero. You realize that the sample size was so large that the results were statistically significant, but they might not be very powerful. Would you still buy gum and have students chew away? Probably not (and we made this example up, anyway).

Understanding the effect size lets us know how powerful a given influence is in changing achievement, the impact for the effort in other words. Some things are hard to implement and have very little impact. Other things are easy to implement and still have limited impact. We search for things that have a greater impact, visible of which will be harder to implement and some of which will be easier to implement. When you're deciding what to implement to impact students' learning, wouldn't you like to know what the effect size is? Then you can decide if it's worth the effort. John was able to demonstrate that influences, strategies, actions, and so on with an effect size greater than 0.40 allow students to learn at an appropriate rate, meaning at least a year of growth for a year in school. Before this level was established, teachers and researchers did not have a way to determine an acceptable threshold, and thus weak practices, often supported by studies with statistically significant findings, continued.

Figure i.1   The Barometer for the Influence of Class Size

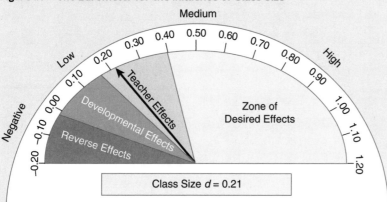

Source: Adapted from Hattie, J. (2012). *Visible learning for teachers: Maximizing impact on learning.* New York: Routledge.

Let's take two real examples. First, let's consider class size. There have been many efforts to reduce the number of students enrolled in a given teacher's classroom. To help people understand effect sizes, John created a barometer so that information could be presented visually. The barometer for class size can be found in Figure i.1. As you can see, the effect size is 0.21, well below the zone of desired effects of 0.40. This is based on three meta-analyses that included 96 studies and a total population of 550,339 students. We don't know a teacher who wouldn't enjoy smaller class sizes, but the evidence suggests that there are more effective ways to improve learning.

Second, let's consider increasing classroom discourse (synonymous with classroom discussion or dialogue). Students would be invited to talk with their peers in collaborative groups, working to solve complex and rich tasks. The students would not be ability grouped, but rather grouped by the teacher intentionally to ensure that there is academic diversity in each group as well as language support and varying degrees of interest and motivation. As can be seen in the barometer in Figure i.2, the effect size of classroom discourse is 0.82, well above our threshold, and likely to result in two years of learning gains for a year of schooling.

STRUCTURE OF THIS BOOK

As authors, we assume you have read *Visible Learning* and *Visible Learning for Literacy* (Fisher, Frey, & Hattie, 2016), so we are not going to recount all of the information contained in those resources. Rather, we're going to focus on aspects of literacy instruction that are critical for students' success. In each chapter, we profile three teachers who have worked to

Figure i.2 The Barometer for the Influence of Classroom Discussion

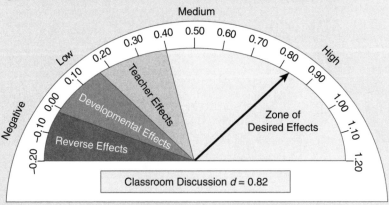

Source: Adapted from Hattie, J. (2012). *Visible learning for teachers: Maximizing impact on learning.* New York: Routledge.

make learning visible for their students and have impacted learning in significant ways. In addition, all chapters have a few things in common:

- Effect size information when available
- Specific teaching tips
- A boxed feature that demonstrates how learning can become visible for students

The characteristics of visible learners are addressed in Chapter 1, but for now know that students should know what they are learning and should have evidence of their learning. Each chapter helps develop this visible learner in literacy.

In the first chapter, we focus on the aspects of literacy instruction that must be included in lessons. We review evidence about the components of effective literacy instruction and note that there is a need to recognize that student learning has to occur at the surface, deep, and transfer levels. These concepts served as the organizing feature of *Visible Learning for Literacy,* and we will briefly review them and their value in learning. This book focuses on the ways in which teachers can develop students' surface, deep, and transfer learning, specifically by providing students with direct instruction, engaging students in dialogic instruction, and facilitating their independent learning. Finally, Chapter 1 contains information about the use of instructional minutes during a given class. We understand that we run the risk of focusing more on the teaching and less on the learning, which is counter to the message in this book, but we decided that it was important to discuss the use of time so that readers don't believe that a given instructional approach can and should consume all of students' learning time.

For example, we are confident that repeated reading is a useful approach, but we wouldn't want that to consume the entire English class period. Importantly, there are numerous approaches that can be used to accomplish a given aspect of learning. When we suggest an average amount of time for teacher direct instruction, through think-alouds and the like, we recognize that there are many, many ways to provide students with this aspect of instruction. Again, there isn't one right way to do this, but there are several wrong ways, which we will explore further in the chapter on direct instruction. Having said that, we add that it is important for teachers to determine the impact of the experiences students have on their learning (and by *their,* we mean both teachers and students). If learning isn't happening, then change the approach by all means!

Following this introductory chapter, we turn our attention to teacher clarity. In this chapter we focus our attention on what students need to know. This requires that teachers understand the grade-level expectations and communicate those learning intentions to students. It also requires that teachers and students understand what success looks like. Teacher clarity is an important aspect of literacy learning, as it sets the stage for challenging tasks, which students appreciate, and provides teachers with actionable information that they can use to make adjustments in the learning environment.

In Chapter 3, we focus on deliberate and direct teaching, because there is considerable evidence that direct instruction works. This does not mean simply telling students what to think or do. We recognize that there are a lot of educators who have negative reactions to the phrase *direct instruction,* so we hope you'll allow us to explain why we have included it in this book. When people first hear the phrase *direct instruction,* many of them think of scripted programs that rely on transmission of information, especially basic skills. They often think of prepackaged curricula that do not take into account the current performance of students or their responses to individual lessons. We don't think of direct instruction in this way. Rather, as John has noted, the essence of direct instruction is actually very common. In his words (2009), "The teacher decides on the learning intentions and success criteria, makes them transparent to students, demonstrates them by modeling, evaluates if they understand what they have been told by checking for understanding, and re-tells them what they have been told by tying it all together with closure" (p. 206). We hope you'll read Chapter 3 with an eye toward these aspects of learning.

In Chapters 4 and 5, we turn our attention to dialogic approaches to learning. Chapter 4 focuses on teacher-led dialogic instruction whereas Chapter 5 focuses on peer-led dialogic learning. In general, these approaches are more effective for deep and transfer learning than for surface learning. That's not to say that direct instruction is only useful for surface learning. We've seen direct instruction lessons on analyzing multiple texts, writing critiques, and public speaking that had demonstrable impacts on students' learning. Dialogic approaches can be teacher-led or peer-mediated, but all require students to interact with their peers and teacher to reach a better understanding. Some of the ideas and examples will likely be familiar to literacy educators while others may be new, as some are drawn from research conducted decades ago. Irrespective of the time frame from which they came, each of these approaches allows teachers and students to

- Explain their ideas and understanding
- Clarify their thinking through examples, nonexamples, and anecdotes
- Reflect on the thinking of others, revising their perspectives along the way
- Use technical language

In Chapter 6, we turn our attention to independent learning. Although we recognize that much of what students learn, they learn with and through others, there are some things that are appropriately learned independently. Importantly, this does not mean assigning students a pile of worksheets to do on their own, but rather inviting students to direct some of their own learning, which is a central tenet of visible learning. Independent tasks can be used to develop students' surface, deep, or transfer learning. Reading the book *Voice of Freedom* (Weatherford, 2015) might contribute to students' surface knowledge about the civil rights movement. As surface knowledge is developed, students move into deeper learning by engaging in more formal discussions and viewing video clips from that period in history. Transfer may occur when students read across multiple texts or when they are asked to analyze a present-day situation, tracing it to the civil rights movement. Teachers use a combination of direct, dialogic, and independent tasks to ensure that learning occurs. And that's the important message here—that learning occurs. If teachers are not having an impact, they should change their approach!

In the final chapter of this book, we focus on literacy assessments that teachers can use to plan instruction and to determine the impact that they have on learning. As part of this chapter, we note the value of feedback and explore the ways in which teachers can provide feedback to students that is growth producing.

In sum, this book contains information on critical aspects of literacy instruction that have evidence for their ability to impact student learning. We're not suggesting that these be implemented in isolation but rather that they be combined into a series of linked learning experiences that result in students reading, writing, speaking, and listening more and better than they did before.

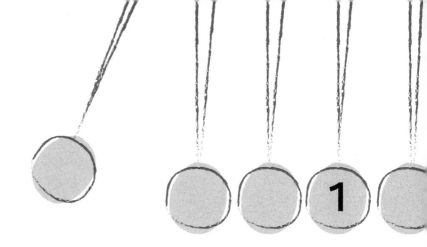

MOBILIZING VISIBLE
LEARNING FOR LITERACY

There are a number of ways that students can tell their life stories. In Sandra Lopez's eleventh-grade English class, students have been reading, writing, and investigating the topic for two weeks. On this morning, she will be conducting a close reading of the poem "My Papa's Waltz" by Theodore Roethke. After the close reading lesson, five students will join her for guided instruction, using the poem to focus on the author's craft. The teacher identified these students as being in need of additional instruction through a preassessment of their ability to write using various tools such as personification, point of view, and rhythm.

© Bob Daemmrich/PhotoEdit

Other students will use the materials in the classroom, including webpages Ms. Lopez bookmarked and several digital articles and videos about effective personal narrative writing that she has loaded into the learning management system. One collaborative group is using an excerpt from *The Story of My Experiments With Truth: An Autobiography,* by Mohandas Gandhi, to develop interview questions for a local author they will be meeting in a digital space the following week. The guest speaker, a blogger who often shares stories from his life, will answer questions about his writing processes and how he selects stories to share. During this unit, students will also read a chapter from Beatrice Nezat's *How to Write a Memoir: The Essential Guide to Writing Your Life Story as a Personal Memoir* about accessing memories and then have time to write about a difficult time in their lives.

Students have choices about how they want to demonstrate mastery of this particular unit of study. Some students, like Rukan, will write poems, using poems they have read as mentor texts (see Figure 1.1). Others will write about events in their lives, while others will blog. The outlet is selected by the students. As Ms. Lopez notes,

> We're working toward achieving our reading and writing goals, but also learning about ourselves and how we can share our own experiences. Of course, students also need to learn to write informational texts and arguments with evidence, but this unit focused on crafting a personal narrative in a genre of choice.

Figure 1.1   Roots by Rukan

You were sculpted

You were planted

You were taken care of

You were healthy

You were patient, so were they

Patiently waiting for your arrival

Finally, you are here!

You are no longer a thought, a vision

You are tangible and fragile

You are exposed to everything

As the years go by your mental and physical appearance change

Morphing into who you are in that moment

What you know in that moment

You are no longer a young mind

You are filled with knowledge and yet still ignorant

You don't know it all but you want to

So you make mistakes

Maybe you repent, maybe you let it go

It's up to you now

To continue what you have been taught

Every tradition, every custom is yours now

No longer guarded by your loved ones

So you subconsciously guard yourself

Learning from your mistakes as you grow

Of course, you have the support of family and friends

Most importantly you have yourself

At a young age you begin to learn from what you see or experience

Your parents have taught you well

You know religion because of them

You know love because of them

You know hate because of them

Truly, cherish them

They aren't long for their world

Yes, *their* world

What goes on behind closed doors and soft whispers

Suddenly you forget everything you've learned

They forget everything they've taught you

No more traditions

No more love

No more smiles and laughter

No more holidays together

Only what is now

And what is now?

It's time for you to grow up!

Become responsible

Take what you have harvested in your mind and use it in reality

Becoming more than your original roots

Passing what is now your knowledge to everyone you meet

First impressions and final goodbyes

Every moment is precious

Every moment was meant to be

Every hardship, every tear, every headache

Every memory, every love, any joy

Was first with them

With your roots

Do not disconnect from this

This is everything

This is what you've been learning from

Still learning from

VISIBLE LEARNING FOR LITERACY

EFFECT SIZE
FOR EXPECTATIONS
= 0.43

EFFECT SIZE
FOR COMPREHENSION
PROGRAMS = 0.60

EFFECT SIZE
FOR PROBLEM-SOLVING
TEACHING = 0.61

EFFECT SIZE
FOR SMALL GROUP
LEARNING = 0.49

EFFECT SIZE
FOR SELF-REPORTED
GRADES/STUDENT
EXPECTATIONS = 1.44

This eleventh-grade teacher is mobilizing the principles of visible learning in literacy in each component of the morning's lessons. She holds high expectations for her students in terms of both the complexity of the content and their ability to deepen their knowledge through investigation. She engages in comprehension instruction using close reading of a complex text, and deepening their knowledge through investigation by presenting a problem for them to address. Ms. Lopez regularly assesses her students for formative purposes such that she can create both teacher-directed and collaborative learning small groups in her classroom. These measures are generated by the students themselves, and are used to inform their goals. She is mobilizing principles of visible learning such that she is consciously aware of her impact and her students are consciously aware of their learning. In other words, she sees the relationship between visible teaching and visible learning (see Figure 1.2).

The literacy practices discussed in *Visible Learning for Literacy* (Fisher, Frey, & Hattie, 2016) highlight effective practices and, importantly, *when* those practices are best leveraged to maximize their impact on student learning. However, we would be remiss if we did not further contextualize their role in quality reading and language arts instruction for secondary-level learners. Understanding how components of such programs interface with the developmental progressions of young adults is vital for accelerating students' literacy learning.

COMPONENTS OF EFFECTIVE LITERACY LEARNING

Teaching Takeaway

Effective teaching requires knowing which approaches work and when they work.

But literacy requires more than reading—it is further expressed through speaking, listening, writing, and viewing. Together these compose the language arts, which are furthered by reading, discussion, and composition of literary and informational texts. Effective literacy instruction fosters student growth through oral language development, composition, investigation, and performance. More specifically, it addresses three major areas (Connor et al., 2014):

- **Linguistic processes,** including language, word knowledge, and academic knowledge

- **Cognitive processes,** including comprehension monitoring, inferencing, and sense-making for self and others

- **Text-specific processes** about how narrative and informational texts are understood and composed

Figure 1.2   The Relationship Between Visible Teaching and Visible Learning

Highly effective teachers . . .	Such that students . . .
Communicate clear learning intentions	Understand the learning intentions
Have challenging success criteria	Are challenged by the success criteria
Teach a range of learning strategies	Develop a range of learning strategies
Know when students are not progressing	Know when they are not progressing
Provide feedback	Seek feedback
Visibly learn themselves	Visibly teach themselves

Available for download at **https://resources.corwin.com/vl-literacy6-12**

In middle and high school, these language arts processes are leveraged to gain knowledge in other subject areas (science, history, mathematics, and the visual and performing arts). Additionally, language arts processes are paired with the study of literature in the English classroom. While the utilization of language arts processes in other content areas is vital, this book focuses specifically on secondary English coursework and the teachers who design and implement lessons and assess their impact.

The College Board's framework for language arts views secondary English as an integrative discipline, in which students learn about themselves and the lives of others, and become "knowledgeable, reflective, creative and critical members of a variety of literacy communities" (2006, p. 14). Of course, these things don't just happen. Their English teachers design instruction that includes modeling, direct instruction, and dialogic learning to foster skills development and analytic thinking.

The indicators for effective English courses are not narrow and prescriptive, but rather can be accomplished using a number of different scheduling structures. However they are organized, the emphasis should be on sustained periods of instruction, including time each day when students

- Read independently

- Talk about their learning with others

- Write about their reading

There is a focus on assessment for the purpose of informing instructional decisions and providing feedback to learners. In addition, skills and strategies at the word and text levels are taught, and all of this is accomplished through making connections between reading, writing, and spoken language. The following assumptions inform our collective understanding about teaching and learning:

- **Assessment occurs throughout the academic year, and the results are used to inform the teacher and the learner.** Each period, time is set aside to understand students' literacy progress and provide feedback to learners.

- **A meaningful amount of time is dedicated to developing literacy processes.** Every day students engage in sustained, organized, and comprehensive experiences with all of the components: reading, writing, speaking, and listening.

- **There is a reading–writing–spoken language connection.** Development of reading and writing proficiency occurs when students have rich reading experiences, opportunities for purposeful writing, and occasions for meaningful interactions with peers and the teacher.

- **Reading and writing occur every class period.** These events occur with the teacher, with peers, and independently.

Ultimately, a successful approach to adolescent literacy is one where reading and writing occurs in all content areas, not just the English classroom. Because literacy learning enhances science, mathematics, social studies, and the visual and performing arts, it is essential to find areas of crossover between the disciplines whenever possible. Having said that, the English classroom is viewed as the primary space for instruction in reading and writing.

ADOLESCENT LITERACY: READING

As any secondary teacher can attest, many students arrive into our care with significant needs in the area of reading. According to a report by the National Council of Teachers of English (NCTE),

> Less than half of the 2005 ACT-tested high school graduates demonstrated readiness for college-level reading, and the 2005 National Assessment of Educational Progress (NAEP) reading scores for 12th graders showed a decrease from 80 percent at the *proficient* level in 1992 to 73 percent in 2005. (2007, p. 1)

In order to effectively combat these decreases in learning, a carefully constructed approach is necessary to close these ever-widening gaps. In the elementary years, students are typically taught the basic elements of reading and writing; by the time they reach middle school, the reading demands of the curriculum require more than just the basics of comprehension—though many students have not even mastered that skill yet. Students must navigate different texts in order to gain content knowledge specific to their courses.

ADOLESCENT LITERACY: WRITING

Writing instruction presents its own unique challenges and opportunities in the secondary classroom despite its close relationship to reading. Because writing calls on students not just to read the words and ideas of others, but to create and construct their own texts in a meaningful way to achieve a specific purpose, different skills need to be taught and developed in addition to those that support reading development. In order to best address student needs, a writing program designed to help students skillfully express their thinking in a variety of circumstances is essential. It is not enough to simply be able to successfully use the conventions of written English; proficient writers must be flexible in their approaches to different writing situations, both in and out of the classroom, and for a wide span of tasks.

KNOWLEDGE OF HOW STUDENTS LEARN

As you can imagine, there is no shortage of ideas, theories, and anecdotes to answer the question about how students learn. The research fields of educational psychology and literacy are dedicated to understanding how learning occurs. Our thinking has been influenced by a number of significant principles, including a developmental view of literacy and the importance of meaningful experiences. These principles help us to answer the question of how students learn.

Developmental View of Learning

Perspectives on learning have moved far from the predominant theories of behaviorism and psychoanalysis of the early 20th century. The developmental work of Vygotsky, Piaget, Montessori, and others has shaped our approach to learning and the educational systems that support it. Clay (2003) asks,

> How do developmental theories influence teachers' assumptions about children? These explanations, particularly in language and cognitive areas, have created for teachers vocabulary and knowledge structures that allow them to think beyond what the child does to what may be occurring in children's heads. (p. 49)

A developmental perspective in learning means that the teacher understands that a student's response is not merely "correct" or "incorrect" but rather a reflection of what is understood at that moment. Therefore, the teacher's role is not simply to evaluate what is correct or incorrect, but instead to recognize that students' response provide opportunities to hypothesize how they are using their knowledge to arrive at an answer. This requires the classroom teacher to understand how young people learn as they grow, especially how they develop literacy knowledge. But adopting a developmental view of learning does not mean that we lock adolescents into rigid stages of development. Their cognitive development is either enhanced or inhibited by the context we create for them. A learning environment should support their explorations, errors, and successes, and provide interactions with more capable peers. They need access to challenging but not defeating topics of study, set within a culturally responsive milieu (American Psychological Association, 2015).

> The teacher's role is not simply to evaluate what is correct or incorrect, but instead to recognize that students' responses provide opportunities to hypothesize how they are using their knowledge to arrive at an answer.

Meaningful Experiences and Social Interaction

A basic premise of learning is that when experiences are meaningful to the learner, the ability to learn increases. For example, your ability to learn the concepts discussed in this book is directly related to the relevancy of learning about literacy teaching in your life. If you were studying to be an engineer, your ability to learn these principles would be somewhat diminished, because the content is not as useful in an engineering degree program. In the same regard, student learning is driven by the questions formulated with and by the learner (Moffett, 1992). Furthermore, learning is social in nature and springs from the interactions we have with others (Halliday, 1975). Therefore, an important role of the teacher is to foster questions and dialogue among students and create meaningful experiences that allow them to interact with one another.

Surface, Deep, and Transfer of Learning

The progression of literacy learning through the secondary years follows a spiral as students move from understanding the surface contours of a skill or concept toward an ever-deepening exploration of what lies beneath. But understanding these progressions requires that teachers consider the levels of learning they can expect from students. How, then, should we define learning, since that is our goal? As John suggested in his 2014 Vernon Wall Lecture (see also Hattie & Donoghue, 2016), learning can be defined as

> the process of developing sufficient surface knowledge to then move to deeper understanding such that one can appropriately transfer this learning to new tasks and situations.

Learning is a process, not an event. The movement from surface learning—the facts, concepts, and principles associated with a topic of study—to deep learning, which is the ability to leverage knowledge across domains in increasingly novel situations, requires careful planning. If students are to deepen their knowledge, they must regularly encounter situations that foster the transfer and generalization of their learning. The American Psychological Association (2015) notes that "student transfer or generalization of their knowledge and skills is not spontaneous or automatic" (p. 10) and requires intentionally created events on the part of the teacher.

> Transfer is more than memorization; it also involves recognition on the part of the learner about what has occurred.

And there is a scale for learning. Some things students understand only at the surface level. While surface learning is often not valued (misconstrued as superficial learning), it should be. You have to know something to be able to do something with it. We've never met a student who could synthesize information from multiple sources who didn't have an understanding of each of the texts. With appropriate instruction about how to relate and extend ideas, surface learning becomes deep understanding. Deep understanding is important if students are going to set their own expectations and monitor their own achievement. But schooling should not stop there. Learning demands that students be able to apply—transfer—their knowledge, skills, and strategies to new tasks and new situations. Transfer is very difficult to attain, and it remains one of our closely kept professional secrets. When was the last time you and your colleagues talked about transfer? Therefore, we often pronounce that students can transfer, but the process of teaching them at this level with the expectation of transfer is too often not discussed.

Teaching Takeaway

The goal of schooling is for students to apply what they have been taught—to transfer their learning to new situations, tasks, and problems.

John uses the SOLO (structure of observed learning outcomes) method developed by Biggs and Collis (1982) to explain the movement from surface to deep learning as a process of first branching out and then strengthening connections between *ideas:*

- One idea

- Many ideas

- Related ideas

- Extended ideas

We'll offer an example from seventh grade to illustrate. Students are introduced to the three rhetorical appeals of *ethos, pathos,* and *logos.* They might study these strategies separately (one idea) as they appear in various media. As their understanding of each individual appeal grows, students begin to see how each operates differently and for different ends. In order to apply this burgeoning knowledge, young adults need plenty of opportunities to examine how ethos, pathos, and logos work individually; the student will eventually be able to *relate* the different instances in which she sees pathos used, for example, and examine how this use of the same concept differs depending on context and situation. In time, her ideas of how each appeal works is *extended* when the student begins to use ethos, pathos, and logos in her own speaking and writing. Transfer is occurring throughout, as she moves from one idea deeper to an extension of ideas. But the transfer of knowledge is not seamless and linear. You see it in adolescents' lack of reasoning in their claims, or in the overuse of one of the appeals at the expense of another.

The ultimate goal, and one that is hard to realize, is transfer. When students reach this level, learning has been accomplished. Transfer occurs throughout surface and deep learning. In fact, *all* learning is really transfer, provided understanding is involved (Bransford, Brown, & Cocking, 2000). By this, we mean that transfer is more than memorization; it also involves recognition on the part of the learner about what has occurred. The seventh grader who *knows* she is using the methods of persuasion is bearing witness to her own transfer of learning. At each phase of learning, specific instructional and curricular methods rise to the top. In other words, it isn't just knowing what works, but rather, what works *best*. Figure 1.3 captures some literacy learning approaches that are especially effective at the surface, deep, and transfer phases of learning.

WHAT STUDENTS NEED

Adolescents are exposed to a barrage of texts—written and otherwise—almost constantly. As the CCNY's report on reading notes, "Literacy demands have increased and changed as the technological capabilities of our society have expanded and been made widely available; concomitantly, the need for flexible, self-regulated individuals who can respond to rapidly changing contexts has also increased" (2004, p. 9). The demands of our society on students are such that they need to be able to understand and respond to a variety of media in an endless array of situations. This requires a person who can recognize how messages work in a variety of forms and contexts. As consumers, creators, and analyzers of print and digital media, adolescents need powerful and purposeful instruction that conveys a sense of urgency about learning. In the framework of a visible learning classroom, we know the following components are crucial in aiding the development of critical readers, writers, and thinkers:

- **Direct, clear expectations** such that students know *what* they are learning, *why* they are learning it, and *how* they will know that they learned it. We need them as active participants in the learning process, but when we fail to communicate

Video 1

The Right Strategy at the Right Time: Surface, Deep, and Transfer Learning

https://resources.corwin.com/ vl-literacy6-12

To read a QR code, you must have a smartphone or tablet with a camera. We recommend that you download a QR code reader app that is made specifically for your phone or tablet brand.

Figure 1.3   High-Impact Literacy Approaches at Each Phase of Learning

Surface Learning		Deep Learning		Transfer Learning	
Strategy	ES	Strategy	ES	Strategy	ES
Wide reading (exposure to reading)	0.42	Questioning	0.48	Extended writing/ writing programs	0.44
Phonics instruction	0.54	Concept mapping	0.60	Peer tutoring	0.55
Direct instruction	0.59	Close reading (study skills)	0.63	Problem-solving teaching	0.61
Note-taking	0.59	Self-questioning	0.64	Synthesizing information across texts	0.63
Comprehension programs	0.60	Metacognitive strategy instruction	0.69	Formal discussions (e.g., debates)/classroom discussion	0.82
Annotation (study skills)	0.63	Reciprocal teaching	0.74	Transforming conceptual knowledge	0.85
Summarizing	0.63	Class discussion	0.82	Organizing conceptual knowledge	0.85
Leveraging prior knowledge/ prior achievement	0.65	Organizing and transforming notes	0.85	Identifying similarities and differences	1.32
Vocabulary instruction	0.67	Cooperative learning 0.59			
Repeated reading	0.67				
Spaced practice	0.71				
Expectations of teacher 0.43					
Teacher clarity 0.75					
Feedback 0.75					
Student expectations of self 1.44					

learning intentions and success criteria to students, we force them to become passive consumers of whatever we're doling out. Students should know and be able to articulate the purpose and goals of their learning, as well as their progress toward these goals. This concept is so elemental to everything else we do, that we have devoted the entire next chapter to communicating expectations—a concept also known as teacher clarity.

- **Complex texts with opportunities for collaboration.** In order to comprehend complex texts, students need plenty of opportunities to work with them alone and with peers in order to further their understanding. Collaboration on the creation of complex texts is equally valuable, as every writer composes orally before laying words down on the page.

- **Consistent, timely, and effective feedback** on progression toward learning goals, so students can adjust their thinking, get more help, or continue on their path. This is especially important in writing; in a process writing approach, students will use this feedback to revise, refine, and republish their writing.

- **Ongoing formative assessments** that are aligned with clearly articulated learning intentions or goals are crucial in identifying opportunities for reteaching or advancement, and to understand the impact on one's teaching on learning. Impact data should rightly be seen as feedback to the teacher from the students.

It's a tall order, to be sure. An ongoing challenge is in making the most of the instructional minutes we have, in order to maximize learning. Most secondary teachers lament that there is never enough time, so it is critical that instructional time within a class period and across the week is aligned with these above-mentioned principles.

Scheduling Instructional Time

The purpose of this book is to address some of the daily concerns of teaching, and logistics is a big one. Organization of an English classroom should allow for students to participate in a model of instruction that allows them to acquire, consolidate, and deepen their literacy skills and strategies on a daily basis. In addition, students read and write every day, collaborate with peers, and work independently. The teacher meets with students as a whole group, in small groups, and individually. While not every student meets with the teacher every day, these meetings occur weekly.

Time Organization

EFFECT SIZE
FOR TEACHER
CLARITY = 0.75

A portion of the instructional minutes is devoted to focused instruction, which consists of time devoted to sharing the learning intentions and success criteria with students. This isn't simply posting the intentions on the board and giving them cursory attention. Instead, students and the teacher engage in dialogue to parse and clarify. The teacher also uses this time to model and think aloud, and to provide any necessary direct instruction that is needed. Before transitioning to the next phase, the teacher returns to the learning intentions and success criteria, and students name or write the goals they have for themselves for the day.

Next, the teacher might meet with small groups of students for needs-based instruction in reading or writing. Students in these groups have been selected based on formative use of assessment information, and are often (but not always) clustered due to similar needs. While the teacher meets for guided instruction, the rest of the class is engaged in collaborative learning.

Collaborative learning may occur in pairs or in slightly larger groups, but all students are working with at least one other person. Depending on the purposes, students may be consolidating previously learned, but still new, knowledge. Conversely, they may be working with peers to deepen their knowledge of a skill or concept. For example, students may be providing peer critiques of each other's writing, or might be engaged in a collaborative conversation about a text they are reading. Later in the period, students are independently reading and writing. This is an opportunity for them to apply what they have been learning, thus further fostering transfer. While students read independently, the teacher meets with individual students to confer, assess, and provide feedback, working with students toward self-reported goals.

Of course, not all instruction necessary for effective practice can be offered in one period. This requires a perspective across the week to see how instruction unfolds. There is flexibility, of course, in how this is implemented on a daily basis. Some days use less time for conferring, as additional time may be devoted to developing writing skills, engaging in extended discussion, or for research and investigation.

Across a Week

This suggested schedule is not meant to be a rigid structure that follows the same pattern day after day. On some days the teacher is collecting assessment information, while at other times he or she meets with individual students to confer about reading and writing. In addition, while small group, needs-based instruction occurs nearly every day, it is not always with the same students. It is critical to plan time for reteaching concepts students may not have mastered the first time. In our experience, well-intentioned teachers do not ever get to reteaching because they do not set aside time to do so. We suggest that time for reteaching be planned each week. If you don't need to reteach anyone during a particular week, you can move on with your curriculum.

We believe that the best teaching is responsive teaching that has an impact on student learning. Good teachers watch their students closely to see how the lesson is going and what students are learning. When teachable moments occur, when a student asks a profound question, when a puzzled look on a student's face suggests she is confused, it's appropriate to

> EFFECT SIZE FOR SMALL GROUP LEARNING = 0.49

> EFFECT SIZE FOR PEER TUTORING = 0.55

Video 2
Assessment and Needs-Based Instruction

https://resources.corwin.com/ vl-literacy6-12

follow the lead. This undoubtedly messes up the carefully crafted lesson. So be it. After all, who's the schedule for? If something has to give on a particular day in order to accommodate these important events, be flexible about it. Don't let the occasional deviations from the lesson discourage you. But it is equally important to remember that expected lapses in schedules do not mean there should be no schedule at all. Learners thrive on knowing what to expect, and teachers find they accomplish far more when a thoughtful schedule is planned and implemented.

SPOTLIGHT ON THREE TEACHERS

To help you further visualize how secondary teachers use the practices highlighted in *Visible Learning for Literacy*, we will follow the practices of three teachers throughout the remaining chapters:

- Simone Okeke is a seventh-grade teacher in Texas. The 34 students in her English classroom represent the rich diversity found in her community, and include many English learners who speak Spanish, Tagalog, or Chinese as a first language. A large portion of her students also speak African-American vernacular English. Ms. Okeke is a teacher-leader in her school, has hosted numerous student teachers over the years, and serves as a teacher-coach for the English department. An important issue for her is building cross-cultural curriculum that supports all of her students and gives them access to rigorous learning opportunities.

  "The immigrant population here in Texas is diverse and vibrant," she noted, "and we as educators have a duty to create learning occasions where our students see themselves reflected in the curriculum. I believe this builds the confidence and self-efficacy needed to take on the challenging situations they will encounter here at school in the world."

- Sandra Lopez is an eleventh-grade teacher in California. She has 35 students in her classroom, and most qualify for free or reduced-price lunch; this qualification is a common measure of socioeconomic status. While some of her students speak English as a first language, a large portion speak Spanish in the home. Ms. Lopez is a national board certified teacher (NBCT) in adolescent and young adulthood language arts.

  When asked about what she sees as being a motivating source in her teaching, she said, "I strive to give my students an education in which their individual needs are addressed, especially in the area of language development." She continued, "But I also want them to develop skills that will serve them outside of the classroom. Since my students will leave the high school environment soon, I want to teach them concepts that transfer from the classroom to the workplace or college environment."

- Charles Peck is a Year 10 teacher in an urban community school in London. Many of his 28 students identify as Indian or Arabic, and they speak Hindi, Arabic, or another non-English language at home. His students are taught using the Key Stage 4 national curriculum, and they are working toward national qualifications, most toward the General Certificate of Secondary Education (GCSE).

"This community had historically high leaving [dropout] rates, but since compulsory education is now required to age 18, we're seeing students changing their goals," he said. With a large student population with diverse needs, "my main concerns are helping my students achieve high levels of success," says Mr. Peck, who is a department chair and mentor teacher. He states, "I see my role as being one who addresses the gaps my students arrive with in order to help remove barriers and empower them to become agents in their own education. My work in the classroom, as well as my mentorship role with developing teachers, is my most powerful tool in doing this."

These three teachers, although in different regions and contexts, operate under three important assumptions:

- Meaningful change occurs when teachers, families, and communities collaborate to strengthen learning.

- Language and cultural diversity is a strength to be leveraged, not a deficit to be corrected.

- Expert teaching requires monitoring student progress, providing feedback, and adjusting lessons based on the learning of students.

In the chapters that follow, you will encounter these three teachers and view the lesson plans they have developed for themselves. In order to establish a predictable pattern for displaying this information, we have adopted a lesson template (see Figure 1.4). Lessons based on the template are not meant to be delivered in a strictly linear fashion, but rather the template is intended to serve as a way to guide your thinking about the elements of the lesson. In addition, you will more briefly meet a number of teachers from other grade levels whose practices illustrate the approaches under discussion. While no book on lesson planning could ever entirely capture every context or circumstance you encounter, we hope that the net effect is that we provide a process for representing methods for incorporating visible learning for literacy consistently in your English classroom.

Video 3
Lesson Planning

*https://resources.corwin.com/
vl-literacy6-12*

Figure 1.4   Lesson Plan Template

Assessed Need: I have noticed that my students need:
Standard(s) Addressed:
Text(s) I Will Use:
Learning Intention for This Lesson:
Success Criteria for This Lesson:
Direct Instruction: Model: Strategies/skills/concepts to emphasize Guide and Scaffold: Questions to ask Assess: These are the students who will need further support
Dialogic Instruction: Teacher-Directed Tools (e.g., anticipation guides, four corners activity, K-W-L, to spark discussion) Student-Enacted Tools (e.g., literature circles, reciprocal teaching, debate, Socratic seminar, that are primarily driven by students) Assess: These are the students who will need further support
Feedback Opportunities:
Independent Learning and Closure:

CONCLUSION

Literacy instruction that capitalizes on visible learning is established upon principles of learning. A developmental approach to reading and writing is utilized to foster increasingly deeper and more sophisticated expressions of literacy. This focus on the individual learner makes this approach ideal for students with language or learning needs. In addition, a visible learning for literacy approach leverages high-impact instruction to accelerate student learning through surface, deep, and transfer phases of learning by engaging them in direct, dialogic, and independent learning tasks. Finally, students learn best when there is a solid organizational structure that allows them to learn in a variety of ways, and with a variety of materials. In other words, learning becomes visible for students. As we will highlight in each chapter that follows, visible learners are students who

- Can be their own teacher

- Can articulate what they are learning and why

- Can talk about how they are learning—the strategies they are using to learn

- Can articulate their next learning steps

- Can use self-regulation strategies

- Are assessment capable—they understand the assessment tools being used and what their results mean, and they can self-assess to answer the key questions: Where am I in my learning? Where am I going? and What do I need to do to get there?

- Seek, are resilient to, and aspire to challenge

- Can set mastery goals

- See errors as opportunities and are comfortable saying that they don't know and/or need help

- Positively support the learning of their peers

- Know what to do when they don't know what to do

- Actively seek feedback

- Have metacognitive skills and can talk about these (systematic planning, memory, abstract thinking, critical thinking, problem solving, etc.)

Video 4

Visible Learners: "What were you learning today?"

https://resources.corwin.com/ vl-literacy6-12

In other words, a visible learner notices when he or she is learning and is proactive in making sure that learning is obvious. As we engage in discussions about literacy learning in this book, we will return to these indicators that students are visible learners to explore how they might look in the classroom.

TEACHER CLARITY

How do you describe a successful lesson? Do you say the lesson was creative? Do you say it used technology in a new way? Do you say that the students really liked it? Or do you say that students learned, and provide evidence to support your claim? We don't have anything against creative and engaging lessons that use technology. In fact, we know that cognitive engagement is an essential component of learning. But visible learning is based on impact. In fact, visible learning assumes that teachers focus their attention on determining the impact that they have had on student learning and they use that information to determine the success of the lesson.

© Bob Daemmrich/PhotoEdit

How do you know whether your students are successful at learning what you wanted them to? How do *they* know whether they're successful? How can students know whether or not they've met the intended learning intentions, or whether they're making progress toward doing so? After completing the monumental feat of studying and consolidating huge amounts of research on quality teaching and learning, John realized that the single most important thing teachers can do is to *know their impact on student learning*.

This impact needs to be assessed daily so that seemingly small yet vital midcourse corrections can be made. In other words, if you're waiting for a project, quiz, or test to find out what your students know, you're waiting too long. These assessments aren't made often enough to provide teachers the information they need to teach their students effectively. The longer the time in between assessments, the less useful the assessments are in helping students achieve. Teachers need tools that allow them to check for understanding frequently. They also need to know when students have met the learning goal so that they can move on. All of this assumes three things:

- The teacher knows what students are supposed to be learning.

- The students know what they are supposed to be learning.

- The teacher and students know what success looks like.

EFFECT SIZE
FOR TEACHER
CLARITY = 0.75

Taken together, these three aspects contribute to *teacher clarity*, which has an effect size of 0.75, and thus remains one of the most robust instructional practices to be described in this book. Fendick (1990) defined teacher clarity as "a measure of the clarity of communication between teachers and students in both directions" (p. 10) and further described it across four dimensions:

1. **Clarity of organization** such that lesson tasks, assignments, and activities include links to the objectives and outcomes of learning

2. **Clarity of explanation** such that information is relevant, accurate, and comprehensible to students

3. **Clarity of examples and guided practice** such that the lesson includes information that is illustrative and illuminating as students gradually move to independence, making progress with less support from the teacher

4. **Clarity of assessment of student learning** such that the teacher is regularly seeking out and acting upon the feedback he or she receives from students, especially through their verbal and written responses

The remainder of this chapter focuses on the first point, what we will call learning intentions and success criteria. *Clarity of explanations* is further described in the chapter on direct instruction and the *clarity of the examples and practice* are explored in the chapters on dialogic approaches. And, as we noted in the introduction, the final chapter focuses on *assessment and feedback*.

Before we explore learning intentions and success criteria further, it is important to note that teacher clarity rests on an understanding of what students need to learn. In other words, teachers have to understand the content and performance standards appropriate for their grade level if they are going to be able to design meaningful learning experiences for students. Lessons should address the gap between what students already know and what they need to know. And this begins with an analysis of the standards.

Lessons should address the gap between what students already know and what they need to know.

UNDERSTANDING EXPECTATIONS IN STANDARDS

A simple read through the standards documents is not sufficient to teach those standards. Knowing the standards well allows teachers to identify the necessary prior knowledge as well as the expectations for students' success. There are entire books written on unwrapping standards (e.g., Ainsworth, 2014), so we won't repeat that information here. Instead, we want to highlight the need to pay attention to the language in the standards that call for transfer of learning. (See Figure 2.1 for a framework for unpacking each standard.) In nearly all cases, the standards themselves articulate outcomes of learning, and often call upon students to apply what they have learned to an ever-widening set of situations and texts:

- **California State Standards for English Language Arts:** Language RI 7.4: Determine the meaning of words and phrases as they are used in a text, including figurative, connotative, and technical meanings; analyze the impact of a specific word choice on meaning and tone.

- **Texas Essential Knowledge and Skills for English Language Arts and Reading 110.31:** (A) Determine the meaning of grade-level technical academic English words in multiple content areas (e.g., science, mathematics, social studies, the arts) derived from Latin, Greek, or other linguistic roots and affixes; (B) analyze textual context (within a sentence and in larger sections of text) to distinguish between the denotative and connotative meanings of words.

- **English National Curriculum for English Language Arts:** Grammar and Vocabulary Key Stage 4: Pupils should be taught to: consolidate and build on their knowledge of grammar and vocabulary through: drawing on new vocabulary and grammatical constructions from their reading and listening, and using these consciously in their writing and speech to achieve particular effects.

We selected these to illustrate that knowledge of vocabulary, for example, deepens both within and across school years, and that the standards themselves call for students to transfer present levels of knowledge to

Figure 2.1   Understanding Expectations in Standards

Standard(s)	
Concepts (nouns)	**Skills (verbs)**
Surface Skills and Knowledge Needed	
Deep Skills and Knowledge Needed	
Transfer: Big Idea or Enduring Understanding	

grade-level contexts. These outcome standards can't be taught in a day or a week, and therefore are developed over many sustained experiences with spoken and written texts. But these long-range outcomes are difficult for children to understand in the context of daily learning. Therefore, we deconstruct these standards in order to articulate daily learning intentions students can internalize.

LEARNING INTENTIONS IN LITERACY

Standards are statements for teachers that identify what students should know and be able to do at a given point in time. Standards are tough for yet-to-be educated students to understand, and they are too broad for students to master in a single lesson. Effective teachers start with a standard, break the learning that standard requires into lesson-sized chunks, and then phrase these chunks so that students will be able to understand them. Each one of these chunked phrases—a daily statement of what a student is expected to learn in a given lesson—is a *learning intention*. Learning intentions can focus on knowledge, skills, or concepts. Effective teachers know where their students are in the learning cycle—at the surface, deep, or transfer level—and design their instruction to foster learning. A teacher who fails to identify where her students are in their literacy learning is likely to undershoot or overshoot expectations for them. The daily learning intentions that are communicated by the teacher are an end product of her careful planning, as she determines the type of expected learning (surface, deep, or transfer) and how to implement instruction for that type of learning. The *success criteria* provide a means for students and the teacher to gauge progress toward learning, thereby making learning visible. Examples of success criteria for products include rubrics and checklists. Success criteria for a given lesson might focus on metacognitive processes used, such as listing the next steps a student will use the following day to complete a task. We will discuss success criteria in more detail in the next section.

Learning intentions (which some people call objectives, learning goals, targets, or purpose statements) are where teacher planning begins. Learning intentions are different from standards. Here are some examples of learning intentions that we have seen in English classrooms:

- Identify transition words that guide the reader.

- Write a summary of the text using key details.

- Compare and contrast ideas from two texts.

- Make inferences from the details in a text.

> **Teaching Takeaway**
>
> Students should know what they're expected to learn each day, and there should be ways to determine if that learning has occurred.

> Effective teachers start with a standard, break the learning that standard requires into lesson-sized chunks, and then phrase these chunks so that students will be able to understand them.

- Identify examples of figurative language and its effects on a text.

- Support your reasons with evidence from the text.

These are common examples of *what* students are expected to learn in secondary classrooms. To our thinking, students should also experience lessons that include *how* they are expected to learn. Some examples of learning intentions that focus on how students might learn include these:

- *Listen carefully to the speakers in your group so you can link your ideas with theirs.*

- *You and your partner will arrive at consensus about the author's underlying message of the text.*

- *Participate in an online discussion to present your ideas and comment on those of your classmates.*

Some teachers might be concerned that statements such as these can rob students of a period of investigation and inquiry. Learning intentions don't have to be used exclusively at the outset of the lesson and should be revisited over the course of the lesson. Teachers can withhold their learning intentions until after an exploration has occurred. And teachers can invite students to explain what they learned from the lesson and compare that with the initial stated learning intention for the lesson. Interesting class discussions about the alignment (or lack of alignment) can provide a great deal of insight on student understanding.

> Learning intentions don't have to be used exclusively at the outset of the lesson and should be revisited over the course of the lesson.

The *VISIBLE LEARNER*

Video 5
Visible Learners: "How do you know what you're supposed to learn?"

https://resources.corwin.com/ vl-literacy6-12

A visitor walks into a ninth-grade classroom and observes students. Gregory, one of the students in the class, explains his learning to a visitor, saying, *"Today, I'm working on using dialogue to help bring more detail and interest to my memoir. I know that memoirs work best when they use a lot of vivid language to paint a picture for the reader, and the ones we have read in class that I like the most had really good lines of dialogue. We all read different models of memoirs and studied how they were structured; we get to choose which structure we want to use. When we're finished we'll share our writing with our classmates and then post it to our class blog so other people in the school can see our stories."*

Visible learners can articulate what they are learning and why.

Learning intentions are themselves evidence of a scaffolded process that unfolds over many lessons. A key to planning a lesson is in knowing where your students currently are in their learning. It would be tough to teach students to write summaries using key details if they did not understand how to identify details. Learning intentions can (and should often) have an inherent recursive element in that they build connections between previously learned content and new knowledge. Savvy teachers embed previous content in the new content. The teacher is not only creating a need and a purpose for students to hone learned skills but also providing opportunities for students to experience those "aha" moments that relate concepts to a previous lesson's content, a sure sign that students are moving from surface to deep learning. There are a few other hallmarks of good learning intentions that Clarke, Timperley, and Hattie (2003) have identified:

Video 6
Teacher Clarity: Learning Intentions and Success Criteria

https://resources.corwin.com/ vl-literacy6-12

- Explicitly share learning intentions with students, so that students understand them and what success looks like. Recognize that not all students in the class will be working at the same rate or starting from the same place, so it's important to adapt the plan relating to the intentions to make it clear to all students.

- Realize that learning does not happen in a neat, linear sequence; therefore, the cascade from the curriculum aim (the standard), through the achievement objective (unit goals), to the learning intention (for a specific lesson) is sometimes complex.

- Learning intentions and activities can be grouped if one activity can contribute to more than one learning intention or one learning intention may need several activities for students to understand it fully.

- Learning intentions are what we intend students to learn, but it is important to realize students may learn other things not planned for, so teachers need to be aware of unintended consequences.

Student Ownership of Learning Intentions

When Doug speaks to teachers and administrators, he tells them to overtly communicate their learning intentions, because this practice has been shown by extensive research to boost student learning and achievement (Hattie, 2012). But he has found that people actually take this advice more seriously when he frames learning intentions as a students' rights issue. Students have a right to know what they're supposed to learn and why they're supposed to learn it. After all, teachers are going to evaluate student performance for transcripts that will last a lifetime. These records can open doors to colleges and careers, or close them. It's only fair that students understand what they're expected to learn if teachers are going to evaluate that learning.

John notes that the New Zealand Privacy Commission ruled that "students owned their data," and this led to major improvements in creating systems for maintaining data where data followed students through school. It is an interesting thought to consider that your students "own" their data (information about what they have and have not yet learned), and one of our roles is to teach them how to interpret what they own. This approach has led to the development of the notion of "student assessment capabilities," which involve teaching students to know when to best assess their knowledge, how to interpret their assessments, and where to go next in their learning process. It also emphasizes the importance of the teacher sharing the learning journey with students, especially the destination—the learning intentions and the success criteria. In other words, these two practices can provide a means for promoting student ownership of their learning, rather than continuing to perpetuate an ineffective system that attends to the act of teaching, rather than the facilitation of learning. In the next section, we will zoom in on learning intentions before turning our attention to success criteria.

Connecting Learning Intentions to Prior Knowledge

The learning intention itself is important—it needs to be based on an agreed upon standard (usually a state, territory, or national organization), phrased in a way that's easy for students to understand, and appropriately constructed around where students are in their learning. But the learning intention should also link to students' prior knowledge. Activating prior knowledge going into a lesson is an important consideration as teachers explain the learning intentions (Bransford et al., 2000). Many teachers begin their classes with a warm-up exercise. Unfortunately, some teachers do this solely for management purposes—taking attendance, making sure everyone has a pencil—thereby squandering an important learning opportunity. Bell work should be an opportunity to cultivate and activate prior knowledge through written work or classroom discourse. An effective teacher uses opportunities like this to assist students in preparing for new knowledge acquisition. You want to be actively engaged with your class so that you can gain a solid sense of what they know, so that you can capitalize on this.

Seventh-grade teacher Steven Patel uses a simple Google Docs form students can submit when they arrive to class and log into their assigned

> Students have a right to know what they're supposed to learn and why they're supposed to learn it.

> Bell work can be a good opportunity to cultivate and activate prior knowledge. The point is to get learners ready to learn the new content by giving their brains something to connect to, or layer onto, their new skill or understanding.

computers. Mr. Patel changes the prompt each morning, but it is always linked to one of his lessons:

- *We're going to learn about Shakespeare's sonnets today. List three things you know about this writer.*

- *We are going to read an article about cell phone tracking devices today. How do you use your cell phone for navigation/location purposes?*

- *Today we will examine rhetorical appeals. Write a few lines about the last advertisement you saw and how it tried to convince you to buy or do something.*

As students arrive each morning, they write their short responses in a form that Mr. Patel can access quickly to see a spreadsheet of his students' names and answers. "This form helps me take attendance quickly because I can see who's not here," said Mr. Patel. "What this is really useful for is in getting the conversation going. I project the spreadsheet of responses," he continued. "They can read what others have to say, and the result is that they ask each other questions. It means I'm not the only one who's leading the inquiry."

Students can write or talk about what they already know about the concept or skill they'll be learning, pose questions about it, or write about concepts they need to understand before they can tackle the day's learning. Bell work can be a good opportunity to cultivate and activate prior knowledge. The point is to get learners ready to learn the new content by giving their brains something to connect to, or layer onto, their new skill or understanding.

Make Learning Intentions Inviting and Engaging

The ways in which teachers talk about learning intentions makes a difference. William Purkey (1992) described four patterns with which students perceived lessons: intentionally disinviting, unintentionally disinviting, unintentionally inviting, and intentionally inviting.

Teachers who were intentionally disinviting were easily recognizable because of their dismissive and harsh tone. Most of us would, thankfully, not be in that category. However, teachers who were unintentionally disinviting were negative and pessimistic about their students' capabilities, and their low expectations were apparent to the learners (and they were often successful in having a low impact on student learning!).

Take, for example, this introduction to a lesson on connotative and figurative meanings of words. The teacher starts by saying, *"Today we are*

> **Teaching Takeaway**
>
> Tie prior learning to new learning intentions by embedding previous content within new content.

going to work on deciphering the meanings of words in different contexts. This is very hard to do, and the majority of you will struggle to understand what the writer is saying and why—this is a lot of work!"

Little does the teacher realize that she has just told the students that they will likely be unsuccessful in this lesson. In addition to being disinviting, this type of introduction elicits a negative response in students, who are thinking, "This is going to be hard and I probably won't be able to do it."

On the other hand, there are a group of teachers Purkey categorizes as unintentionally inviting. They are energetic and enthusiastic, but they lack a plan for their journey. Students like being with them but don't benefit as fully as they could from instruction because it is inconsistent and naïve. An unintentionally inviting teacher might begin the same lesson by saying, *"Good morning everyone! Today we're going to spend our time studying how an author uses words in different ways. It's exciting to unravel a mystery and I think you'll find this to be a fun and interesting process!"*

This is unintentionally inviting because the teacher is all about getting students excited and interested in the lesson, but notice how the statement doesn't talk about exactly what students are going to learn or why it is important. It may not take long before the students realize that despite their enthusiasm, they have no idea of what is going on.

The final category, those who are intentionally inviting, are consistently positive and are sensitive to the needs of students. They take action and promote a growth mindset. Most of all, they are purposeful and effectively transmit a sense of instructional urgency. As teachers set the learning intentions, they also set the tone for their classroom.

Seventh-grade teacher Simone Okeke's students have been learning about writing narrative texts in order to explain natural phenomena, a topic they have explored through reading folktales in class as well as through studying myths from other civilizations in their world history class. However, she has determined that the narratives they are writing lack a strong main idea and supporting details. Therefore, she has decided that she will have them compose a class folktale on how the stars came to be in the sky.

"My students, through their study in their world history course and the legends we have covered in class, are very knowledgeable about this topic, so I can help them focus more on how to organize what they know in a meaningful, logical manner versus doing more research," she said.

Ms. Okeke knows that she doesn't want to tell students they aren't succeeding at organization and cause them to shut down. Instead, she motivates them to work on the project by saying, *"You've learned so much about how cultures create and pass down myths to explain the world, and I am so excited to have you share your stories. Since we have been partnering with a second-grade class this quarter, I thought it would be a good idea to write a class folktale to share with them on our next meeting to show how much we understand this storytelling style."*

After explaining what a class book would look like (pairs of students compose individual pages, which are assembled as a coherent book) and discussing the qualities the students would like to see in their final product, she turns to the learning intention for the lesson.

> *You've said that it's going to be important that our young friends not only understand the natural event our folktale is trying to explain, but also really "see" the story in their minds, so we will need to make sure the purpose of our story is really clear and has lots of vivid details.*

Ms. Okeke continued,

> *Let's use one of the stories we read together, called "The People Could Fly." Remember this one? One of the reasons it is such a great example of a legend is because the author does a great job creating a vibrant story for us while also being very clear about what the story is trying to explain. I'm thinking we can annotate and reverse outline this folktale to see how the author organizes her ideas and uses details to compose a strong message to her readers. We will then want to make sure our class folktale does the same thing so our young readers and families really understand the point of our legend.*

Ms. Okeke ably communicated the learning intention, to be sure, but she took the extra step of making sure it was inviting by including mention of their families as their readers. "The class is so proud to show what they know, and linking this work to an authentic audience is even more motivating." See Ms. Okeke's complete lesson plan in Figure 2.2.

Social Learning Intentions

Since high-quality lessons involve a good deal of collaboration, it makes sense for teachers to set social learning intentions as well. Social learning intentions are those that focus on the social skills that foster effective collaboration and communication. Nancy saw one frustrated teacher post the social goal, "Raise your hand before talking!" This is *not* the type of social goal that we mean here. However, a social goal of "taking turns while speaking and tracking the speaker" is a valued skill in small and large group work. It makes sense to attend to the social skills of students as they learn. After all, Vygotsky (1962) and others have certainly shown us that

Video 7
Teacher Clarity:
Social Intentions

*https://resources.corwin.com/
vl-literacy6-12*

Figure 2.2   Lesson Plan for Seventh-Grade Organization in Writing

Assessed Need: I have noticed that my students need: To clarify their purpose in narrative writing and include specific details.
Standard(s) Addressed: TEKS Grade 7:   (14) Writing/Writing Process. Students use elements of the writing process (planning, drafting, revising, editing, and publishing) to compose text. Students are expected to: (A) plan a first draft by selecting a genre appropriate for conveying the intended meaning to an audience, determining appropriate topics through a range of strategies (e.g., discussion, background reading, personal interests, interviews), and developing a thesis or controlling idea.
Text(s) I Will Use: "The People Could Fly"
Learning Intention for This Lesson: We will reverse outline this story to examine how the structure helps establish a clear purpose.
Success Criteria for This Lesson: We will make our own outline for our class folktale.
Direct Instruction: Model: Strategies/skills/concepts to emphasize   Model and think aloud about what I expect to learn from this book, based on the text features. They have read this story before and are familiar with the content. I will model the reverse outlining process with a section or two.   Guide and Scaffold: Questions to ask   1. What would our readers expect to learn in folktale titled "The People Could Fly"?   2. How can I be sure my readers know what natural phenomena my story is trying to explain? When should I establish this?   Assess: These are the students who will need further support   Pair Victor with Brian, as they speak the same dialect and can broker language.
Dialogic Instruction: Teacher-Directed Tools   Assigned partners share ideas and write them on their whiteboards.   Student-Enacted Tools   Partners will first verbally compose their sections, and then write on their assigned topic in the next segment of this lesson.   I will need to review the rubric for narrative writing with them.   Assess: These are the students who will need further support   N/A
Feedback Opportunities: We will analyze our story outline to see if we have met the learning intention of planning our class book. I will also meet with Arjun, Nicholas, Sarah, and Lola to look at the items they generated for this lesson.
Independent Learning and Closure: Students will meet with their writing partners to begin composing their sections for the class book. They will also review their drafts and compare them with the learning intentions.

all learning is a social endeavor. The ways in which peers interact and work with one another, and with their teacher, are an engine in the classroom.

Social learning intentions can include things like

- *Ask your teammates for help.*

- *Listen to really understand what your group members are saying.*

- *Explain your reasoning.*

- *Give helpful feedback to others.*

These and other communication skills contribute to a sense of classroom cohesion, which Hattie (2009) describes as "the sense that all (teachers and students) are working toward positive learning gains" (p. 103). As with other learning expectations, social learning intentions should be based on what teachers learn from their students as they watch them work and review individual and group products. Listening to and observing the interactions of students in small and large group settings is essential for making such decisions.

During the second week of the school year, eleventh-grade English teacher Sandra Lopez asks her students to create a list of class norms they will agree to as they work together throughout the school year. *"It's so important that we're able to talk about our ideas, thoughts, and perspectives in ways that allow for voices to be heard, while maintaining a respectful level of discourse,"* Ms. Lopez began. She stated that the learning intention focused on developing some norms that aligned with these expectations. She posted several key phrases featured in the speaking and listening standards for Grades 11–12 on charts hung around the room:

- "Civil, democratic discussions and decision-making"

- "Thoughtful, well-reasoned exchange of ideas"

- ""Ensure a hearing for a full range of positions on a topic or issue"

- "Clarify, verify, or challenge ideas and conclusions"

- "Promote divergent and creative perspectives"

After reviewing each, she invited students to travel in small groups to each chart, and add behaviors and norms that would represent these ideals. *"I've placed markers at each for you to write on the charts. Please talk about and then add your ideas to the chart. When you arrive at the next chart, please read what your peers have already written before adding new ideas."* For the next 20 minutes, Ms. Lopez's students used this gallery walk (a student-enacted form of dialogic instruction, because conversations are student-led) to chart their ideas. When they were finished, she

EFFECT SIZE FOR CLASSROOM COHESION = 0.53

Teaching Takeaway

Social goals can include things like "Ask your teammates for help," "Listen to really understand what your group members are saying," "Explain your reasoning," or "Give helpful feedback to others."

invited them back to their tables to review and discuss each. Through extended discussion, the third period class reached consensus. Here are the norms they developed:

1. We will communicate our ideas as clearly and accurately as we can.

2. We will listen closely when others question our ideas, because new knowledge is generated when we do so.

3. While we might disagree with another speaker, we can't lose sight of the respect we have for each other.

4. Complicated issues don't have easy solutions. But if we don't consider lots of ideas, we can't arrive at new solutions.

"I'm really proud of the norms they developed," Ms. Lopez said later. "Each period has a different spin, but the basic ideas are there. These are young adults. They don't need the simple 'rules of discussion' they used as little kids," she explained. "Civil discourse is vital in any democracy, and unfortunately there's been precious little of it in politics, on the Internet, and even on TV. But that doesn't need to be the case in this classroom."

As the year progressed, students added other norms to this list. Introducing the norms set the tone when discussions were challenging or involved a controversial topic. When needed, Ms. Lopez could refer back to their agreements about the norms that had been decided by the entire class, allowing the students to take a greater degree of responsibility for the quality of their discussions. Ms. Lopez's lesson plan can be viewed in Figure 2.3.

SUCCESS CRITERIA IN LITERACY

Effective teachers establish not only the learning intentions but also the success criteria. In addition to knowing what they're supposed to learn, students should know *how* they will know they've learned it, and how they can assess themselves along the way.

Success Criteria Are Crucial for Motivation

The good news about learning intentions and success criteria is that they have been shown to increase students' internal motivation. And a very convincing case could be made that internal motivation to succeed is one of the most important things your students can learn.

Success criteria work because they tap into principles of human motivation (Bandura, 1997; Elliot & Harackiewicz, 1994). People tend to compare their current performance or ability to a goal that they have set, or

---

> In addition to knowing what they're supposed to learn, students should know how they'll know they've learned it, and how they can assess themselves along the way.

EFFECT SIZE
FOR CLASSROOM
MANAGEMENT = 0.52

Figure 2.3   Lesson Plan for Eleventh-Grade English

Assessed Need: I have noticed that my students need: To develop agreed-upon norms for civil discourse in our class.
Standard(s) Addressed: CCR SL.1: Prepare for and participate effectively in a range of conversations and collaborations with diverse partners, building on others' ideas and expressing their own clearly and persuasively.
Text(s) I Will Use: Key phrases from the standards: • "Civil, democratic discussions and decision-making" • "Thoughtful, well-reasoned exchange of ideas" • ""Ensure a hearing for a full range of positions on a topic or issue" • "Clarify, verify, or challenge ideas and conclusions" • "Promote divergent and creative perspectives"
Learning Intention for This Lesson: To develop a list of class norms to reflect how we will achieve these ideals.
Success Criteria for This Lesson: We will come to consensus to develop a list of norms for civil discourse.
Direct Instruction: Model: Strategies/skills/concepts to emphasize Read the standard (display on document camera) and highlight key phrases. Then watch a short film clip of two politicians engaged in an insult-laden argument (a nonexample), and ask the class to compare it to our standard Guide and Scaffold: Questions to ask 1. How is a discussion different from a verbal confrontation? 2. What can happen in a discussion where the norms are disregarded? 3. What do you consider to be the most essential elements of each norm, and why? Assess: These are the students who will need further support Nya may need redirection to gain her attention.
Dialogic Instruction: Teacher-Directed Tools After the gallery walk (below) we will return to the tables and review each of the charts. I will facilitate the discussion to help the group arrive at consensus, and I will record their evolving ideas on a displayed Google Doc to capture ideas. Student-Enacted Tools Use a gallery walk process so that students can meet in small groups in front of each poster. Students will be given colored markers to write statements they consider to be essential. Assess: These are the students who will need further support Check in with Nasir frequently to make sure he is following the discussion.
Feedback Opportunities: Students will write a short exit slip about the process we used, so I can address any individual concerns.
Independent Learning and Closure: Students will apply norms with my assistance for the next week, and we will revisit these after this time period to revise as needed. For closure, students will be asked to review major aspects of the lessons and identify what they learned from each.

that a caring teacher has set with them. When there is a gap between where they are and where they want to be, it creates cognitive dissonance. Students are motivated to close the gap and get rid of the dissonance by working and learning. The more explicitly and precisely they can see the goal, the more motivated they will be.

It may seem obvious that teachers should know whether or not their students are learning what they're supposed to. But students need to know whether they're on the right track, too. Self-reported grades reflect the extent to which students have accurate understandings of their levels of achievement and can evaluate. It matters that students can describe their current performance accurately, whether that performance is high or low (Hattie, 2012). When we think about it, though, it's hard for learners to know whether they are learning something without having some criteria against which they can measure themselves. Teachers should have success criteria in mind for the lesson. Put simply, success criteria describe what success looks like when the learning goal is reached. They are specific, concrete, and measureable.

> **EFFECT SIZE FOR SELF-REPORTED GRADES/STUDENT EXPECTATIONS = 1.44**

Suppose that a teacher establishes a learning intention that students should compose a response to a writing prompt. How would a student know whether she can do this? Would writing three sentences be enough? Should students compose the response independently, or as part of a team? What if her spelling and conventions are correct, but she forgets to use evidence from texts to support her opinion? Each of these questions can guide teachers in determining what success looks like for their students. In writing, for instance, success is demonstrated by more than simply writing a certain number of words or sentences. Teachers who focus only on the correctness of a student's use of conventions do

The *VISIBLE LEARNER*

Tenth grader Nick was reviewing a personal narrative he had just received with feedback, and he wrote in his English journal, "*I will include at least three sensory details when I am creating a 'scene' in my writing.*" When asked about this, Nick said that he already included dialogue to flesh out his writing and that having a new goal keeps him focused. In Nick's mind, "*Having a goal in mind helps me to focus my efforts. I like to have a target to reach so I know whether I am successful or not.*" Nick understands that writing is more than adding detail to sentences and has identified other areas for mastery, including "*making sure my writing matches the audience I am writing it for*" and "*changing up my sentence lengths to create an interesting rhythm in my writing.*"

Visible learners can set mastery goals.

so at the peril of misunderstanding the student's conceptual understanding of the topic and the purposes of writing.

Without clearly defined criteria, teachers and students are not sure what type of learning has occurred, if any. As we noted earlier, some learning intentions focus on surface learning, and thus the success criteria should be aligned with that level of learning. Other times, the learning intention focuses on deep or transfer levels of learning, and the success criteria need to align with those levels.

Students are much more motivated to work toward success criteria if those criteria are specific (Locke & Latham, 1990). Criteria such as "Do your best" and "Try hard" are not very clear or actionable. Criteria such as these are more likely to produce results:

> "I will be able to clearly support arguments in my writing with evidence from the text."

> "I vary sentence length and structure to maintain reader interest."

The more specific the learning intentions and the criteria for reaching those intentions, the more likely it is that your students will achieve them. Learning intentions should be proximal (Bandura, 1997). In other words, they shouldn't be too distant in the future. This is important to keep in mind when assigning long projects—it really is worth establishing daily success criteria that your students can keep in mind as they work on long-term projects and units of study.

Success criteria for longer projects often come in the form of rubrics and checklists, but more common ones are specific to the individual lesson and are used many times:

- List how you checked your work before turning it in.

- I ask questions about terms I don't know in a text and strategize how to resolve them.

- Be sure your essay includes a clear thesis and ends with a statement that reiterates the thesis.

- I use examples of indirect characterization to illustrate the protagonist's major dramatic question.

- I fully explain and connect evidence to my thesis.

Success criteria can be developed with students, and this is especially effective because it ensures that you are truly using student-friendly language, which is especially important in the earlier grades.

> Success criteria describe what success looks like when the learning goal is reached. They are specific, concrete, and measureable.

Year 10 English teacher Charles Peck has created checklists of success criteria for analyzing various aspects of narrative and informational text during the first semester. "They've seen checklists I've created," he explained, "but now I want to push them a bit more to be more aware of how they analyze." He said he was interested in increasing their opportunities to think metacognitively. "They can do this with a checklist I give them, but I really want to draw their attention to their thinking by having them create and test one themselves."

Using a previously read and discussed passage from an article read by the class, Mr. Peck explained that the learning intention was to *"identify the ways we determine an author's main message by looking at what he says and how he composes,"* and that today's success criterion was to *"develop a checklist we can use to analyze similar informational texts."* He began by modeling and thinking aloud while the passage was displayed on the document camera, inviting students to record the questions he asked himself. "The amount of academic language they used to describe what they saw was very impressive," he remarked later.

Using questions to further scaffold their thinking, he queried them about how the structure and writing techniques a writer employs can help readers understand the writer's main purpose. Mohamed commented, *"If I can't figure out the message, I don't know why the author wrote what he did,"* and Janelle added, *"One of the first things I do when I get lost in a reading is to see if I can find clues to point me to the author's purpose for writing this in the first place."*

Together, the students and Mr. Peck created the following checklist:

To locate the author's purpose:

☐ Look for statements about what the writer is doing. Does the writer use language that suggests she wants to inform, persuade, or convey an experience?

☐ Figure out what the author thinks is important and why she says it is.

☐ Check to see if there are text features that can give you a clue.

☐ Examine the rhetorical structures used by the writer. Is it primarily *ethos*, *pathos*, or *logos*?

☐ Does the writer state her own beliefs, or are you left to infer beliefs?

☐ Does the writer attempt to demonstrate relationships between concepts?

Using the checklist they developed, students then did a "test drive" using another reading passage to see if their suggestions worked. *"These statements and questions are a good start, and we can edit them during the next week until we have a solid checklist. When we're ready, I'll post it on the LMS* [learning management system] *with the other success criteria we've created,"* Mr. Peck told his class. His lesson can be seen in Figure 2.4.

Figure 2.4   Lesson Plan for Year 10 Success Criteria

Assessed Need: I have noticed that my students need: *To internalize their own success criteria for analyzing a document.*

Standard(s) Addressed: *Key Stage 4 Reading: Understand and critically evaluate texts through (1) reading in different ways for different purposes, (2) summarizing and synthesizing ideas and information, and (3) evaluating their usefulness for particular purposes.*

Text(s) I Will Use: *Passage we read yesterday*

Learning Intention for This Lesson: *Identify the ways we determine an author's main purpose by looking at what the author says and how the author writes.*

Success Criteria for This Lesson: *We will develop a checklist we can use to help us locate these in other informational texts.*

Direct Instruction:

Model: Strategies/skills/concepts to emphasize

I will think aloud about how I determine a writer's purpose.

- *I look at the title and opening paragraph to see if the writer has explicitly stated the purpose.*
- *I consider common purposes for writing, such as explaining and persuading.*
- *I look for evidence, such as citations.*
- *I examine the source of the article. Is it credible?*
- *I look to see if the writer has posed questions to consider, and whether they are rhetorical or actionable.*

Guide and Scaffold: Questions to ask

- *Why is it essential for a reader to know the writer's purpose?*
- *In what ways is a reader vulnerable when he doesn't understand the purpose?*

Assess: These are the students who will need further support

Scott and Fatima were absent yesterday and have not read the passage. I will need to discuss it with them before the lesson.

Dialogic Instruction:

Teacher-Directed Tools

Students will work in groups of four with another passage and their draft checklist to see if they can locate the writer's purpose.

Student-Enacted Tools

N/A

Assess: These are the students who will need further support

Check for understanding with Scott and Fatima to see if have further questions.

Feedback Opportunities: *I will meet with Kiara, Tevin, Jake, and Jamie for guided instruction so they can get feedback about how successfully they are using the checklist.*

Independent Learning and Closure: *Students will use the checklist we develop in their independent reading, and then we will discuss what worked and what didn't work for them. We will also revisit the learning intentions and success criteria, providing students time to consider their own learning.*

Available for download at **https://resources.corwin.com/vl-literacy6-12**

CONCLUSION

Learning intentions and success criteria contribute greatly to teacher clarity, but only if they are adequately and consistently communicated to students. There is another benefit from spending time figuring out what you want out of a lesson, and that is in its contribution to your planning processes. As we have stated before, this book is not about writing extensive lesson plans that consume huge amounts of precious time. However, if we cannot articulate what we are pursuing in our lessons, how will our students ever know? And without coherent learning intentions and success criteria, how would we ever know our impact on learning?

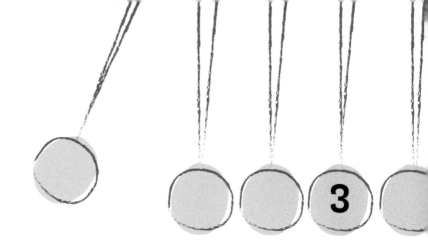

DELIBERATE AND
DIRECT TEACHING

3

"Is rejection a sign of great innovation?" Year 10 teacher Charles Peck asks his students. The students in his London classroom have been studying Ayn Rand's novella *Anthem* and tracking the main character's evolution. The class has just read a chapter in which the main character has presented a new invention to his society, only to be persecuted for it. Mr. Peck has selected an informational article that illustrates a complementary psychological phenomenon: that people often react negatively to new ideas because of fear of the unknown. He wants his students to have a better

© Bob Daemmrich/PhotoEdit

understanding of what motivates the characters in the text, so he chose to provide them with an outside source to consider.

Mr. Peck recognizes that simply assigning a book and wishing for the best isn't likely to have the impact he wants. The article he selected is a challenge for these 15-year-olds, and the author has a decidedly strong point of view, one that might cause students to simply go with the author's opinion, rather than question it. The teacher knows that direct instruction is an essential aspect of his teaching, and he plans on using an element of the approach, called teacher modeling, to demonstrate to students how he interrogates a text to determine the author's opinion. "Based on past evidence of impact that I've collected about my teaching, students tend to accept Rand's perspective at face value. The question

3

isn't a matter of validity of argument, but rather whether a critical reader digs underneath assumptions to query positions." He continued, "I've learned that I need to be deliberate about modeling and thinking aloud using a critical reading stance. She's such a talented author, and many readers hesitate to read against the text, not just with the text." (Mr. Peck's full lesson plan can be found in Figure 3.1.)

Figure 3.1   Lesson Plan for Year 10 Using Texts in Context

Assessed Need: I have noticed that my students need: *To evaluate texts by looking for loaded language to determine an author's opinion.*

Standard(s) Addressed: *Key Stage 4 Reading: Understand and critically evaluate texts to distinguish between statements that are supported by evidence and those that are not, and identify bias and misuse of evidence.*

Text(s) I Will Use: *"Why Rejection May Be a Mark of Great Innovation"*

Learning Intention for This Lesson: *We will consider the author's message and point of view in relation to the structure so that we can evaluate the information presented.*

Success Criteria for This Lesson: *I will write a response to this information that includes my opinion and supporting evidence, and compare or contrast it with the author's point of view (use argumentation rubric).*

Direct Instruction:

Model: Strategies/skills/concepts to emphasize

Use of structure to convey opinion

Name the strategy, state its purpose, explain its use: Use title to set the author's purpose (bold statement with corresponding headings). I am modeling how I look for structural cues that suggest the author's point of view. When I am reading an opinion piece, I look carefully for terms and examples that show the author's opinion.

Analogy: Strategic organization is like a commercial in the sense that all the most convincing evidence is up front, while the less convincing "fine print" is always at the end (and stated really, really quickly!).

Demonstration: Reverse outline the paragraphs and note the headings: Blame it on the brain stem; No point of reference; No trust.

Errors to avoid: I have to be careful that I don't form my own opinion too soon and stop reading altogether just because I might disagree. I need to keep reading and give the author time to make his case, before I settle on my opinion.

Assess the skill: Write at least one question in the margin of each paragraph that challenges the author's message.

Guide and Scaffold: Questions to ask

1: How does the author use different techniques for conveying her message?

2: The author claims the reptilian brain causes us to fear change. What evidence might refute her idea that this part of our brains is no longer useful?

3: What do you want to independently verify in this paragraph? What statements might you challenge?

Assess: These are the students who will need further support

Eugene, Alyssa, and Mandy will need me to support them through the second paragraph, while the rest of the class is reading independently.

Dialogic Instruction:

Teacher-Directed Tools

N/A

Student-Enacted Tools

After reading, students will meet in Four Corners to determine similar opinion groups (strongly agree, agree, disagree, strongly disagree), and then work together to list arguments in favor of or opposed to the idea that rejection is a mark of great innovation.

Assess: These are the students who will need further support

Amir, Tevin, and Stephanie

Feedback Opportunities: I will meet with the smallest group first so that they receive feedback about their list. Given a smaller number, they may need further support.

Independent Learning and Closure: Students will write an exit ticket that provides their opinion with evidence, using the argumentation rubric as a way to self-assess before submitting. As part of the closure, I will summarize the main points of the lesson and foreshadow the next lesson.

Available for download at **https://resources.corwin.com/vl-literacy6-12**

The *VISIBLE LEARNER*

When asked about reading challenging texts, eighth grader LaShunna said, *"It's not always easy for sure, but it does keep things from getting boring. I like when the teacher gives a little clue on what to read for; then it's my job to find those things. Having to dig for certain things keeps it fun and keeps me thinking pretty hard, but it feels like I can do it."*

Similarly, twelfth grader Terrence said, *"My teacher is always giving us things that she says she read in college, and since that's where I know I want to end up, I want to try to understand the reading. I'm motivated to do it because we practice all the time and keep getting better."*

The visible learner seeks, is resilient to, and aspires to challenge.

To be sure, direct instruction has gotten a bad rap in some quarters. In fact, it might be one of the most misunderstood instructional approaches out there. Impressions about direct instruction usually cluster into three categories:

1. It is scripted and didactic.

2. It is inflexible.

3. It devalues teacher judgment.

Yet walk into virtually any effective classroom and you will see direct instruction in action. Don't believe us? Interview colleagues you have identified as being highly successful with their students, and ask them to reflect on the methods they frequently employ. You might ask,

- When planning, do you have a clear idea about your learning intentions?

- Do you consider it important for students to know what the criteria for learning success are, and to be held accountable for their learning?

- Is it important to draw students into the lesson by appealing to their interests, curiosities, and wonderings?

- Are modeling and demonstrating skills and concepts part of your repertoire?

- Does checking for understanding have a place in your lessons?

- Should a lesson include guided instruction such that learners can practice new skills and concepts, with feedback from the teacher?

- How important is it to close a lesson with a summary to organize student thinking and consolidate learning?

- Should students have time to try on new learning independently in novel situations?

Chances are good that the talented teachers you identified affirmed that each of these actions is vital for students' learning. Adams and Engelmann (1996), in their meta-analysis of direct instruction, named each of these as necessary components of direct instruction. To limit one's understanding of direct instruction to highly scripted programs is to overlook the practices that make it highly effective for developing surface level knowledge. With an effect size of 0.59, direct instruction offers a pedagogical pathway that provides students with the modeling, scaffolding, and practice they require when learning new skills and concepts. John notes that

> when we learn something new . . . we need more skill development and content; as we progress, we need more connections, relationships, and schemas to organize these skills and content; we then need more regulation or self-control over how we continue to learn the content and ideas. (Hattie, 2009, p. 84)

In other words, whether we are 5 or 45, we follow a trajectory that moves from surface learning to deeper learning, and we transfer some of that learning such that we can utilize it in lots of new and seemingly dissimilar situations. It is quite possible that you have applied a teaching technique or two over the years to your own unsuspecting family members, even though no one told you to do so.

Perhaps you are still reluctant to entertain the possibility that direct instruction might be effective. We invite you to try it and evaluate it yourself using your students' learning as a measure. We would be remiss, and would fail to convey the full message of visible learning, if we did not restate that knowing your impact on your students is the truest yardstick you'll ever possess (Hattie, 2009). We don't mean your gut instincts, or your impressions, or your anecdotes, but the fact that you determine the impact of your teaching on your students and adjust accordingly. Finding out what they know and don't know at the beginning of a unit of study, teaching, and then assessing again at the end of the unit furnishes feedback to you about the impact of your teaching.

EFFECT SIZE
FOR DIRECT
INSTRUCTION = 0.59

To limit one's understanding of direct instruction to highly scripted programs is to overlook the practices that make it highly effective for developing surface level knowledge.

Figure 3.2   Questions About Direct Instruction in Your Lessons

- When planning, do you have a clear idea about your learning intentions?
- Do you consider it important for students to know what the criteria for learning success are, and to be held accountable for their learning?
- Is it important to draw students into the lesson by appealing to their interests, curiosities, and wonderings?
- Are modeling and demonstrating skills and concepts part of your repertoire?
- Does checking for understanding have a place in your lessons?
- Should a lesson include guided instruction such that learners can practice new skills and concepts, with feedback from the teacher?
- How important is it to close a lesson with a summary to organize student thinking and consolidate learning?
- Should students have time to try on new learning independently in novel situations?

Available for download at **https://resources.corwin.com/vl-literacy6-12**

Imagine meeting a seventh grader who didn't know how to write a two-part thesis. It is hardly appropriate, then, to ask him to write a two-page persuasive paper with a clear controlling idea. Of course giving students a thesis to write with instead of having them develop their own wouldn't provide an opportunity for mastery either. They also need to practice and receive feedback. Telling students what a two-part thesis does and showing them how it works with a model text would help them begin to break the code for unlocking this type of writing. For example, let's say that there is a small group of students in class who struggle to find the thesis or controlling idea in the texts they read. The teacher might say, "*Today we are going to learn how to find an author's main idea, in other words, her thesis.*" Reading the text aloud, the teacher could model, saying, "*When I see the title of this article, I realize that this can provide me with a heads-up of what this text might mostly be about. I also know that most writers will tell me their main idea in the first few lines or paragraph of their writing.*"

The teacher might then provide students with opportunities to read the text together and collect other clues about the author's main purpose: "*Let's look at the main idea in each paragraph. Do they seem to have a com-*

mon theme? Can we find a line that 'sums up' what all these paragraphs seem to be about?" "Yes, this sentence seems to cover all of our paragraphs." Over time, and with practice, the students will recognize how a thesis controls the body paragraphs of a text.

But that's not writing a thesis; it's learning how one works. To write one, students will need to see how their own writing should follow a logical organization centered around one controlling idea. Following the recognition of how a thesis works in a model, students could try to write a "thesis" for a one-paragraph response. For example, teachers might propose a topic and model how they might develop a paragraph around an idea related to this topic. Through direct instruction, the teacher may model what details to include and which to leave out. The teacher could then propose a new topic and have students try out the same process alone or in groups. After the students practice a bit, the teacher might change the topic again to practice the method again. The role of direct instruction cannot be minimized (see Figure 3.2).

Although this chapter is not about writing instruction per se, we seek to profile the many ways teachers provide direct instruction for students who are learning a wide range of skills, strategies, or concepts. Because the first two steps in the list—learning intentions and success criteria—have already been examined in the previous chapter, we will confine our discussion in this chapter to

- Relevance

- Modeling

- Checking for understanding

- Guided instruction

- Closure

- Independent learning

RELEVANCE

All learners, whether they are 16 years of age or 36-year-old educators, crave relevance. By that, we mean that an important driver of learning is in understanding *why* the acquisition of a new skill or concept is important in one's life. Think about all of those ubiquitous how-to videos on YouTube. Quite frankly, many of them are boring, unless you actually have a need and desire to learn something. Figuring out how to tie a necktie, or making the new tortilla iron work (something Doug had to figure out one evening), makes those videos infinitely more interesting, because there's a reason to learn something.

Video 8
Relevance
https://resources.corwin.com/ vl-literacy6-12

Importantly, relevance facilitates intrinsic motivation, and those who are intrinsically motivated to learn tend to persist in their learning when they confront challenges (Meece, Anderman, & Anderman, 2006). Relevancy doesn't mean that all your lessons need to ensure success in a career, but rather that learners can see how the learning intentions apply in their lives. Why are writing conventions important? It helps us communicate with precision and accuracy. Why are literary devices important? Knowledge of them helps us interpret the underlying meaning of a text.

Tenth-grade teacher Theodore Taylor knows that relevancy is key for his students. For instance, at the beginning of a lesson on identifying how an author uses counterclaims, Mr. Taylor set the learning intention and success criteria and then said, *"It's always important that we think about why we are learning something. If you're not sure, you should always ask, 'Mr. Taylor, why are we learning this?' I want to make sure we can always explain why we are learning something."* He then points to the board and reads his purpose statement: *"Today we are working on identifying how an author uses counterclaims for a specific audience in order to understand how arguments change depending on their audience."* After noting the success criteria for this learning target, he then goes on to explain, *"Skilled writers anticipate counterclaims and address them. Your use of counterclaims prevents others from punching holes in your argument."*

> Relevance facilitates intrinsic motivation, and those who are intrinsically motivated to learn tend to persist in their learning when they confront challenges.

The VISIBLE LEARNER

Kaitlin, a student in Mr. Taylor's class, asks his teacher during a small group conference, *"I know counterclaims are really important, but I'm wondering if they can ever 'undo' the hard work I put into my argument. Is there a way I can use them to show I know what the audience is thinking?"* Mr. Taylor responds, *"That's a really important point, Kaitlin. I think we should keep this in mind as we look at how different writers do this before we start writing our own counterclaims. How confident do you feel in pointing out the counterclaims in this text?"*

Kaitlin responded, *"I think I found, one, but I know there are more in there. I'm looking for signal words or phrases that we learned earlier, so I think I'm on the right track. I'll check in with Shayna [another student] after I finish annotating this to make sure I didn't miss any."*

Visible learners can articulate their next learning steps.

TEACHER MODELING

There was a fascinating series of studies that began with neuroscientists in the 1990s who noticed something surprising. When they measured brain cell activity of monkeys that were watching the movements of other monkeys, such as picking up a banana, they found that specialized brain cells called motor neurons in the observing monkeys were active, even though these observing monkeys were sitting still. Interestingly, these were some of the same neurons that became active when the observing monkey was the one doing the motion. So, the monkey *watching* and the monkey *doing* used a lot of the same brain cells, and the cells were similarly active (Rizzolatti & Craighero, 2004). Later, researchers showed that these mirror neuron systems in the human brain function similarly to understand the intentions of others (Iacoboni et al., 2005). When you observe someone else doing something, you use many of the same neural pathways as when you perform the same action yourself. These mirror neuron systems may help explain the power of teacher modeling, not to mention how babies learn and why fads and trends spread so quickly.

Teacher modeling processes can trigger similar responses in observing students. Through modeling, students can be taught to think aloud about their own cognitive decision making and problem solving, providing teachers with further insight into students' grasp of skills and concepts. Providing examples of thinking is useful, but effective modeling includes an explanation of *why* teachers are doing what they are doing, so that students understand *how* the teacher was able to think, not just *what* the teacher was thinking.

Pair With Think-Alouds

When teachers explain their expert thinking in a way that students can understand, students are better able to imitate the thinking of their teachers. We're not looking for students to simply replicate the work of the teacher but rather to explore the ways that other people think. Thinking is invisible, so teachers have to talk about their thinking. By listening to a teacher think, students are guided through the same cognitive processes that the expert uses, as if they were apprentices. Teachers who open up their minds to describe their cognitive and metacognitive processes for their students call these narrations *think-alouds* (Davey, 1983). As noted in Figure 3.3, there are common steps in teacher think-alouds (Fisher, Frey, & Lapp, 2009). Of course, teachers don't use all of these each time they think aloud. They pick and choose the aspects of the think-aloud necessary to build students' strategic thinking.

> **Teaching Takeaway**
>
> Model for students such that they can approximate the thinking of an expert.

Video 9
Modeling

https://resources.corwin.com/vl-literacy6-12

Figure 3.3   Design a Think-Aloud

Possible Features to Model	Features You Plan to Model
1. Name the strategy, skill, or task.	
2. State the purpose of the strategy, skill, or task.	
3. Explain when the strategy or skill is used.	
4. Use analogies to link prior knowledge to new learning.	
5. Demonstrate how the skill, strategy, or task is completed.	
6. Alert learners to errors to avoid.	
7. Assess the use of the skill.	

Source: Adapted from Fisher, D., Frey, N., & Lapp, D. (2009). *In a reading state of mind: Brain research, teacher modeling, and comprehension instruction.* Newark, DE: International Reading Association.

 Available for download at **https://resources.corwin.com/vl-literacy6-12**

The "I" and "Why" of Think-Alouds

Think-alouds use "I" statements. A lot of teachers say "we" or "you" in their explanations, but "I" statements—using a first-person pronoun—do something different and more powerful for the brains of students. They activate the ability—some call it an instinct—of humans to learn by imitation. We have worked with teachers who actually think that they are using "I" statements, when they are saying the word "you" (a second-person pronoun) in their explanations. Or, they will start their think-alouds with "I" and then switch to "you" at some point in their explanation. The second-person pronoun is directive; the first-person pronoun signals the sharing of intentions.

These people are not delusional. Rather, teaching is such a complex skill that it can be difficult for teachers to use the exact words that they'd planned on using, or to remember exactly what they said at a time when they were also thinking about 32 (or more) young people, considering formative evaluation results, wondering whether they'd been talking for too long, and thinking as an expert, all simultaneously. Allowing teachers to video- or audio-record their think-alouds, and then giving them the opportunity to watch or listen to the recording, has been very useful in helping teachers over this hump. Knight (2014) and his colleagues at the University of Kansas have analyzed the work of teachers and instructional coaches as they interacted with video- and audio-recordings of lessons, and found that these tools propelled improvements in instructional quality more effectively than lesson debriefing alone. Similar effects were seen with individual teachers who coached themselves by watching videos of their own teaching. Advancements in digital technology have made it possible for teachers to wear a small device that remotely signals the video camera to turn and follow them as they teach, eliminating the need for another person to operate the camera.

Another strategy is for teachers to use written notes that include the word *because*. It's important to explain *why* you're thinking what you're thinking. If you don't, students experience an example but do not know how to do what you're doing on their own. Using *because* reduces the chance that students will be left wondering how you knew to do something or why you think a certain way.

For example, while modeling the comprehension strategy of predicting, the teacher might say, *"Based on what I just read in this paragraph, I'm anticipating what might come next. I expect the writer to explain [insert content] because she referred to it but didn't provide an explication yet."*

A teacher modeling word solving might say, *"When I encounter a word or phrase I don't know, I look first for structural cues, such as affixes to figure out the part of speech, and derivations, such as Latin and Greek root words."*

Including the *why* or *because* while modeling increases the chance that students will be able to imitate the expert thinking they have witnessed, because they are provided with examples and the reasons for those examples. Thinking about your thinking is a metacognitive act, and students will start to think more metacognitively when they hear others, including their peers, do so.

Seventh-grade teacher Simone Okeke's students have been working on analyzing how elements of a story interact to create meaning. This is a complex skill that is developed over many lessons, so Ms. Okeke routinely models how she applies this comprehension skill using the many texts they read. The previous few days, she read the opening chapter from *Roll of Thunder, Hear My Cry*, a novel about racism in America during the Great Depression. The story features a family of sharecroppers and follows the experiences of Cassie Logan, a nine-year-old girl. As Ms. Okeke reads the chapter aloud, students became acquainted with the struggles Cassie and her classmates encounter when they are given

"I" statements do something different and more powerful for the brains of students. They activate the ability—some call it an instinct—of humans to learn by imitation.

EFFECT SIZE FOR METACOGNITIVE STRATEGIES = 0.69

subpar materials to learn from. Once the students have a foundational knowledge of the conflict of the story, Ms. Okeke returns to the chapter to model and think aloud about how she connects this isolated experience the characters have to the time and place of the novel (her full lesson plan can be found in Figure 3.4 on pages 58–59). After establishing the learning intention and success criteria, she begins,

> *Today I'm going to model and think aloud about how I understand clues from a text and what they tell me about the effect the setting has on the characters in the story.* [names strategy]

> *We've done this before, and today I'm going to use it with part of* Roll of Thunder, Hear My Cry, *the novel we're currently reading. Understanding how setting drives a story helps me to understand deeper themes of the book.* [describes purpose]

> *Authors don't usually tell us directly how the setting affects the characters, because if they did the book would be really long and seem like an informational article rather than a story. Most authors give us subtle clues to find. That's what I mean by reading like a detective. I need to find the clues to unravel the mystery about the choice of setting.* [provides analogy]

> *The clues I'm looking for are words, actions, and details about the setting or objects in the story.* [explains use]

Ms. Okeke reads aloud a section consisting of six lines from the selected passage, and then she demonstrates where she locates clues.

> *As I'm reading I keep track of clues like a detective, to see how the environment my characters are in might affect them. One clue I am noticing is here* [points to passage]. *The narrator says Little Man is sucking in his breath and throws down his school book. I know he's upset and it has to do with the books, but I wonder why? I know this book must have something to do with the way the children feel they are treated, because the narrator also makes a point of telling me the books are dirty. I know if I was given something damaged or dirty, I would feel upset, but I'm still not sure why the children actually received the books this way. I'll keep looking.*

Rereading, she pauses on the phrase "stamped on the inside cover was a chart that read. . . ." [Cassie sees that the book has been used and given to them after it has been discarded by classes of White children].

> *That's a huge clue! The author was hinting that something was wrong with the books, but now I know why. Not only were the*

students given subpar materials, I see now that it is because the children are African American. I know I would be so upset if I was treated unfairly because of how I looked, and this is what is happening to the children in the story. I would probably act very poorly, actually. What do you think will happen to Little Man after he throws the book?

Ms. Okeke continues, now demonstrating how she makes connections between the setting and the characters' behavior.

It says now that Little Man is getting whipped for acting out. Now, that might have been expected at the time this story takes place. It's the 1930s, and hitting a child might have been seen as a just punishment for throwing a book, but now I see why Little Man did it. Is he just a brat?

[The class responds with a resounding *"No!"*]

Right. He was reacting to something unjust, which is a product of the time he lives in. I feel like I understand him, and where he lives, much better.

She then explains that she needs to put these clues together to avoid an error:

When I read, I sometimes just want to follow the plot of the story without asking myself why the author made certain choices, but I know there is much more to learn about how elements like a setting shape how characters act, like in the part where we discover why Little Man is so upset. [rereads] Now that I know the why, I can reread the beginning of that scene and really understand why Little Man appears to be acting like a brat. It also gives me insight into Cassie and Miss Crocker, and I can compare how racism affects them similarly to or differently from the way it affects Little Man. [assess the skill]

In the next part of her lesson, she will use questions to scaffold their learning, in order to check for their understanding of the comprehension strategy she modeled for them.

STUDENTS SHOULD THINK ALOUD, TOO

Have you ever had a student come to the front of the room to show how she figured out a solution, only to watch her explain it in a way that guarantees nobody else will learn from it? Students leading the class

If you want students to explain their thinking or their solution, you will need to teach them how to do this explicitly.

Figure 3.4   Lesson Plan for Seventh Grade Inferring the Affect of Settings on Characters Using Multiple Clues

Assessed Need: I have noticed that my students need: To connect setting with character development.
Standard(s) Addressed: EKS Grade 7: (6) Reading/Comprehension of Literary Text/Fiction. Students understand, make inferences and draw conclusions about the structure and elements of fiction and provide evidence from text to support their understanding. Students are expected to: (A) explain the influence of the setting on plot development.
Text(s) I Will Use: Roll of Thunder, Hear My Cry
Learning Intention for This Lesson: We will look for character reactions and plot details to assess how setting influences character development.
Success Criteria for This Lesson: I can find and explain evidence of how setting affects characters in a graphic organizer.
Direct Instruction: Model: Strategies/skills/concepts to emphasize   Use the passage where Little Man throws the book to model my thinking about the word clues I find about how setting influences the character's actions. Since we read the entire chapter this week, this will be a "zoom in" on the text.   <u>Name the strategy, state its purpose, explain its use</u>: Authors don't directly tell us when parts of a story are related--that would be boring and take too long. They expect the reader to infer the character's feelings by using words, actions, and pictures. I am going to look closely at the first part of the schoolhouse scene to find these clues.   <u>Analogy</u>: When I read, I am always looking for clues like this, just like a detective does when she's solving a mystery. I gather up the clues to figure out what might be happening.   <u>Demonstration</u>:   Actions to model: "Little Man bit his lip. . . ."   Relation to setting: "The blank lines continued down to line 20 and I knew that they had all been reserved for black students."   <u>Errors to avoid</u>:   If I just read for plot points, I may think Little Man is just being a brat, when in fact he is rightly upset.   <u>Assess the skill</u>: Read the passage again using the correct vocal tone.   Guide and Scaffold: Questions to ask   1. What are the words, actions, and picture clues that tell us how Little Man is feeling? How Cassie is feeling?   2. What clues are we given as to why Little Man and Cassie are so upset? How does this relate to the surroundings they live in?

3. Miss Crocker is upset with the students now, but why? What words and actions, by her and the children, help us understand this?

Assess: These are the students who will need further support

I will reread the text with Aubrey, Ignacio, David, and Alexis because they struggled with the fantasy element of the story yesterday when we read it for the first time.

Dialogic Instruction:

Teacher-Directed Tools

Students will complete a simple graphic organizer about Little Man, Cassie, and Miss Crocker, listing three pieces of evidence + inferences about how the setting is related to the actions of the characters.

Student-Enacted Tools

Students may use the graphic organizer provided or one of their own choosing.

Assess: These are the students who will need further support

Marla seems to have trouble with the graphic organizer--check if it is a misunderstanding about the tool or the text. Also, Jacqueline and Brandon both lacked evidence in their last submission.

Feedback Opportunities: I check for understanding with students at tables 2, 4, and 5 to listen to their evidence. These same students will then partner with classmates at tables 1, 3, and 6 to share their evidence.

Independent Learning and Closure: Students are finding evidence on their own, and after meeting with partners, will add any new examples. They will be provided opportunities to reflect on this experience and ask questions about areas of confusion and what they still would like to learn.

Available for download at **https://resources.corwin.com/vl-literacy6-12**

through their solution paths can be very powerful, and the way this is done shouldn't be left to the pedagogical skills of an untrained child. Rather, if you want students to explain their thinking or their solution, you will need to teach them how to do this explicitly. One way to do this is to debrief after your think-alouds, explaining what you did. Figure 3.5 includes a checklist useful in self-assessing aspects of a think-aloud. If you use this checklist to debrief your think-alouds, your students can use it as a guide when they are leading. Other students can hold the demonstrator accountable for following the guidelines, and, ideally, they will hold you accountable when you do yours as well.

Figure 3.5   Student Think-Aloud Checklist

☐ Let your listener(s) read through the entire question or text before you begin your think-aloud.

☐ Use "I" statements.

☐ Summarize the text/comments/claims briefly.

☐ Speak loudly enough for your partner(s) to hear.

☐ Don't go too fast or too slow.

☐ Locate contradictions when possible and resolve them.

☐ Identify areas for more research.

☐ Make sure your think-aloud doesn't go on for more than five minutes.

Available for download at **https://resources.corwin.com/vl-literacy6-12**

The eleventh-grade students in Sandra Lopez's class have been reading Richard Hofstadr's "Abraham Lincoln and the Self-Made Myth," a selection from *The American Political Tradition*. In this piece, Hofstadr challenges widely held beliefs about Abraham Lincoln in order to compel his readers to think about how we understand history. Ms. Lopez and her class have read all of the selections previously, and she wants her students to use the think-aloud checklist to explain their thinking when faced with a text that invites questioning and extra research.

To refresh their memories, she reviews the checklist using one of the readings from the book. "I selected Luis to be my partner because of his distractibility. Being in the fishbowl with me will keep him focused," she said.

After completing the teacher think-aloud, Ms. Lopez hosts a short discussion, using questions to guide students' thinking in order to circumvent possible difficulties. She asks students, *"When I lost meaning in the second paragraph, what did I do to regain understanding?"* and *"How did Luis use the headings to keep himself on track?"* After the class discussion, she has each student partner with another student to think aloud about a section from the text. Ms. Lopez's lesson is in Figure 3.6 on pages 62–63.

Greg and Maritza choose Part IV, the section about Lincoln's visit to a New Orleans slave auction. Greg speaks first:

EFFECT SIZE FOR
SELF-VERBALIZATION
AND SELF-
QUESTIONING = 0.64

Okay, so this part is basically about the famous legend that Abraham Lincoln saw slaves being sold and felt like he was pierced in his heart. Essentially, he swears he will get rid of slavery if he ever gets the chance. But, Hofstadr is saying that isn't true! I can't believe it, but the guy who was supposedly with him wasn't ever there. According to this. I personally would like to research this a little bit because I'm just not convinced yet that this huge part of the Lincoln legend is a lie.

Now Maritza continues:

When we looked at this part earlier, we were told to look out for any sort of language that would show the author's bias. I agree that the part where Hofstadr says, "We know that he refused to denounce the Fugitive Slave Law, viciously unfair though it was," shows that the author is upset. I'd like to investigate more where Hofstadr got his information so I can really trust him.

The pair then evaluates each other's performance, agreeing that they both used "I" statements, spoke loud enough to be heard, and identified areas of the text that they had questions about for further research. *"We also were right to the point and didn't drag it out too much,"* said Maritza.

The *VISIBLE LEARNER*

Video 10
Visible Learners
Support Their Peers

https://resources.corwin.com/vl-literacy6-12

Greg and Maritza, students in Sandra Lopez's eleventh-grade class, do not tell each other answers. Rather they support each other through questions and prompts. They provide hints to one another, much like their teacher has modeled. For example, when Greg gets frustrated with a section of the text, Maritza says, *"It's okay, let's just think about what we know already about this guy and his ideas and see if we can't figure the rest out. It's kind of fun to see how annoyed he is with the Lincoln legend."*

Visible learners positively support their peers' learning.

CHECKING FOR UNDERSTANDING

Effective teachers check for understanding throughout their lessons, using a variety of approaches, especially by examining the oral and written language of their students. The most common method is in posing questions to students, especially to gauge comprehension (Durkin, 1978/79). However, the type of question posed signals to students what kind of knowledge is of value, and what is not. Studies of the knowledge

Figure 3.6   Lesson Plan for Student Think-Alouds

Assessed Need: I have noticed that my students need: To use academic language to express ideas.

Standard(s) Addressed: 11–12.1.D: Respond thoughtfully to diverse perspectives; synthesize comments, claims, and evidence made on all sides of an issue; resolve contradictions when possible; and determine what additional information or research is required to deepen the investigation or complete the task.

Text(s) I Will Use: Passage from "Abraham Lincoln and the Self-Made Myth."

Learning Intention for This Lesson: We will use spoken language and visuals to share ideas with others.

Success Criteria for This Lesson: Think-aloud checklist

Direct Instruction:

Model: Strategies/skills/concepts to emphasize

Review the student think-aloud checklist to reinforce knowledge of elements.

<u>Name the strategy, state its purpose, explain its use:</u>

I am going to model how I use the think-aloud checklist to help me remember all the things I should do when I think aloud for a partner. When I remember to do these, I help my partner understand

<u>Analogy:</u> When I go to the grocery store, I have a list so I don't forget to buy something I need. The think-aloud checklist helps me remember everything.

<u>Demonstration:</u> Think aloud using sections from "Abraham Lincoln and the Self-Made Myth." I am going to think aloud today with Luis. First, I will read the checklist to myself to make sure I remember everything I am looking for. I know I need to let my partner read first, so he knows what I am talking about. Next, I will use "I" statements to summarize what I think the section is about. I will point out areas that I find to be particularly effective, keeping in mind that I also want to identify areas where I am left with questions. For example, this passage makes it sound like the author is jealous: "No man ever had an easier time of it in his early days than Lincoln. He had . . . influential and financial friends to help him; they almost fought each other for the privilege of assisting Lincoln. . . . Lincoln was a pet in his family." I wonder if there is a way to confirm this statement. Maybe I could do more research.

<u>Errors to avoid:</u> One mistake would be to talk too softly. It would be hard for my partner to hear if I am too quiet.

<u>Assess the skill:</u> I will check with my partner to ask how I have done. Luis, can you give me feedback using the checklist?

Guide and Scaffold: Questions to ask

What can be hard about thinking aloud?

How will you know you have been successful?

If you are having a difficult time, how could you get help?

Assess: These are the students who will need further support

I am thinking aloud with Luis as my partner so he can be more actively engaged in this lesson.

Dialogic Instruction:

Teacher-Directed Tools

Students will complete the checklist with their partners to rate how they did.

Student-Enacted Tools

N/A

Assess: These are the students who will need further support

David, Kenny, Angelica, Omar, and Kimberly need to be monitored for use of the checklist.

Feedback Opportunities: I will listen to the think-alouds that Scott, Miteesha, Jacque, and Thomas perform with each other. The rest of the class will get written feedback on their checklists.

Independent Learning and Closure: Students will select a section of "Abraham Lincoln and the Self-Made Myth." They will receive feedback from their peers using the checklist and note at least one area in which they would like to grow.

Available for download at **https://resources.corwin.com/vl-literacy6-12**

type needed to answer the majority of teachers' questions are discouraging, as the evidence suggests that the majority require only recall and recognition, the lowest order of critical thinking (Bintz & Williams, 2009; Zohar, Schwartzer, & Tamir, 1998). In order to engage in deeper levels of thinking, students need questions that scaffold and probe, rather than interrogate.

Use Questions to Probe Student Thinking

Questions that check for understanding are a crucial aspect of direct instruction. But the best teachers probe deeper, for more specific information. They don't just want to know whether or not a student understands something. If the student does understand, they want to see if the student can explain their thinking and apply what is understood. If the student doesn't understand, these teachers probe deeper to find the point at which a misconception, overgeneralization, or partial understanding led her astray. Lurking in the back of the teacher's mind is the question, "What does this child's answer tell me about what he or she knows and doesn't know?"

Video 11

Checking for Understanding

https://resources.corwin.com/vl-literacy6-12

The purpose of the question matters, that is, it matters what kind of knowledge you are hoping to surface. Closed questions that constrict student speculation limit student thinking to trying to determine what the "right" answer might be. (Doug calls it, "Guess what's in the teacher's brain.") A series of closed questions strung together is called a *funneling* pattern, because the purpose is to lead the student through a procedure, without adequate attention to connections (Herbal-Eisenmann & Breyfogle, 2005). In contrast, open questions require students to notice their own thinking, and a string of these is called *focusing questions*. The difference at times may seem subtle, but it is the outcome that is more telling. A series of funneling questions result in channeling the student toward the predetermined correct answers, with little room left for students to consider possibilities and notice their thinking. On the other hand, a series of focusing questions can open up students' thinking and provide you with more insight into their thought processes.

Eighth-grade teacher Matthew Stewart worked with his grade-level colleague Briana Taylor, a second-year teacher, to develop focusing questions that would open up student thinking. After examining questions Ms. Taylor had developed to use with the following day's reading, she and Mr. Stewart discussed the concepts of funneling and focusing questions. Then they changed her questions just enough so that the revised ones might prompt richer responses (see Figure 3.7). After school the

> Effective teachers don't just want to know whether a student understands something, they want to see if the student can explain their thinking and apply what is understood.

Figure 3.7   Funneling and Focusing Questions

Funneling Questions	Focusing Questions
What did the character mean when she said, "I need a change of scenery"?	The character said he needed a "change of scenery." What might have caused him to say that?
What two problems is the character facing at this point in the story?	Are there any connections you could make between that remark and any problems the character might be having?
Which problem would be solved if the character left town? Which problem would be made worse?	Would a change of scenery solve the character's problems or make them worse? Why do you say so?
Can you predict what the character will do next?	Based on what you know about the character so far, what might he do next? Do you believe that is a wise thing for him to do? How would you advise him?

Available for download at **https://resources.corwin.com/vl-literacy6-12**

next day, Mr. Stewart came back to Ms. Taylor's room, and she said, "I got much richer responses from students when I used some of the questions we developed. It was much easier for me to ask follow-up questions that were meaningful, because I had more student ideas to work with. It was so much better than when I felt like I was pulling teeth to get ideas out of them."

Teaching Takeaway

Use questions to better understand student misconceptions or partial understanding.

GUIDED INSTRUCTION

Using focusing questions is an excellent way to begin guided instruction, because it has the potential of expanding, rather than constricting, student thinking. Direct instruction requires that the teacher scaffold—only as much as needed—through strategic questions, prompts, and cues, with the goal of elevating students' learning. It does *not* involve giving students the answers, or telling them how to solve a problem. Many teachers default to a pattern of questioning that has been labeled initiate-respond-evaluate, or IRE for short. In an IRE pattern, a teacher asks a question, a student provides an answer, and the teacher decides whether the answer is right or wrong. This is Durkin's (1978–79) major criticism of teachers' questioning—that it too often consists of interrogation, rather than activation of thinking.

EFFECT SIZE FOR QUESTIONING = 0.48

One of the problems with IRE is that students tend to stop thinking the minute you tell them they're right (Cazden, 1998). More damaging, however, is that giving students feedback that is limited to the correctness of their answers or methods hurts their long-term understanding and prevents them from transferring their knowledge to new situations (Schroth, 1992). Most harmful of all, however, is feedback that is limited, infrequent, and focused on the personal attributes of the student, rather than on the task, process used, and ability to influence their own learning. It takes away their ability to self-regulate (Hattie & Timperley, 2007). When you're guiding students' learning using questions, prompts, and cues, let students do as much cognitive work as possible to evaluate their own learning—especially if they're correct. When they ask you, "Is this right?" reply, *"Tell me why you think it's right and I'll listen."*

Video 12

Guided Instruction

https://resources.corwin.com/vl-literacy6-12

Effective teachers pose strategic questions to prompt the learner to move beyond answering the "what" by considering the "how." Strategic questions prompt students "to think deliberately: What do I do next? How can I best approach this next step, this next challenge, this next frustration? What thinking tool is most apt to help me here?" (McKenzie, 1997, p. 4) One way to develop skills in this area is to video-record your

Teaching Takeaway

Structure the feedback so they have the space to hypothesize, reflect on their own learning, and evaluate their own approaches as well as those of their peers.

own teaching and then watch the video later, ideally with another person, so that you can analyze your moves and determine if you are guiding students, using direct explanations, or telling them what to think. Structure the feedback so they have the space to hypothesize, reflect on their own learning, and evaluate their own approaches as well as those of their peers.

At times, of course, student responses are incorrect or show only a partial understanding of the concept or skill in question. This is the point of departure that separates expert teachers from novices. Nonexpert teachers respond more often with corrections, rather than asking another question or two to uncover students' thinking. The knee-jerk reaction is to give students the right answer—"No, that word is *flout*"—rather than being confident enough to explore why the student might have misread a word. When the teacher says, "Read that sentence again and think about the meaning. Does what you read—*flaunt*—work in the context?" You're posing a question, one that should cause the student to think. At the same time, you're providing a prompt (a reminder) for the student to monitor sense-making while reading.

If that isn't sufficient, and the student is still stumbling, then provide him with a cue, which is a more overt signal designed to shift his attention to a physical space or cognitive task (e.g., pointing to the dictionary app on the tablet when a student is stuck on a term). Based on the student's next move, you now have a lot more information to work with: Is the difficulty because he isn't monitoring his understanding, or he doesn't have a good schema of the topic, or possibly that he doesn't know how to repair his errors when the meaning is lost? These are the "pivotal events" that Ross and Gibson (2010, p. 197) attribute to expert teaching—the ability to rapidly hypothesize what instructional move should come next to move student learning forward. Simply correcting errors over and over isn't going to result in learning that lasts. However, getting students to think metacognitively, although it takes a bit longer, will.

Formative Evaluation During Guided Instruction

The benefit of noticing errors and misconceptions is that it allows for additional instruction. By observing and taking notes, you'll know which groups or individual students are stuck or need help, which ones are flying and need enrichment, and who misunderstands the concepts or lacks foundational knowledge that you will need to scaffold for them. When you do move in to guide the learning, you will be able to do so in a strategic way that provides the right amount of feedback, differentiation, and support that your students need—and not the excessive scaffolding that takes the rigor and engagement out of your tasks.

As the seventh reading comprehension lesson evolved, Ms. Okeke transitioned from modeling and thinking aloud to guided instruction, using a series of questions to probe her students' thinking and monitor their understanding. She had prepared a few of these scaffolding questions in advance, primarily focusing ones to draw her students' attention to incidents in the book when Little Man and Cassie react badly to their circumstances in school:

1. *What are the direct and indirect characterizations that tell us how Little Man is feeling? How Cassie is feeling?*

2. *What clues are we provided as to why Little Man and Cassie are so upset? How does this relate to the surroundings they live in?*

3. *Miss Crocker is upset with the students now, but why? What words and actions, by her and the children, help us to understand the source of her anger?*

She uses these questions to check in with students sitting at tables 2, 4, and 5. They'll later "pollinate ideas" as Ms. Okeke calls it, by partnering with students at tables 1, 3, and 6.

INDEPENDENT LEARNING

The learning continues, and in fact deepens, when students are able to employ what they have been learning. This can occur in four possible ways (Fisher & Frey, 2008):

- Fluency building

- Application

- Spiral review

- Extension

Fluency Building

Fluency building is especially effective when students are in the surface learning phase and need spaced practice opportunities to strengthen automaticity. For instance, students who play online vocabulary games, or who read books independently, are engaged in fluency-building independent learning.

EFFECT SIZE FOR SPACED VERSUS MASS PRACTICE = 0.71

Application

Application is arguably the most common approach to independent learning. Students engaged in application of learning are consolidating their knowledge through the transfer of skills to contexts similar to the situation in which they initially learned. As an example, Mr. Peck's Year 10 students wrote an exit slip using evidence to either support or deny the claim that society rejects innovation out of fear of the unknown. Like the author, they are applying similarly loaded language to support their positions.

Spiral Review

Spiral review, a third approach to independent learning, is one in which students revisit previously mastered content in order to prevent learning recidivism due to infrequent use. For instance, eighth-grade teachers Matthew Stewart and Briana Taylor keep the learning alive by requiring that their students use previously read class novels to compare with their current readings.

Ms. Taylor said, "Matthew was the one who suggested this. He's been doing it himself for several years. By revisiting previous readings, they deepen their understanding. For instance, when I teach about a literacy device like the use of a particular archetype, I want them to see how it has been applied in so many stories, even if archetypes weren't an instructional emphasis when we read a story a few months ago."

Teaching Takeaway

Use spiral review to foster transfer.

Ms. Taylor's students, she noted, end up consulting texts read earlier in the year to locate examples. "It's like watching light bulbs going off over their heads. They can recognize the situational archetype of the quest in a book like *The Lightning Thief*, when I teach it. But when they revisit *Keeping the Moon*, which we read last quarter, now they see that the quest archetype was there all along, even though they didn't initially notice it."

Her colleague, Mr. Stewart, added, "Just teaching about archetypes and literary devices can consume an entire school year, and if I tried to stuff all that content into one book, we'd only get to a few titles a year. When we cycle back to books we've already read, they can analyze them and gain a new understanding."

Extension

Extension is a fourth kind of independent learning in which students are asked to use what they have learned in a new way. This often requires that they research on their own and find additional information. The text-dependent question: "What does this text inspire you to do?"

(Fisher & Frey, 2014b) is an organizing tool that can be used to design extension learning. Independent learning through extension includes

- Writing

- Presenting information to peers

- Participating in debates and Socratic seminars

- Engaging in investigations

This is especially effective when the text has been utilized over multiple lessons, including those that require close and critical reading. Eleventh-grade teacher Sandra Lopez did just that as an extension of the study her students did with *Abraham Lincoln and the Self-Made Myth*. Her students are still learning how to critique arguments, so Ms. Lopez curated websites using Diigo to tag resources her students might benefit from.

"I had them research other examples of critiques like Hofstadr's," she said. One team investigated the argument that Shakespeare the man remains a mystery.

One member, Theo, said, *"The Mark Twain piece 'Is Shakespeare Dead?' was hilarious and also gave us another great example of how an author uses rhetorical techniques to challenge these 'larger than life' people."*

His friend Roberto added, *"Mark Twain is harsh! I would not want to be on his bad side because he makes valid and funny points to make his opposition look ridiculous."*

CLOSURE

A robust lesson will fall short of its full potential if the lesson doesn't include a solid closure. This is the time to return to the learning intention and success criteria in order to reestablish purpose and consolidate new knowledge. Importantly, it doesn't necessarily mean the temporal end of the lesson. Rather, consider it to be a time when you are checking for understanding more globally and inviting students to consider their own learning so far. Lesson closure can include a combination of the following:

- Revisiting the learning intention and success criteria

- Reviewing the key points of a lesson

- Posing a question that asks students to summarize (e.g., "Tell me the three most important ideas you learned this morning")

- Inviting students to draw conclusions or to notice similarities and differences based on the learning

- Asking students to rate their level of understanding (e.g., a fist-to-five method displaying the number of fingers that correspond to the level of understanding)

- Inviting further clarifying questions from students

- Previewing future learning opportunities and lessons

- Exhibiting evidence of student learning

- Creating a smooth transition to the next lesson

Using a direct instruction approach, Charles Peck has led his Year 10 students through modeling with think-alouds, guided instruction, and peer collaboration as they read and discussed the informational article on whether or not genius ideas are rejected because they are innovative and therefore frightening to society. Satisfied with their progress through frequent checks for understanding, he will soon be releasing them to further independent learning as they compose an exit ticket summarizing the author's use of loaded language in the informational article, using evidence from the text. However, before he does so, he spends a few minutes on closure to further consolidate their learning and invite self-assessment of progress toward goals. He begins with questions about the content, asking them for the most surprising facts they learned, before turning his attention to the learning intention, which concerned looking for loaded language to determine the author's point of view.

"Could you summarize, please?" he asks.

Jessica responds, *"Authors want to get their point across as strongly as possible, and their wording and structure gives you a clue as to what they think. This author in particular uses headings and strong, direct statements like 'We're literally programmed to be afraid of something we don't understand.'"*

After fielding a few more responses, he tells his students, *"Consult the writing goals you developed for yourself for this term. Since we're going to be doing some timed writing in class next, now's an excellent time to check in with them."*

CONCLUSION

Direct instruction has a solid track record for promoting acquisition, consolidation, and transfer of learning through intentional lesson design that uses an explicit approach. Although sometimes narrowly

The *VISIBLE LEARNER*

It is important for students to know what they are learning and why, but equally important is for students to know *how* they are learning. If students are able to articulate the strategies that they are using to learn, they are more likely to try those approaches again when the learning gets hard.

Arturo, a sixth grader and English learner, is developing the habit of summarizing as he reads and annotates. Although he knows how to summarize when prompted by his teacher, he does it less often when reading independently. Arturo says, *"I know I'm supposed to make some notes to summarize what I'm reading, but I don't always do it. I'm reading Crossover right now, and a bunch of my friends are reading it, too. But I kept getting the two twins confused. My friend Hector showed me how he's got a chart going in his notebook to keep the two straight."* Arturo smiled as he said, *"When I met with Ms. Rivas about my independent reading, I showed her my chart. She said what I'm doing is a form of summarizing! I can see how this is something that helps me understand, and not just something you do for school."*

Visible learners can talk about how they are learning—the strategies they used to learn.

defined as a heavily scripted program, direct instruction has elements that trace their roots to Madeline Hunter's (1982) model of mastery learning. These elements of instruction include clear statements about the learning intention and success criteria, teacher modeling and think-alouds, guided instruction through scaffolding, checks for understanding, closure, and independent learning. These practices form a solid set of practices for making skills and concepts clear to learners. However, we do not suggest that these are the only valuable teaching practices. In the next chapter, we will turn our attention to the value of dialogic teaching, instruction that requires the effective use of talk to accomplish the learning. You might be wondering about the difference between direct and dialogic approaches, given that there has been a lot of talking described in this chapter. In the next chapter, we hope you'll see a different type of talk, one in which the discussions rely on argumentation and inquiry.

4

TEACHER-LED DIALOGIC INSTRUCTION

© Michael Newman/PhotoEdit

Sixth graders Salma and Mason meet to discuss their online discussion board responses to informational articles on the foster care system, posted by their English teacher, Dawit Hussein. Each student has read and written a response to a different article. Mr. Hussein, who is facilitating peer critique sessions with his students, begins by orienting the pair and reviewing the process, and then asks them to begin.

"Remember that your goal is to give the writer useful feedback about his or her posting. I'm here to help," he said, *"but otherwise this is your time to conference with each other."*

"I'll go first," said Salma, turning to Mason, who had written a short discussion board post. *"I read your post about the system, even though parts were really sad,"* began Salma. *"I didn't know how the system can affect kids so differently."*

"Why did you like that in particular, Salma? Can you be more specific?" said Mr. Hussein. *"This will be useful for Mason to hear."*

"Yeah," said Salma. *"I was really surprised to read how different everyone's stories were in the article you read. You said that the trauma of being in foster care can contribute to mental illness later on. But the article I read tells about*

how the foster care system rescued this girl from abuse and saved her life. So what I liked was that your discussion board post gave me a different angle."

"Were there some questions you have that Salma should explain?" said Mr. Hussein, now addressing Mason, the writer.

Mason asked Salma, *"How can I improve my posting?"*

Salma offered, *"Yeah, here's one. So you said that when really little kids have lots of trauma in their lives, it can mess up their lives. But you could explain why it's worse when it's little kids,"* said Salma. *"Now you go. Can you tell me about mine? Sometimes when you retell it, it helps me figure out if I got something wrong."*

Mason comments, *"Okay, you said that the foster care system was initially put in to place to help homeless and neglected children, but that the results have been mixed throughout the years. Can you say more about that, Salma?"*

"Yeah, the article I read had personal stories from people who have gone through the system and had different experiences—both good and bad," offered Salma.

"You told me about a girl that was better off because she was in foster care," Mason said, *"but you didn't include that in your summary. It would be stronger to have a success in there, too, since you said it's mixed. If you only have a failure, then it doesn't balance."*

Mr. Hussein has been listening and is pleased with the dialogue between the students. *"I have one more question for both of you,"* he said. *"Can you give feedback about the feedback? In other words, can you tell each other how this conversation was helpful to you as a writer?"*

As the school year progresses, these middle school students will eventually be able to offer peer critiques on their own, without the teacher serving as the facilitator. But a teacher's presence in a discussion can serve as a scaffold for deepening dialogue. While Mr. Hussein's plan is to fade his support as students take over the conversation, he understands that teacher-led dialogic instruction is needed to build their communication skills. "The interesting thing I find," he said, "is that as their dialogic skills develop, their writing gets more sophisticated. That link between talk and writing? Can't be stated enough times."

Many teachers state that student discussion is critical for learning, yet despite all the talk about talk, the discouraging news is that it isn't as prevalent as one would like to believe. One review of the research on student discussion reported that its use in middle and high school classrooms varied from 14 seconds to 68 seconds per class period (Wilkinson & Nelson, 2013). Discussion time in elementary classrooms is somewhat longer. However, here the dominant talker remains the teacher, who

> Despite all the talk about talk, the discouraging news is that it is not prevalent. One review of the research on discussion reported that its use in middle and high school classrooms varied from 14 seconds to 68 seconds per class period.

relies primarily on a repertoire of recitation (question–answer sequences asking students to furnish information that is already known) and exposition (explaining and imparting information) (Alexander, 2008).

If you're questioning the results of these published studies and thinking to yourself, "Well, that's not me!" that may be entirely true. However, we challenge you to use a timer for yourself for one week to measure the amount of time you allot to discussion. To do so, use Applebee, Langer, Nystrand, and Gamoran's definition of discussion: "a free exchange of information among students and/or between at least three participants that lasts longer than 30 seconds" (2003, p. 700).

The dearth of meaningful discussion about texts, ideas, and concepts is especially unfortunate for students who are not making expected progress. Ironically, they are the ones who seem to profit most from discussion, as measured by improved reading comprehension (Murphy Soter, Hennessey, & Alexander, 2009). As we noted in the previous chapter, direct instruction is an essential instructional practice. However, it should not come at the expense of discussion. In fact, the benefits of classroom discussion, with an effect size of 0.82, are even stronger than the benefits of direct instruction. As is the case for most good things in life, though, there should always be a healthy balance between them.

EFFECTIVE TALK, NOT JUST ANY TALK

Just because students are chattering away doesn't mean they're learning. Most will do that with little prompting—on the quad, waiting in line, or sharing lunch. Those interactions are of value, especially as they develop the social and communication skills needed in everyday life. But classroom talk differs from social exchanges, and in fact represents a specific language register—what Joos (1961) describes as the *consultative mode*. This consultative mode is one of five registers he has identified—each of which sits along a broader continuum of formality:

- **Fixed or frozen:** Unchanging speech, such as reciting the Pledge of Allegiance each morning in class

- **Formal:** As in delivering a presentation to the class, where interruption is not expected or elicited

- **Consultative:** The academic discourse of the classroom, where information is exchanged and background information is provided. The consultative register is regularly used in work settings as well.

- **Casual:** The informal exchanges between friends, where prior knowledge is assumed due to shared experiences

- **Intimate:** Private exchanges among family members and the closest of friends

Students arrive to school already immersed in the intimate and casual registers, but the others are first learned in school. Of the three others (fixed, formal, and consultative), it is this last one that should occupy the greatest amount of time. However, in truth students seem to spend more time on the receiving end of the formal register, listening to the uninterrupted speech of the teacher. Yet what lies within the consultative register are some of the most significant functions in which school-aged pupils engage. Specifically, they use oral language to do the following:

- Share facts and information (e.g., "Not all the pilgrims who came to the New World were motivated by religion.")

- Speculate or find out about something (e.g., "What did the non-religious pilgrims come for? Were these settlers hoping to profit from this new endeavor?")

- Think imaginatively (e.g., "If I were a pilgrim, my biggest fear might be the witches that people said lived in the surrounding countryside. Everything was so foreign and unknown!")

Talk, in this case, serves as a platform for written expression. After all, if students don't get to verbally explain, pose questions, and narrate routinely, it's going to be much more difficult for them to do so in writing. Therefore, students must be taught how to engage in productive discussions that build and extend their knowledge, and strengthen their ability to organize their thinking using logic and rhetoric.

Teachers who create space for students to pose questions, wrestle with complex issues, clarify thinking, speculate, probe, disagree, resolve problems, and reach consensus are employing a dialogic approach to instruction. Unlike the initiate–respond–evaluate cycle of teacher questioning and student recitation (Cazden, 1988), this form of instruction assumes a higher level of authority on the part of the learners, who coconstruct knowledge under the guidance of a teacher who facilitates the discussion rather than presents information. Dialogic instruction assumes many forms, including those that are facilitated primarily by students (the subject of the next chapter), such as reciprocal teaching and peer tutoring. However, many other forms of dialogic instruction are led by the teacher, who remains the chief mediator of the discussion. Using the collective knowledge of the learning community, students consolidate, deepen, and extend their learning.

> Teachers who create space for students to pose questions, wrestle with complex issues, clarify thinking, speculate, probe, disagree, resolve problems, and reach consensus are employing a dialogic approach to instruction.

FOSTER DEEP LEARNING AND TRANSFER

Discussions can have a profound effect on shaping and transforming the understanding of a student. You'll recall that in Chapter 1 we discussed that the process of progressing from surface to deep, and from deep to transfer learning involves students moving initially from one idea to many ideas. The deepening really accelerates when students begin to transform concepts such that they see how ideas are related. In the transfer phase of learning, students are extending ideas to new and novel situations.

How does this deepening actually occur? It is accomplished in a multitude of ways:

- At the surface phase of learning, students figure out what they already know about a topic, and determine where their gaps may lie.

- They share their opinions with one another and listen to those who agree and disagree with them.

- This acquisition and consolidation of knowledge continues as learners deepen their understanding, especially as they find connections and further organize their thinking.

- They read with texts and then against them, thinking critically about what is told and what is not. They consider bias and question the commonplace.

- They further deepen their knowledge as they read *across* texts, especially those that offer contradictory perspectives.

Discussion, in small groups and with the whole class, is fodder for thinking. But meaningful discussion doesn't just spontaneously happen, or at least not without a teacher's intention to cultivate a climate where exchange is expected.

If we could sum up our advice to teachers who want to encourage classroom discussion, we would say, "Teachers, stop talking so much." This signals to students that they have a hand in controlling the conversation. As John has noted many times, we would never tolerate a personal conversation that adhered to the same rules as much of the classroom talk encountered worldwide. Would you ever want to spend time talking to someone who decided what could be discussed and when it would end, asked questions but rarely gave you space to do the same, and spent most of the time interrogating you to find out if you were paying attention? Yet that's the dynamic in too many classrooms, for too many

> Deep learning really accelerates when students begin to transform concepts such that they see how ideas are related.

instructional minutes. No wonder so many students become progressively more disengaged the longer they attend school. They figure out that we're not listening.

LISTEN CAREFULLY

When was the last time you read research on teacher listening? If your response is "never," it's possibly because there is very little on the topic, despite its importance in classroom discussion. Much of the research on adult listening in schools skews toward empathetic listening as a counseling tool to be employed when a student is troubled or upset. Empathetic listening—maintaining eye contact, using body language that signals acceptance, revoicing student statements—is of great value in these situations.

Video 13
Teacher Listening
*https://resources.corwin.com/
vl-literacy6-12*

Yet these tools can be applied in discussions of academic content, too. A teacher's nonverbal signals and compassionate listening can encourage students to take risks, publicly speculate, ask questions, and pose arguments. Teacher listening during student discussions is challenging because we're simultaneously doing two things—we are listening *to*, and listening *for*. Listening *to* a student is the act of locating identity within her utterances. In doing so, we consider how her insights and questions in turn inform us about who she is as an individual. At the same time, we are listening *for* the turns in the conversation that signal content understandings and misconceptions. It's awfully difficult to do both, and requires self-discipline. Parker (2010) offers that a self-disciplined listener in the classroom operates under three guidelines—reciprocity, humility, and caution:

- **Reciprocity** is giving the speaker the floor in order to represent herself, rather than falling prey to the assumption that you can do it better since she is an adolescent and you are the adult.

- **Humility** is adopting the assumption that one cannot know another's experiences and point of view, and that it may take time for this to be revealed.

- **Caution** is suppressing the urge to chime in with every thought that may be passing through your head.

> Providing a forum where someone can speak without interruption, using nonverbal language that communicates receptiveness, and allowing silences to happen are all deliberate actions on the part of the teacher.

Listening, of course, isn't passive. Providing a forum where someone can speak without interruption, using nonverbal language that communicates receptiveness, and allowing silences to happen are all deliberate actions on the part of the teacher. These are paired with conversational moves that facilitate discussion.

Video 14
Facilitate and
Guide Discussion

*https://resources.corwin.com/
vl-literacy6-12*

FACILITATE AND GUIDE DISCUSSION

Students are still emerging adults, and they have to learn how to have focused academic conversation. The prompts that propel a discussion that is lagging often need to come from the teacher. Over time, students incorporate these moves into their conversations with peers. These conversational teacher moves are intended to organize ideas and ensure productive discussion (Michaels, O'Connor, Hall, & Resnick, 2010, pp. 27–32):

- Marking conversation: "That's an important point."

- Keeping the channels open: "Did everyone hear what she just said?"

- Keeping everyone together: "Who can repeat . . . ?"

- Challenging students: "That's a great question, Rebecca. What do the rest of you think?"

- Revoicing: "So are you saying that . . . ?"

- Asking students to explain or restate: "Who disagrees or agrees, and why?"

- Linking contributions: "Who can add on to what he said?"

- Pressing for accuracy: "Where can we find that?"

- Building on prior knowledge: "How does this connect . . . ?"

- Pressing for reasoning: "Why do you think that?"

- Expanding reasoning: "Take your time. Say more."

- Recapping: "What have we discovered?"

These conversational moves should be punctuated by wait time, both after posing a thought provoking question (Wait Time 1) and again after a student responds (Wait Time 2). The first wait time allows students to process and contemplate the question, while the second wait time provides the speaker with the space to elaborate on his answer. Although less readily recognized, the practice of ensuring wait time also allows the teacher to process the conversation, and results in increased quality of teacher questions (Rowe, 1986). Equipped with the tools to listen carefully to children, to facilitate and guide discussion, and to provide them the space and time to think, teachers can leverage dialogic instruction to deepen knowledge.

In the next section of the chapter, we will elaborate on the first of two facets of dialogic instruction. The first are the *teacher-led approaches* that

Teaching Takeaway

Challenge yourself by using a timer for one week to measure the amount of time you allot to discussion. Use Applebee and colleagues' definition of discussion: "a free exchange of information among students and/or between at least three participants that lasts longer than 30 seconds" (2003, p. 700). See if you can increase the amount of time you devote to effective discussion using the techniques described above.

The *VISIBLE LEARNER*

When teachers engage students in the type of accountable talk described in this section, students begin to use these approaches on their own. In fact, the conversation markers that teachers use can become students' self-regulation strategies. There are a number of tools that students can use to self-regulate, and the discussion markers can be some of those.

Cody, a student in ninth grade, was overheard saying to herself, *"Is this credible and accurate? I need to keep looking."* When asked about this, she responded, *"I found some information that looked good, but I wanted to make sure it was actually right. So, I checked it against other information I had and realized that yes, it was."*

Visible learners can use self-regulation strategies.

are primarily directed by the teacher, but with the intention of promoting student discussion. These are more formally structured than other aspects of dialogic instruction, and the teacher plays an active role in propelling conversation. The second fact, which is the subject of the next chapter, comprises the *student-led tools* that allow the teacher to step back further as teens share the responsibility in directing these interactions (Caughlan, Juzwik, Borsheim-Black, Kelly, & Fine, 2013). While we have assigned them to one category or another, in practice these tools are used more fluidly, as teacher and students respond to one another.

TEACHER-LED TOOLS FOR DIALOGIC INSTRUCTION

Teachers utilize a number of tools to apprentice students into engaging in meaningful dialogue and discussion with one another. In addition, these tools activate, build, and extend knowledge, using children's thinking as the fulcrum, rather than the teacher's presentation of information. Anticipation guides, which are described in more detail in the section that follows, are a form of advance organizers specifically designed to provide students with statements that cause them to question. These can be used as an effective tool for activating prior knowledge.

> EFFECT SIZE FOR BEHAVIORAL ORGANIZERS/ ADJUNCT QUESTIONS = 0.41

Anticipation Guides

An anticipation guide is a teacher-prepared list of statements based on a specific text or unit of study. The purpose is to activate prior knowledge, encourage predictions, and stimulate curiosity about a topic (Head & Readence, 1986). However, an anticipation guide can be used for more than just cataloging current understanding of a topic. These guides are useful for promoting class discussion, because they can spark debate and foster the inevitable need to consult other sources of information. The steps to creating a guide are fairly simple:

1. **Identify the major concepts.** What are the main ideas in the passage or unit of study?

2. **Consider your students' prior knowledge.** What misconceptions are they most likely to hold?

3. **Write five or ten statements pertaining to the unit.** Don't make them all factual—be sure to create open-ended statements as well. Look again to your major concepts to make sure you are creating statements that relate to larger concepts rather than isolated facts. For example, for a reading about drama in literature, the titles of various plays would not be useful.

Video 15
Teacher-Led Questioning

https://resources.corwin.com/ vl-literacy6-12

Markita Jones used an anticipation guide to introduce her tenth-grade students to their study of the Holocaust, a cross-curricular topic the entire grade level has been studying. Ms. Jones prepared the anticipation guide (see Figure 4.1) to encourage her students to begin thinking about the content. Before the class had read about, discussed, watched videos, conducted Internet searches, and carefully examined the topic, they used the anticipation guide to formulate questions.

The discussion portion of the lesson was an essential component. Although the teacher didn't provide the correct answers at the outset, she did want her students to consider what they did and did not know, and how they might learn more to confirm or disconfirm their thinking. After completing the anticipation guide and tallying the responses for each item, they began to debate the second one in particular, concerning the causes of the Holocaust. Several students said they answered *false* because they believed only Jewish people were targeted by Hitler's regime. Without revealing the answer, Ms. Jones said, *"I can see there's disagreement. How would we go about learning more about this? I can write down your ideas for sources and research ideas."*

Within a few minutes, her students listed (1) locating books and articles from credible sources about the Holocaust, (2) consulting museums and other agencies about the topic, and (3) asking their great-grandparents (if available) about their memories from that time. From time to time, she would ask students to elaborate further on their statements, saying, *"Tell us more about your idea"* or *"What hunches do you have about this question?"*

When the class finished, she posted their suggestions on the class's learning management system and said, *"As you explore this subject in this class and your other content classes, keep in mind the sources of information you're looking for. This list is going to be a good beginning as we fact-check."*

Ms. Jones later said that the anticipation guide served as a good preassessment of their knowledge. "I'll readminister this at the end of the unit to assess growth," she said. "This is a good tool for me to use to measure my impact on learning."

Figure 4.1   Anticipation Guide for Holocaust Interdisciplinary Unit

Name: _____ Date: _____

Anticipation Guide for the Holocaust Unit

Directions: Read each statement and write a "+" for true statements and a "–" for false statements.

Statement	Before Our Study	After Our Study
The Nazi movement involved only willing participants.		
The Holocaust occurred in Germany.		
The main purpose of concentration camps was to kill people quickly.		
Jews were the only people targeted by the Nazis.		
Outside of Germany, few countries were affected by the Holocaust.		
People with disabilities were targeted by the Nazis.		
The Treaty of Versailles was good for Germany.		
Ghettos were safe houses for Jewish people.		
Hitler's hatred for Jewish people was based on religion.		
No one helped victims of the Holocaust.		
America was not affected by the Holocaust.		

Available for download at **https://resources.corwin.com/vl-literacy6-12**

Pinwheel Discussions

This approach comes to us from one of our favorite teachers, Sarah Brown Wessling, a high school English teacher and 2010 National Teacher of the Year. As we have stated before, meaningful discussion requires that students understand the demands of true participation. In a pinwheel discussion, students are divided into four teams, with the purpose of comparing and contrasting previously read text. The first three teams address issues of content (e.g., three different poets), and the fourth team is what Wessling calls "the provocateurs." In our example, the three content teams meet to consolidate their knowledge of the topic. For instance, a team assigned to Robert Frost's poem "Nothing Gold Can Stay" meet to review, while the team assigned to Dylan Thomas's "Do Not Go Gentle Into That Good Night" review their assigned poem. The third group, assigned to William Carlos Williams's "Landscape With the Fall of Icarus," prepares to represent this poem. As they prepare, the teacher meets separately with the provocateurs, whose job it will be to lead the questioning and discussion.

After the teams have prepared, the first group of four—one member representing each of the four teams—sits in the center of the room. Each representative's teammates sit just behind their representative. The discussion begins, led by the teacher and the provocateur. After a proscribed period (usually 7 to 10 minutes), the teams "pinwheel" as a new representative from each of the four teams takes the center chair. This continues until all students have had a turn in the discussion. Importantly, the teacher's role is an active one. The teacher poses questions when the provocateurs falter, revoicing and restating as needed when team representatives make a point that is in need of clarification. In addition, the teacher keeps a tally on the board of the conversational moves of the participants, noting each time a student

- Makes a connection.

- Proposes a new idea.

- Poses a follow-up that propels the discussion.

- Uses textual evidence to support a position.

These active visual reminders assist all the students in recognizing when valuable turns in the discussion take place, and signal to them when particular conversational moves are lacking. We use this version of pinwheel discussions to prepare students for fishbowl discussions, which are more student directed. We will expand on fishbowl discussions in the next chapter, but keep pinwheel discussions in mind as a method for preparing students for student-led fishbowls.

Opinion Stations

Adolescents are full of strong opinions about virtually everything, although they don't necessarily have all the evidence they need to support their claims. Opinion stations can assist students in determining where they stand on an issue, and then in listening closely to the positions of others. This is where discussion is of great value. We use opinion stations often, but then always follow up with whole class discussion, allowing students to change their opinions when persuaded by the arguments of others. In other words, we want to develop students' critical thinking and listening skills, not just their ability to identify their own opinions.

Sandra Lopez uses opinion stations regularly in her eleventh-grade English class to organize extended discussions. (Her lesson plan can be found in Figure 4.2.) Posted in the four corners of her classroom are signs reading, respectively, "Strongly Agree," "Agree," "Disagree," and "Strongly Disagree." Her class has been reading the Lorraine Hansberry play *A Raisin in the Sun* and comparing it to the Langston Hughes poem that gave the play its title, "Harlem (A Dream Deferred)." They have reached the point in Act III when the dreams of the main characters are colliding. Ms. Lopez poses an opinion question to the students and asks them to write independently for three minutes before choosing a station. *"Please give thought to this statement,"* she asks. *"Hansberry chose this title to express how sweet a longstanding dream can be when it is finally achieved. Do you agree? Disagree? Write about that."* Ms. Lopez then directs students to spend the next few minutes writing about their opinion, listing reasons and evidence to support their claims. After the students have finished writing, she displays the opinion prompt again and asks them to move to their corner of choice. *"Don't forget to take a copy of the play and the poem with you, as well as something to write with. You'll want to take notes,"* she says.

After revisiting the learning intention and success criteria, she directs them to discuss their opinions with their like-minded peers. *"You'll need to accomplish three things during this preparation phase,"* Ms. Lopez tells them. *"The first is to record the evidence and reasons you'll be using on the chart paper I've posted in your corners. That's means you'll need to select someone to record for your group. The third decision is that you'll also need to select two spokespersons to represent your group's position."*

During this time, the teacher checks in with each group to gauge progress, and checks in with Kendra, who uses a smartpen, so that she can record the discussion. After the groups have signaled that they are ready, Ms. Lopez tells them that she will also record each group's major points as they emerge throughout the discussion that will follow. *"This is exactly*

> We want to develop students' critical thinking and listening skills, not just their ability to identify their own opinion.

Figure 4.2   Lesson Plan for Opinion Stations in *A Raisin in the Sun* by Lorraine Hansberry

Assessed Need: I have noticed that my students need: An opportunity to make connections between Hughes's poem and the title of the play.
Standard(s) Addressed: SL.11–12.4. Present information, findings, and supporting evidence (e.g., reflective, historical investigation, response to literature presentations), conveying a clear and distinct perspective and a logical argument, such that listeners can follow the line of reasoning, alternative or opposing perspectives are addressed, and the organization, development, substance, and style are appropriate to purpose, audience, and a range of formal and informal tasks. Use appropriate eye contact, adequate volume, and clear pronunciation. RL.11–12.9. Demonstrate knowledge of 18th-, 19th-, and early 20th-century foundational works of American Literature, including how two or more texts from the same period treat similar themes or topics.
Text(s) I Will Use: <u>A Raisin in the Sun</u> and "Harlem (A Dream Deferred)"
Learning Intention for This Lesson: We will formulate our opinions in writing and in collaboration with others, and listen to the arguments put forth by opposing groups.
Success Criteria for This Lesson: I use evidence to form opinions and demonstrate flexibility of thought through a willingness to remain open to other possibilities. This will come in the form of a short constructed written response exit ticket at the end of the class period.
Direct Instruction: Model: Strategies/skills/concepts to emphasize   Students have used opinion stations before, but briefly review directions for using them. Remind students that when we reach the stage where groups voice their opinions, they will be free to change stations to reflect their changing opinions.   Guide and Scaffold: Questions to ask   Ask, "Do you agree or disagree with the statement that Hansberry selected this line from Hughes's poem as a message that a dream deferred, and then achieved, is sweeter for the wait? Students will be directed to write independently for three minutes, listing reasons and evidence that support their opinion.   Assess: These are the students who will need further support   Make sure that Kendra has her smartpen charged so she can capture the discussion as she makes notes.
Dialogic Instruction: Teacher-Directed Tools   Opinion stations: Display the following statement: "Hansberry chose this title to express how sweet a longstanding dream can be when it is finally achieved." After students write and then self-select the opinion station that best reflects their thinking (SA, A, D, SD), prompt the groups to hold a discussion and list their reasons/evidence on chart paper. The groups should select two spokespersons to share with the class.   • Direct the first group's spokespersons to lay out why their group holds a particular position, using the collective notes they have gathered (five minutes).   • Direct members of other groups to pose clarifying questions, but do not allow them to attempt to persuade students to adopt their position instead (three minutes).   • Vote with your feet: Invite students to change groups if they have been persuaded   Repeat the process for each of the remaining groups.   Student-Enacted Tools   N/A

Assess: These are the students who will need further support

Watch for Jessica's participation as she typically stands in the middle of the room and does not join a group. Hector had difficulty with the speed of the interactions and may need some translation.

Feedback Opportunities: I will record major points made by each group and review positions.

Independent Learning and Closure:

Closure: Remind students of learning intention and success criteria. Revisit writing criteria for evidence and persuasive devices before they write in their journals.

Independent Learning: Based on the opinion stations discussion, revisit your independent writing from the beginning of the period. Using the same prompt, explain your opinion using evidence shared in the discussions (small group and whole class). This is a 10-minute timed writing of a short constructed response, and it will be your exit ticket for today's lesson.

Available for download at **https://resources.corwin.com/vl-literacy6-12**

what careful and critical listeners do during a discussion," she said. *"They mentally, and sometimes physically, list the salient points."*

The Strongly Disagree group is asked to present their argument first. During the next several minutes, Stefan and Ofelia serve as their group's spokespersons and outline the following points:

- The production of raisins requires that all of the moisture of the grape is lost, leaving a dried fruit that is small and shriveled compared to its original state.

- Walter Lee's monologue in Act II, Scene 3 about his refusal to go to work for three days indicates how aimless and without direction his life has become.

- Beneatha says in Act III that she stopped caring about her dream of being a doctor because "it was a child's way of seeing things— or an idealist."

- Mama says that people would tell her when she was young that she "aimed too high all the time." She goes on to say with resignation that "me and Big Walter never learned right."

After the Strongly Disagree group finishes, she invites the other three groups to ask any clarifying questions. *"Remember though, you're not arguing back. You'll have time to state your positions, too."*

Several students ask for page numbers so they can annotate their scripts, and one student asks for confirmation that Beneatha's remark came during an exchange with Asagai. After closing out this portion of the discussion, Ms. Lopez says, *"Okay, now vote with your feet. If you are persuaded by their argument, please join them. If you are resolute or want to hear more, remain where you are."*

This pattern continues for three more rounds as each group presents their opinions and supporting evidence. Next will be the Strongly Agree group, followed by the Disagree and Agree groups.

"These last two groups tend to have a more nuanced view, so I save them for later in the discussion," she explains.

Teaching Takeaway

Scaffold students with structured discussion before asking them to write and claim a final opinion.

Ms. Lopez interjects as needed to maintain the structure of the discussion and ask additional clarifying questions. Each round ends with another reshuffling as students vote with their feet. Because the groups' composition changes slightly with each round, she checks to see if new spokespersons are needed. In the meantime, she records major points made by each group. At the end of the fourth round of discussion, students return to their tables, with poems and scripts further annotated. *"In the remaining 15 minutes of class, you're going to complete a short constructed response that will be your exit ticket for the period,"* says the teacher. *"Take a look at what you wrote at the beginning of class. Has your opinion changed, or has your original opinion strengthened? Please address that question first, and then write a justification of your opinion using evidence cited in the small group discussions, or in the whole class discussion."*

With that, students turn back to their independent writing, now bolstered by the discussion that took place over the last hour.

CLOSE AND CRITICAL READING

EFFECT SIZE FOR QUESTIONING = 0.48

EFFECT SIZE FOR REPEATED READING PROGRAMS = 0.67

The instructional practice of close reading has been used with older students for a century (Fisher & Frey, 2012). The purpose is to build the habit of reading closely to ascertain deeper comprehension. What is especially powerful about close reading is that it draws upon several high-impact instructional routines, typically with text that is more complex relative to the reader's independent reading level, and it is meant to stretch the student's reading comprehension through a questioning and rereading protocol. In addition, close reading requires students to annotate text. Importantly, the intent is to spur critical analysis of text using a teacher-led dialogic approach, and not simply to show or tell students what to think. For this reason, we often choose texts that have the potential to spark rich discussion.

Because the nature of close reading involves careful inspection of text, it can be time consuming if the text is too long. This is not to say that long-format novels and informational books can't be used. Rather, key passages are chosen in order to focus students on denser passages where deeper meaning might otherwise be lost. However, these insights will not be reached if we simply tell students why a passage is meaningful. We shudder to think how many books we have ruined in our own teaching careers because we were so eager to tell them why it was so meaningful, rather than providing the space for students to engage critically with the text. On the other hand, it is not sufficient to simply hand them a complex text and then hope for the best. A close reading protocol, led by the teacher, can build the mental habits needed to understand complex texts. Figure 4.3 contains elements and conditions of a close reading.

Charles Peck's Year 10 students are reading a class text, the novella *Anthem* by Ayn Rand, in their collaborative reading groups. The novella is set in a dystopian society where individuality and new ideas

> EFFECT SIZE FOR
> STUDY SKILLS = **0.63**

> EFFECT SIZE FOR
> CLASSROOM
> DISCUSSION = **0.82**

Figure 4.3   **Characteristics of Close Reading in Upper Grades**

Elements	Close Reading in Upper Grades
Text Selection	Text complexity is slightly higher than in texts the student takes on during other phases of reading instruction.
Initial Reading	Students are more likely to read the text independently, although they are not fully grasping its deeper meaning.
Annotation	Students familiar with annotation practices are marking text independently, and adding to their annotations throughout class discussions.
Repeated Readings	Students are rereading independently or with minimal support. Students may also have access to audio supports (a poet reading her poem, a teacher reading dialogue, a peer reading a key sentence).
Responding to Texts	Students write collaboratively and independently. They investigate, research, discuss, and debate compelling questions.

Source: Fisher, D., Frey, N., & Lapp, D. (2015). *Text complexity: Stretcher readers with texts and tasks* (2nd ed.). Thousand Oaks, CA: Corwin.

 Available for download at **https://resources.corwin.com/vl-literacy6-12**

are outlawed. The struggle of the main character, Equality 7-2521, to create an identity for himself has sparked a number of discussions about individuality and conformity. The previous day, Mr. Peck read aloud the short passage where Equality 7-2521 is reflecting on the newfound personhood he received only by leaving his society and learning to read. Mr. Peck and the class processed this scene, which is complex not only in its ideas but also in a shift in narrative style, as the main character switches from using plural to singular pronouns in describing himself.

Today, they are resuming the story and will read about the main character's reflection on his identity as an individual in a society he is founding with his partner, the Golden One. Therefore, Mr. Peck has chosen to use this passage for a close reading lesson. (His lesson can be found in Figure 4.4 on pages 90–91.) This chapter is a turning point in the text and reveals much of the meaning in the novella. Mr. Peck structures his questions to foster comprehension through four phases of deepening understanding (Fisher, Frey, Anderson, & Thayre, 2015):

- What does the text say? (literal)

- How does the text work? (structural)

- What does the text mean? (inferential)

- What does the text inspire you to do? (interpretive)

Mr. Peck invites his students to read the passage silently to themselves, and then read it a second time to make notes to themselves about questions or observations they have. (He had photocopied these pages from their books so they could annotate directly on the text.) After asking several literal questions to ensure they understood what the text said, he moves to the second phase, which focuses on organizational structures and word choice. *"Take a look at the narration—what has changed in how Equality refers to himself?"* he asks.

Several students immediately answer "I" (which is right there in the sentence), and Mr. Peck continues, *"So why is that important? The author put that in there, and we know by now she doesn't waste words."*

Shelley answers, *"Well, before it was just 'we,' but now he's read books and learned the word 'I.'"*

One of her classmates, Kauzee, expands on this idea, saying, *"That's true, but it seems like more than just learning a new word—his ideas about himself seem different. The tone is different."*

Mr. Peck asks Kauzee to show where he sees the tone shift, and Kauzee points out the line: *"The word 'We' is as lime poured over men, which sets*

A close reading protocol, led by the teacher, can build the mental habits needed to understand complex texts.

and hardens to stone, and crushes all beneath it, and that which is white and that which is black are lost equally in the grey of it."

The students ponder this section while Kauzee offers, *"I don't really get how a lime fits in, but the words* crushes, black, grey, *and* lost *seem dark and negative to me."* Several students express agreement with Kauzee and also some confusion at Rand's word choice. Mr. Peck says, *"It seems as though we are in agreement about Rand's tone, so let's take a look at this word,* lime. *Is it possible she's talking about a real lime?"* Most of the students look at one another shaking their heads. *"Do we know any other uses for this word,* lime?"

Kassandra raises her hand and says, *"I remember a lab from science class where we watched a short video about lime dissolving things, but it looked like a powder, so maybe lime is also a type of powder that destroys thing?"*

Mr. Peck surveys the class, *"Would that make sense?"* Most of the class nods.

He transitions to the third phase (What does the text mean?) and says, *"Let's consider that line again. What type of literary device is that?"* Nicholas, seated in the back, raises his hand and says, *"Oh, it's a metaphor! She's saying 'we' is like this stuff that breaks people down."*

Mr. Peck considers this and asks, *"Well, what do you all think? Could the word 'we' be so powerful it destroys men?"*

Now Sumanta enters the conversation. *"I don't know if it's so much the word, but the idea from his society that no one can be individual—that's what breaks people down. So, we should never work with others because they might bring us down."*

"What do we think?" asks Mr. Peck. *"Could this be what Rand is trying to tell us?"*

"Well, I don't think always, because she says, 'And we shall join our hands when we wish, or walk alone when we so desire.' So I think it's alright to work together sometimes, as long as it doesn't take away from our individuality. I think Rand is saying it should be our choice when we work together and when we go alone," Thomas observes.

Mr. Peck signals for quiet and repeats Thomas's statement. *"It should be our choice when we work together and when we go alone. . . ."* He lets that linger in the air.

Sumanta speaks next. *"Yeah, I can see that, actually. It seems like she is okay with what individuals do with themselves as long as* they *decide, because she says 'I shall choose only such as please me.' Still though, she calls 'we' evil, so it's hard to see her being okay with all kinds of working together."*

Mr. Peck smiles and says, *"I can see you're all puzzling over this. Take a look at the line toward the end when Equality says, 'I am done with the monster of*

Figure 4.4   Lesson Plan for *Anthem* by Ayn Rand

Assessed Need: I have noticed that my students need: *To examine more carefully how Rand's choice of shifting pronouns communicates the novella's message about identity.*
Standard(s) Addressed: *Key Stage 4: Reading: Understand and critically evaluate texts, drawing on knowledge of the purpose, audience for and context of the writing, including its social, historical and cultural context and the literary tradition to which it belongs, to inform evaluation.* *Seeking evidence in the text to support a point of view, including justifying inferences with evidence.* *Analyzing a writer's choice of vocabulary, form, grammatical and structural features, and evaluating their effectiveness and impact.*
Text(s) I Will Use: *Anthem*
Learning Intention for This Lesson: *Examine the shift in Equality-2521's shifting use of pronouns to describe himself, and link that to the author's message about identity.*
Success Criteria for This Lesson: *I will write a timed response explaining Rand's stance about individual and collective identities, using evidence from Part 12 to support claims.*
Direct Instruction: Model: Strategies/skills/concepts to emphasize *Review conclusions from yesterday's collaborative discussions, and model annotation in the first paragraph of today's close reading (Part 12).* *"I am highlighting and noting in the margin that the act of reading brought Equality to tears, which he had never known before. The connection I am making is that the act of reading is <u>eye opening</u>, and his discovery of the word 'I' is triggering this imagery for me as I associate the word 'I,' the eye that sheds a tear, and an eye-opening moment in his life."* Guide and Scaffold: Questions to ask *Are there any words or phrases that are confusing to you?* Assess: These are the students who will need further support *Christina and Ben have been absent this week; give them time to catch up with the story prior to the lesson.*
Dialogic Instruction: Teacher-Directed Tools *Close reading questions for discussion:* *What does the text say? (literal)* • *Who is the speaker?* • *Where is this excerpt located in the context of the story? How do you know?* *How does the text work? (structural)* • *What is the tone of the excerpt? Note specific words or phrases that informed your thinking.* • *Where does the author use metaphor? To what end?* *What does the text mean? (inferential)* • *What does the author mean when she says, "Let each man keep his temple untouched and undefiled"? "Then let him join hands with others if he wishes, but only beyond his holy threshold."*

• Reword this phrase: "It [we] is the word by which the depraved steal the virtue of the good, by which the weak steal the might of the strong, by which the fools steal the wisdom of the sages."

What does the text inspire you to do? (interpretive)

What do you think Rand's attitude toward working together is? Is she against all versions of "we"? Based on what we discussed, what do you think she would say about voluntary teamwork? Be sure to tell me why you are making that conclusion using evidence from the excerpt.

Student-Enacted Tools

Students should be encouraged to develop their own questions about the text.

Assess: These are the students who will need further support

AJ, Kalid, and Stephanie need support with vocabulary.

Feedback Opportunities: Use questions, prompts, and cues to facilitate conversation. Phrases that I want to be mindful to use include these:

• "Tell us more about that."

• "How does your remark link to _____'s?"

• Repeat especially insightful statements by students to generate further discussion.

Independent Learning and Closure:

Closure: Remind students of learning intention and success criteria, and refer them to the writing rubric we use for short pieces.

Independent Learning: What do you think Rand's attitude toward working together is? Is she against all versions of "we"? Based on what we discussed, what do you think she would say about voluntary teamwork? Be sure to tell me why you are making that conclusion using evidence from Part 12.

*"We," the word of serfdom, of plunder, of misery, falsehood and shame. . . . '
What do you think Rand's attitude toward working together is? Is she against all versions of 'we'? Based on what we discussed, what do you think she would say about voluntary teamwork? Be sure to tell me why you are making that conclusion using evidence from the excerpt."* With that, his students begin to write, analyzing what Ayn Rand might say about teamwork.

SCAFFOLDED READING WITH SMALL GROUPS

Small group scaffolded reading instruction has long been a hallmark of the effective literacy teacher's classroom. While it has been called various names throughout the previous century, including high/middle/low ability reading groups (Gray, 1925), directed reading activity (Betts, 1946), or three-to-five groups (Marita, 1965), the central concept has always been to teach small needs-based groups of students to comprehend a text based on the skills and strategies they are developing. It's not tracking or ability grouping in that the groups are not permanent, but rather based on the needs of the students at a moment in time. There's a big difference. Scaffolded reading is part of the overall structure and fabric of the English school classroom and allows teachers an opportunity to observe their students reading and thinking so that they can make appropriate adjustments in instruction. Scaffolded reading in middle and high school classrooms serves three purposes: (1) preview a later reading, (2) build the skills of a specific group of students, and (3) extend a close reading (Fisher, Frey, & Lapp, 2015).

Scaffolded reading lessons are typically between 10 and 20 minutes in length and occur while the rest of the class works collaboratively. Because secondary teachers don't have the same number of instructional minutes as their elementary colleagues, English teachers might only meet with one small group of students each day. Although scaffolded reading lessons do not need to follow a rigid sequence of instruction, several components are generally recognized and recommended. First and foremost, scaffolded reading includes discussion between the teacher and the students. The small group format allows for a more focused conversation based on the text that has been read. If the whole class can engage in the reading and discussion, a close reading protocol might be more useful.

Seventh-grade English teacher Simone Okeke is devoting her scaffolded reading time on this day to build the skills of five students related to their ability to locate evidence in the text. Her lesson plan is featured in Figure 4.5.

Figure 4.5   Scaffolded Reading Lesson for "Charles" by Shirley Jackson

Assessed Need: I have noticed that my students need: I noticed that Julia, Willy, Carmelo, Kevin, and Anissa need more time to discuss the role of the narrator in shaping our understanding of the text and its surprise ending.
Standard(s) Addressed: TEKS Grade 7 (6) Reading/Comprehension of Literary Text/Fiction. Students understand, make inferences and draw conclusions about the structure and elements of fiction and provide evidence from text to support their understanding. Students are expected to: (c) analyze different forms of point of view, including first-person, third-person omniscient, and third-person limited.
Text(s) I Will Use: The short story "Charles" by Shirley Jackson
Learning Intention for This Lesson: We will look for evidence specific to the narrator that demonstrates the mismatch between her perceptions of her son and his true nature.

Success Criteria for This Lesson: I will gather and use textual evidence in our discussion about a mother's blind spot when it comes to her child, and write a short response speculating on the conversation that might occur between the two main characters after the ending of the story.

Direct Instruction:

Model: Strategies/skills/concepts to emphasize

After they reread the last page of the story, I will model and demonstrate how I locate words and phrases that give me insight about the mother's perception of her son, Laurie, and her opinions about Charles.

Have students work together to construct a t-chart of the mother's opinions of Laurie and Charles.

Guide and Scaffold: Questions to ask

Ask them to reread the last page of the story to refresh their memories about the surprise ending.

Assess: These are the students who will need further support

Anissa was disengaged from the lesson yesterday, and this may continue today. Bring her into the discussion early by addressing the first question to her.

Dialogic Instruction:

Teacher-Directed Tools

Discussion questions:

- What evidence do you find that the mother thinks Laurie is a sweet boy?
- What evidence do you find that Laurie's actions aren't as innocent as his mother might think?
- Why would his mother kept changing the subject whenever Laurie was disrespectful to his father?
- How does the mother envision Charles's mother? Why would she have this image?
- Why do you believe Laurie thought it was necessary to create a fictitious classmate, Charles?

Student-Enacted Tools

Remind students to generate questions as they read.

Assess: These are the students who will need further support

Provide annotation support for Kristen, Ashley, Frankie, and Nicholas.

Feedback Opportunities: I will start the t-chart for them, and then have them work on it collaboratively to log evidence for use in the discussion. This will give me an opportunity to observe how accurately they write and spell.

Independent Learning and Closure: Closure: Remind students of learning intention and success criteria.

Independent Learning: When they return to their tables, have these students write a response on the class discussion board about "Charles." What might his mother say to Laurie after returning from the PTA meeting, now knowing that Charles is not real?

"I selected these students based on the formative information I collected from yesterday's lesson—their written responses," she explained. Using the previous day's text, "Charles" (Jackson, 1949), she has them first reread the last page of the short story to remind them about the surprise ending. There are two key reasons for doing this:

- Engaging in repeated readings of the same text builds fluency: the ability to read smoothly, accurately, and with expression.

- Rereading aids in students' ability to recall information and in their ability to incorporate new information into their thinking—both of which are important when reentering a partially read text.

Following the rereading, Ms. Okeke opens the discussion with some brief modeling about how she locates words and phrases that give her insight about the narrator.

"As we discussed yesterday in the close reading, we as readers were led astray by the mother's beliefs about her little boy, Laurie. When I reread the opening paragraph, I saw two clues that set up the contrast: She described her son as a 'sweet-voiced nursery school tot replaced by a long-trousered, swaggering character, who forgot to stop at the corner to wave goodbye to me.' I'm going to set up a t-chart contrasting her perceptions so I can keep track of the evidence."

Soon Ms. Okeke has her students join in constructing the t-chart, looking for evidence of the mother's beliefs about her son as well as her beliefs about Charles, the classmate her son keeps talking about.

"After we set this up, we'll have a discussion about this topic," says the teacher. *"So let's start,"* Ms. Okeke begins after the students have completed the t-chart. *"My first question is this: What evidence did you find that the mother thinks Laurie is a sweet boy? Anissa, I'd love to hear your thoughts about this."* Referencing the chart they have constructed, Anissa offers, *"Well, she said that Charles was a bad influence on Laurie."*

"Can you read where you found that?" asked Ms. Okeke. *"It's a great example."* Anissa finds the passage and reads it to the group. *"That's a good example,"* Ms. Okeke said. The discussion continued as the teacher asked a number of other questions to guide their thinking:

- What evidence do you find that Laurie's actions aren't as innocent as his mother might think?

- Why would his mother kept changing the subject whenever Laurie was disrespectful to his father?

- How does the mother envision Charles' mother? Why would she have this image?

- Why do you believe Laurie thought it was necessary to create a fictitious classmate, Charles?

Whenever possible, Ms. Okeke steered the discussion toward the other students and away from herself. *"You're not just answering my questions. I'd like to observe how you resolve these questions with each other."* By the end of the scaffolded reading lesson 15 minutes later, her students had a clearer vision of the narrow perspective of the narrator. Following the discussion, the students were asked to write in response to their reading. *"Log into the discussion board on 'Charles,' and now imagine what the conversation at home would be like after the mother returns from the PTA meeting,"* said Ms. Okeke. *"She now knows that Charles is not real. This isn't just guessing what the conversation might be. Back up your narrative with reasons and evidence in the text that support it."*

The *VISIBLE LEARNER*

During a small group lesson, Travis responded incorrectly to a question his teacher asked. They had been reading the poem "Daddy" by Sylvia Plath. When asked, "Why does Plath include allusions to Nazi Germany?" Travis said that he thought it was because Plath might be German herself.

In response, Rocio, another student in the group, said, "I don't think I agree, Travis." The tenth-grade English teacher, Markita Jones, said, *"Okay, that's fine. There's a difference of opinion here, which means it's something for us to clarify together. Good with you, Travis? Rocio, can you tell us why you disagree?"*

Rocio responds, noting that the references seemed to support the theme of oppression more than a literal reference to the German heritage of Plath's parents. *"We know that the 'Meinkampf look' is a reference to Hitler, and I doubt Plath would want to relate herself to him. I think she's trying to show how rigid and unforgiving her dad was."*

"Oh, I see what you mean," Travis said. *"And, I know we have been talking about allusions and symbols in class, so that makes sense. And from what I know about Hitler, I get a really good idea of what her dad was all about."*

"Or at least how the poet perceived him to be," says Ms. Jones. *"Not all poems are strictly autobiographical."*

"That's true," Travis said. *"Her [Plath's] own father died when she was a little girl, and her dad was a professor in Boston who specialized in bumblebees."* He continued, *"So maybe my first comment was too literal and too easy."*

Visible learners see errors as opportunities and are comfortable saying that they don't know and/or need help.

CONCLUSION

Discussion provides students with a chance to consider the perspectives of others. It's not the only way that students learn, but it's an important way. In this chapter, we focused on teacher-led or teacher-mediated dialogic approaches to learning. In each case, the teacher guided, facilitated, and questioned students as they engaged in literacy tasks. That doesn't mean that the students talk only with the teacher, but rather that the teacher is paying close attention to the flow of ideas in the group or classroom. Teacher-led dialogic approaches to learning can be used in whole class or small group settings. In the next chapter, we turn our attention to *student-led* dialogic approaches to learning, which are especially useful when the teacher is meeting with a small group of students who need targeted learning support.

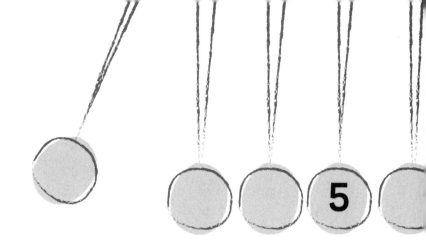

STUDENT-LED
DIALOGIC LEARNING

"Well, I thought I knew what I thought. Now I'm not so sure anymore."

That was the honest statement issued by Abdi, a tenth-grade student in Megan Clarke's class. It came during a small group discussion about the merits and drawbacks of fining or jailing parents of truant students. The group had read two conflicting passages on the subject. One pointed out the merits, including the decreased amount of absences in certain districts enacting the penalty, as well as evidence that truant students are more apt to begin criminal activity. The second article argued that a study showed

© Bob Daemmrich/PhotoEdit

that poorer families are unfairly targeted with this legislation, as well as inconclusive evidence that it is effective on a large scale. The article also stated that enforcement of this policy is erratic and difficult to formalize, making it inconsistent and unfair overall.

Abdi was in agreement with the author who argued that mandatory truancy laws were effective in curbing absence rates. However, Makaila sided with the argument that they were unfair. Using the discussion protocol developed by Ms. Clarke for grounding collaborative conversations, they expanded their rationale using their own experiences as evidence. Makaila argued that according to the articles the class read, most truant students are over the age of 14, saying, *"By this age, we do things that aren't our parents' fault. Think about all the choices you make that wouldn't be fair to punish your parent for!"* That's when Abdi's thinking began to shift. *"Well, I thought I knew what I thought. Now I'm not so sure anymore. So tell me more about that,"* he said.

THE VALUE OF STUDENT-TO-STUDENT DISCUSSION

We imagine everyone reading this book has been struck silent at a profound comment made by a student who wisely stated what should have been obvious to all, yet wasn't. To be sure, not everything they remark upon reaches this same level, but it is important to note that without a forum for speaking, the wise observation can never be heard. This is especially true when it comes to the learning that can occur through student-led collaboration and discussion. Adolescents have a way of making themselves understood by their peers. The American Educational Research Association (2016) explains:

> Because their understanding is deep, based on either the underlying principles or structure of a domain or topic, expert teachers cannot always explain in a manner that allows students to integrate their explanations in a meaningful and helpful way. . . . There is a lack of correspondence between the ideas and concepts referred to by the expert teachers and the superficial concepts and entities that students refer to in their understanding.

In other words, students' thoughts and explanations can propel the learning of others. In turn, the collaborative act of peer-assisted learning is reciprocal, with both benefiting from the exchange (Daiute & Dalton, 1993). In student-led dialogic learning, the role of the teacher is to organize and facilitate, but it is the students who are the ones that lead the discussion.

Another theoretical grounding of collaboration among young people is the work of Piaget's sociocognitive theory (1932). Although this theory is often associated more readily with children's intellectual development, Piaget's final stage, formal operational thought, extends into adulthood and is marked by the ability to entertain increasingly abstract concepts. Manning (1995) explains

EFFECT SIZE FOR PIAGETIAN PROGRAMS = 1.28

> that young adolescents advance from Piaget's concrete operations stage to the formal operations; that they develop the ability to think hypothetically, reflectively, and abstractly; that they develop the ability to make reasoned ethical and moral choices; that they develop personal attitudes and perspectives

toward other people and institutions; and that they develop cognitive skills that allow them to solve real-life problems. This cognitive development can be addressed using opportunities for a core of common knowledge and integrated approaches, for higher-order thinking, for developing skills for life-long learning, and for collaboration, cooperation, and communities of learning. (p. 98)

Exposure to the knowledge, ideas, and perspectives of others, particularly when these do not align with those of the person being exposed, fosters cognitive growth when given the space and tools for sense making. Therefore, these interactions should be understood more broadly as sophisticated enactments of cognition and not simply as a mercantile for the trading of ideas.

Peer-assisted dialogic learning describes a constellation of instructional methods that allow learners to teach and learn from one another. The array of peer-assisted learning routines ranges from small group collaborative discussions among students to more formal structures such as whole class Socratic seminars. A specialized form of peer-assisted learning, called peer tutoring, designates one student as the tutor and one or more as the tutees. In all cases, students assist one another in learning through completion of academic tasks. The root of collaborative learning is in an aspect of the work of Vygotsky and the zone of proximal development (1978), which posits that learning occurs through interaction with a more competent other. While in many cases this is an adult, Vygotsky and others since have argued that peer collaboration is of value for two reasons: (1) The more knowledgeable peer is better able to recall his or her own learning path and can therefore share it more ably, and (2) the interaction itself benefits the more competent peer because it reinforces and clarifies his own knowledge.

THE SOCIAL AND BEHAVIORAL BENEFITS OF PEER-ASSISTED LEARNING

The social and behavioral benefits of peer-assisted learning, especially for young adults, are important as well. Spend time in the company of learners, and you will witness the development of the social and language processes needed to successfully negotiate the dynamics of a group. While adults adjust their behavior and language to meet adolescents where they are, this doesn't occur to the same degree with classmates. The ability to set goals and deadlines with peers, hear a full range of perspectives (especially those that don't align with their own), and resolve contradictions comes in part from direct experiences with peers.

Consequently, if a majority of interactions are mediated by adults, gains in these crucial communication skills would be inhibited. Classroom peer interactions need to be taught, of course, but students also need lots of opportunities to put these into action.

Bowman-Perrott, Burke, Nan, and Zaini (2014) conducted a meta-analysis to examine the nonacademic benefits of peer-assisted learning for students in Grades K through 12. They found good effect sizes related to social skills outcomes (ES = 0.39) and reducing disruptive and off-task behaviors (ES = 0.60). Importantly, the effect sizes were similar whether the peer-assisted learning was reciprocal (students tutoring one another) or nonreciprocal (tutor and tutee). These results make sense, in that adolescents, according to Piaget, are able to engage in formal operations of intellectual development (marked by increasingly logical thought) and become better at interpreting the behaviors and motives of others. In other words, they are becoming better attuned to one another and are strengthening their capacity to explain concepts to others. This need is certainly evident in the various content standards, such as

- Listening and responding in a variety of different contexts, both formal and informal, and evaluating content, viewpoints, evidence and aspects of presentation. (English Programmes of Study, Key Stage 4).

- Work with peers to promote civil, democratic discussions and decision-making, set clear goals and deadlines, and establish individual roles as needed. (California Grade 11)

- Students work productively with others in teams. Students are expected to participate productively in discussions, plan agendas with clear goals and deadlines, set time limits for speakers, take notes, and vote on key issues. (Texas Grade 7)

Sixth-grade teacher Stephen Cheng begins working on these communication skills at the start of the academic year. Over the course of the first month, his students learn about the importance of working productively with one another. "It's really the heart of this English class," explained Mr. Cheng. "So much of what gets accomplished in here is due to my students' abilities to push each other's thinking." Mr. Cheng uses a simple rubric he has constructed for guiding communication.

"The rubric gives them a reminder of what aspects of speaking and listening we are focusing on for that week," explains Mr. Cheng. To encourage listening and questioning skills, they play games that require careful listening and questioning. "I play a sort of modified 'Who am I?' game with specified themes. Students have a sticky note with a person or object written on it, and they must ask questions of their partner to determine

---

Classroom peer interactions need to be taught, of course, but students also need lots of opportunities to put these into action.

EFFECT SIZE FOR SOCIAL SKILLS PROGRAMS = 0.39

'who' the partner is. It's a fun way to get students to review content and get comfortable asking each other questions and assisting one another."

For instance, for their poetry unit, Mr. Cheng distributed sticky notes labeled with important poets they had read. "They get to ask 10 questions in total, and the student with the note can give two helpful hints, if needed. This activity really stretches their listening and language skills, as well as requiring them to draw on knowledge from our unit of study. After they have each taken a turn, they provide feedback to one another about what was helpful and what was confusing. My purpose is to get them thinking about techniques they use when assisting a peer to clear up a confusion," said Mr. Cheng.

FOSTERING COLLABORATIVE DISCUSSIONS

Increasing the amount of time students talk using academic language has been a priority in schools for decades. Simply said, students need practice with academic language if they are to become proficient in that language. Said another way, students must learn to speak the language of science, history, mathematics, art, and literature if they are to become thinkers in those disciplines. But the use of academic language is more than just teaching them the vocabulary of the subject. Success in using collaborative discussions requires knowing exactly how you want them to grow in their interaction skills.

Video 16
Prepping Students for Student-Led Dialogic Learning

https://resources.corwin.com/ vl-literacy6-12

The most obvious instructional implication relates to the use of time. Students need time every day to practice their collaborative conversations. That's not to say teachers should simply turn over their classrooms for students to talk, but rather that there are expectations established for student-to-student interaction, and that students are held accountable for these interactions.

An easy way to do this is to use a conversation roundtable. Students can simply fold a piece of paper like the one in Figure 5.1. As students read a selected text, they take notes in the upper left quadrant of their own paper. After the students have composed notes on their own paper, they each take a turn at discussing the text. As each student speaks, the listeners make notes about the content being shared, using the other three quadrants of the paper. So at the end of the collaborative discussion, they have their own notes in the first quadrant and notes about each other speaker's thoughts in the remaining three quadrants. Now they turn their attention to the rhombus in the center of the paper. Students independently write their own response in the center. Depending on the task assigned by the teacher, they might be summarizing their understanding of the text, identifying the theme, or posing additional questions in the area in the center. Importantly, their response should be influenced by the collaborative discussion. This

Figure 5.1   Template for Notes for Conversation Roundtable

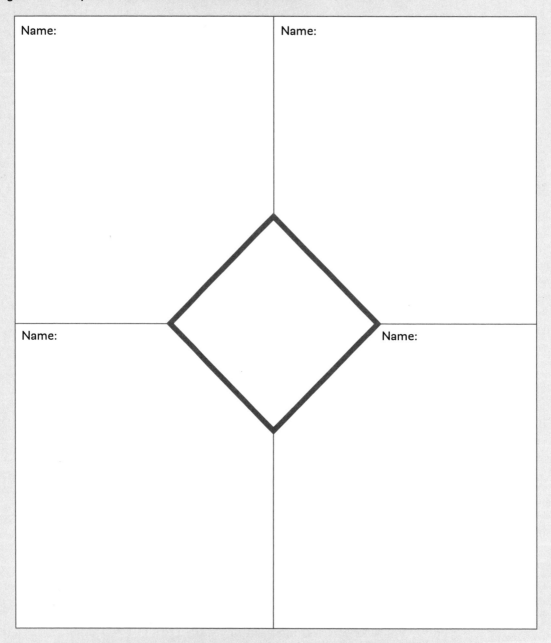

activity accomplishes two important purposes. The first is that it provides you with a record of the quality of the discussion, because each student has constructed notes about the information each member shared. The second purpose is that it gives you insight into each student's deepening comprehension. When reviewing these conversation roundtable notes, we are most interested in examining the changes in the student's thinking from their initial understandings before the discussion (Quadrant 1) and after (their independent writing in the center of the paper).

> Students need time every day to practice their collaborative conversations.

It's also important to provide students with instruction in how to engage in a collaborative conversation. They may need sentence starters at first to begin using argumentation in their discussions. For example, ninth-grade teacher Patrice Adams provided her students with the following frames when they wanted to offer a counter claim:

- I disagree with _____ because _____.
- The reason I believe _____ is _____.
- The facts that support my idea are _____.
- In my opinion _____.
- One difference between my idea and yours is _____.

In addition, students need to be taught the rules of a conversation, so Ms. Adams teaches her students the following (Blyth, 2009):

1. Avoid unnecessary details.
2. Don't ask another question before the first one has been answered.
3. Do not interrupt another while he or she is speaking.
4. Do not contradict, especially if it's not important.
5. Do not do all the talking.
6. Don't always be the hero of your story (but have a hero).
7. Choose a subject of mutual interest.
8. Be a good listener.
9. Have a conversation that is in harmony with the surroundings.
10. Do not exaggerate.
11. Do not misquote.
12. Cultivate tact.

"I think it's critical to review the rules of conversation," said Ms. Adams. "By the time they get to high school, most of them seem to think they already know how to do this, but they don't really listen to one another. I guess adults are like that, too," she chuckled. "But, the concern raises the discussion of why I think we still need them. It opens up the possibility to them that these easy skills are easily forgotten and need to be practiced," she explained.

She said that the discussion about misquoting is an important one. "With social media, misquoting others has an exponentially greater effect than when I was a teenager," said Ms. Adams. "I play the old telephone game with them, and we discuss how rumors get started." (The telephone game involves a student whispering a statement into another student's ear, who then whispers it into a third student's ear. It is inevitable that the message will get mangled with each successive student.) Ms. Adams does this as a fishbowl with a group of ten students in the middle of the room. When the last student in the circle has received the whispered message, he or she announces it to the class, while the originator displays the message in written form. "It gives us license to discuss the fact that misquoting is often unintentional, although it can be perceived by others as malicious," said Ms. Adams.

Another rule is *cultivating tact*. "How you share the message is as important as the message itself," explained Ms. Adams. "We discuss peer critiques and feedback, and methods for being able to provide constructive feedback that doesn't demoralize the receiver."

TEACH STUDENTS TO DEVELOP THEIR OWN QUESTIONS

The peer-assisted learning that can come from collaborative discussions will fall short of your expectations if attention is not given to the development of student questions. While most students know how to obtain information, it is more challenging to pose questions that move the conversation forward. Since many of the student-led dialogic learning is centered on text, we make sure to teach older students a simple frame for seeing the relationship between questions, texts, and themselves, using a classification system of questions described by Pearson and Johnson (1978):

- *text explicit* (the answer is a direct quote from the text);

- *text implicit* (the answer must be inferred from several passages in the book);

- *script implicit* (requires both the text and prior knowledge and experiences).

See Figure 5.2 for a table describing this questioning taxonomy.

> The peer-assisted learning that can come from collaborative discussions will fall short of your expectations if attention is not given to the development of student questions.

Figure 5.2   Taxonomy of Questions

Category	Description
Text explicit	The question is asked using words from the text, and the answer is directly stated in the reading.
Text implicit	The questions are derived from the text and require the reader to look for the answer in several places and to combine the information.
Script implicit	The question elicits an answer to come from the reader's own prior knowledge and experiences. The text may or may not be needed to answer the question.

Source: Pearson, P. D., & Johnson, D. D. (1972). *Teaching reading comprehension.* Boston: Cengage Learning. © 1978 South-Western, a part of Cengage Learning, Inc. Reproduced by permission. www.cengage.com/permissions.

 Available for download at **https://resources.corwin.com/vl-literacy6-12**

Students use this model to generate their own questions about a text. For example, students can write text-explicit and text-implicit questions for one another to check on their understanding of the passage. This inquiry interaction promotes more personal involvement than using only teacher-generated questions. As well, script-implicit questions invite the reader to integrate personal experiences and prior knowledge into their responses. These inferential and evaluative questions require the reader to make connections between concepts and ideas. As they generate these questions, the students developing them are deducing, inferring, connecting, and evaluating. Self-generated questions are of great value to students, with an effect size of 0.64.

EFFECT SIZE FOR SELF-VERBALIZATION AND SELF-QUESTIONING = **0.64**

To initially introduce this questioning taxonomy, we advise the teacher to use a think-aloud process:

1. Read aloud a small segment of text.

2. Ask a question about what was read.

3. Reflect aloud on the selection and answer the question, using a think-aloud process in front of the class.

4. Identify the *type* of question and the *source* of the answer.

As students learn to classify questions and locate answers, they also learn to recognize that comprehension is influenced by both the reader and the text. Soon, students are ready to formulate original questions in response to text.

The purpose of teaching students a questioning taxonomy is so that they can apply the technique in small group discussions with peers. For example, after a small group of Stephanie Torres's ninth-grade students read a chapter of *Of Mice and Men,* the students asked one another a series of questions about the chapter they had just finished. When asked a question, the respondent first indicated which type of question it was and then provided the answer with evidence. At one point in the conversation, Gregory said to Tina, *"I'm a little confused about the relationship between Lennie and George. It seems like maybe Lennie needs George to care for him, but I'm not sure, because they seem to be similar ages."*

Tina responded, *"I think this is a text-implicit question, because the author really doesn't tell you exactly why George and Lennie are together, but there are clues in the book. I think Lennie maybe needs extra help because he seems so childlike—when he talks about the mouse it seems like maybe he isn't focused on what an adult might be; George kind of treats him like a father or older brother."*

STUDENT-LED TOOLS FOR DIALOGIC LEARNING

The flow from direct instruction to teacher-led dialogic teaching to student enactments of learning is always recursive, as students' conceptual knowledge, communication skills, and capacity to think critically are continually under construction. So in no way do we mean to suggest that direct instruction happens during the first part of the school year and is replaced by teacher-led dialogic instruction at the midpoint, and that only during the latter part of the school year do students ever get to lead discussions. Although there is always going to be a period during which students learn about the structure of such activities, the goal is to move them forward in taking steps toward becoming their own teachers. Some of the ways teachers can do this are discussed next.

> The flow from direct instruction to teacher-led dialogic teaching to student enactments of learning is always recursive.

Fishbowl

Students benefit from bearing witness to quality student-led discussions. One method for doing so is the fishbowl. You'll recall that in the previous chapter we offered pinwheel discussions, which are more teacher-directed, as a prelude for fishbowl discussions, which are led by students. Here's how a fishbowl discussion works:

1. The teacher hosts a small group of students in the center of the room for a discussion, while the other students observe the interaction.

2. After introducing the purpose and the topic, the teacher is primarily an observer, interjecting only as needed to forward the discussion, usually by posing a new question.

3. The inner circle of participants (those in the fishbowl) debate the topic, while those in the outer circle listen and take notes.

4. A member of the outer circle can temporarily join the inner circle to comment, occupying an empty chair placed in the inner circle.

5. After the first round of discussion, members of the outer circle exchange places with those in the inner circle, and the discussion continues.

6. After all the students have participated in the inner circle, the teacher takes a more overt role in the discussion, asking questions that encourage students to synthesize their thinking.

7. The teacher asks students to comment on the process and their own learning.

8. Teachers can take a smaller role or eliminate themselves from the process as students become more skilled in participating in the fishbowl.

Video 17
Student-Led Discussion

*https://resources.corwin.com/
vl-literacy6-12*

Eleventh-grade teacher Sandra Lopez is midway through a unit on storytelling. "This unit is important because it explores fundamental human experiences in the context of how we create stories about them," she explained. "But I also want them to think critically about what we are reading, and to question texts and ideas." Her school explores essential questions every quarter, and the current question being explored is "How does where you live affect how you live?"

"We have been reading *The Things They Carried* this quarter and just finished the chapter 'The Sweetheart of the Song Tra Bong,' which the students always enjoy because the ending is so shocking," said Ms. Lopez. "The transformation of the main character really generates a lot of discussion about how environments can affect behavior." The subject of the chapter, Mary Ann, is smuggled into the country by her boyfriend, an American soldier in the Vietnam War, so she can keep him company. However, she embraces Vietnam, discovering that she has an adventurous and thrill-seeking temperament. She disappears, having gone out on patrol with other soldiers. When she emerges three weeks later, she is wearing a necklace made of tongues and is condemned by her boyfriend. "This story, coupled with the informational texts we have been reading about ethics and the psychological consequences of war, make

Figure 5.3   Lesson Plan for Eleventh Grade Using a Fishbowl Technique

Assessed Need: I have noticed that my students need: Extended discussion experiences to explore complex storylines.
Standard(s) Addressed: SL.11–12.1. Initiate and participate effectively in a range of collaborative discussions (one-on-one, in groups, and teacher-led) with diverse partners on grades 11–12 topics, texts, and issues, building on others' ideas and expressing their own clearly and persuasively. RL.11–12.3. Analyze the impact of the author's choices regarding how to develop and relate elements of a story or drama (e.g., where a story is set, how the action is ordered, how the characters/archetypes are introduced and developed).
Text(s) I Will Use: "Sweetheart of the Song Tra Bong" from _The Things They Carried_ by Tim O'Brien
Learning Intention for This Lesson: We will analyze the character's motives and responsibilities using an ethical framework.
Success Criteria for This Lesson: After listening and participating in the fishbowl, you will write in response to a timed writing prompt addressing the major questions under discussion.
Direct Instruction: Model: Strategies/skills/concepts to emphasize Set the purpose: Form an opinion and supply evidence to address the question. What is the role of the environment in Mary Ann's transformation? What are her responsibilities in a time of crisis and war? Provide a review of the fishbowl technique, modeling active listening and discussion behaviors. • Inside circle and outside circle will be used, and everyone will have a turn in the inside circle. • Review how to tap in / tap out of the inner circle to join and exit the discussion. • Demonstrate listening behaviors (track the speaker, don't interrupt). • Demonstrate discussion behaviors, and remind students of sentence frames we have been using: (Examples: I agree/disagree with _____ because _____. I would like to add on to _____'s idea _____. Can you tell us more about your idea?) Guide and Scaffold: Questions to ask Central question: How do the surroundings influence Mary Ann? What is her responsibility for her actions in times of crisis and war? Assess: These are the students who will need further support Alex and Hailey have modified versions of the text
Dialogic Instruction: Teacher-Directed Tools N/A Student-Enacted Tools Fishbowl discussion: Brian and Fernando are the moderators for this discussion. Make sure they have a list of possible clarifying questions to ask when needed. They will keep time (10 minutes per circle session) until all students have participated in the inner circle. I will sit with the outer circle to encourage student leadership of this discussion. Assess: These are the students who will need further support Listen and watch for any students who are having difficulty in explaining themselves, and prompt the moderators if needed to pose additional questions.
Feedback Opportunities: Keep track of the number of times each student contributes to the discussion. If there are students who have not yet contributed near the end of their fishbowl, let them know and prompt them to participate.

Independent Learning and Closure:

Closure: Moderators Brian and Fernando will summarize the fishbowl discussion at the end and provide a list of points that were discussed. I will then review the learning intention and success criteria for the lesson, and move students back to their tables for independent writing.

Independent Learning: Write a 300-word essay that

- Addresses the central questions: To what extent does the environment play a role in Mary Ann's transformation? Are her decisions ethical, given that her changes may be for the better or the worse?
- Provides evidence from the text, as well as additional evidence from the article on ethics, to support your answers.

Available for download at **https://resources.corwin.com/vl-literacy6-12**

determining 'right' and 'wrong' difficult; I want my students to grapple with these ideas and really take a look at what they think and why." Her lesson plan can be found in Figure 5.3.

Ms. Lopez's students have participated in other fishbowl discussions so she is turning over more of the responsibility to students. Brian and Fernando are moderators and will regulate the discussion, including timekeeping (each fishbowl group will have 10 minutes) and asking follow-up questions. Ms. Lopez has given them a short list with suggested prompts, such as *"Can you tell us more about your idea?"* and *"Why do you think that?"*

Ms. Lopez begins by explaining the learning intentions and success criteria for the lesson; then she reviews the fishbowl discussion process with her students. Ms. Lopez then joins the outer circle, further signaling that her role is participatory rather than directive in nature.

The moderators begin by referring to the chapter under discussion, which they read earlier in the week. All the students have their annotated copies in front of them. *"Our discussion question for today is, 'How do surroundings influence Mary Ann? What are her responsibilities for her behaviors in times of crisis and war?'"* says Brian.

Fernando invites nine students to join the inner circle to begin the discussion. (A tenth chair is empty so that members of the outer circle may temporarily join to add to the discussion.) The first group relies heavily on listing examples from the chapter, chronicling how drastically Mary Ann has changed once she has spent time in Vietnam, rather than examining why. Soon Brian calls time and invites a second group to the inner circle, and he reminds them of the central question about environment and *all* types of behaviors in general. By now the class is warming to the topic.

"At first it seemed like Mary Ann was trying to fit in to the environment," Trevor says, *"'because it is so different from where she is from and she needs to adapt."* Fernando invites him to elaborate, saying, *"Say more about that."*

"Well, when she first got there, she was just trying to be a good girlfriend. But soon she got more interested in Vietnamese culture than her boyfriend ever did. But maybe it's because he was there as a soldier, and she was there because she saw it as an adventure. So right there the decisions they each made were bound to be different."

"Hmm, that's very insightful, Trevor, and thank you for sharing that," says Ms. Lopez.

The other students looked at one another, and then Karla quietly said, *"I think she was discovering what feminism was really about. It was the 1960s and the women's movement was starting. Mary Ann made a decision to drop all the trappings of being a traditional girlfriend. She wanted to be her own person and take risks, and her boyfriend didn't like it at all."*

Brian called time, and by now nearly all the remaining students were vying to join the inner circle. What ensued was a deeper discussion about ethical dilemmas faced by Mary Ann, who cuts her hair, spends time with an indigenous mountain tribe, and refuses to return to the United States when her boyfriend orders her to do so. *"How much do environments change us, and when they change us for the worse, who is responsible? What do we do?"* asks Ms. Lopez.

When the fishbowl discussions concluded, the moderators shared the t-chart they had been constructing. On one side were listed some of the arguments that supported Mary Ann's decisions; on the other were those that were critical of her decisions. Ms. Lopez continued with the closure, returning her students' attention to the learning intention and success criteria.

"Now's the time to write. You've read this chapter and participated in the fishbowl. Fernando and Brian, thank you for the summary you developed. I'd like you to write about 300 words, and include three parts." She pointed at the success criteria displayed on the document camera:

1. Address the central questions: To what extent does the environment play a role in Mary Ann's transformation? Are her decisions ethical, given that her changes may be for the better or the worse?

Teaching Takeaway

Display these accountable talk prompts prominently in the classroom so that students can use them in many other lessons.

2. Provide evidence from the text, as well as additional evidence from the article on ethics, to support your answers.

3. Use at least one other example that came from the fishbowl discussion.

For the next 50 minutes, her students wrote quietly, rarely breaking the silence as everyone worked. Ms. Lopez provided further brief guided instruction as needed for individual students. "Examining this chapter through the lens of ethical dilemmas is causing them to think beyond story and plot," she said. "I'm looking forward to reading what they've written."

The fishbowl is a method for fostering habits associated with extended discussion. In middle and high school classrooms, these often take place in table groups. Simply locating six students and a text at a table is not going to be sufficient. But when students are regularly involved in the use of accountable talk, and their teacher uses conversational moves to model reasoning and argumentation, they begin to internalize this type of thinking. Ted Kramer's ninth-grade students have been regularly using student-directed dialogic methods since the beginning of the school year.

> When students are regularly involved in the use of accountable talk, and their teacher uses conversational moves to model reasoning and argumentation, they begin to internalize this type of thinking.

"I'm most interested in introducing them to literature that gives them a window to other experiences beyond ones they have had," he said. The teacher began the school year with Sandra Cisneros' *House on Mango Street*. "The format of this text was helpful: We discussed the different themes that occur within each chapter, and we used the themes as springboards to write and talk about our own lives," Mr. Kramer explained.

As the year progressed, his class considered other big questions through texts:

*   Can we always trust the narrator? Why or why not? (*The Cask of Amontillado*)

*   How is justice truly served? (*The Lady or the Tiger?*)

*   What do Walter's daydreams tell us about him? (*The Secret Life of Walter Mitty*)

"I want to build their capacity to read a wide variety of texts in order to think critically, not just follow a plot or enjoy a story. If they can explain their thinking and reasoning to another person, they have truly shown mastery of this skill," Mr. Kramer said.

Gallery Walks

Student-led dialogic learning routines such as fishbowl discussions still have an adult presence, albeit one that takes a backseat as students direct the experience. Other routines, like gallery walks done in small groups or pairs, are performed away from the company of an adult. Paired and small group collaborative discussions of this nature tend to be a bit more informal, and the structure of the talk is left a bit more in the hands of students. Gallery walks are one example, and the purpose is to elicit knowledge in a shared environment such that students can build on the observations of one another. Here's how gallery walks work:

1. Three-dimensional items, photographs, or language charts are placed at stations throughout the room.

2. Small groups of students rotate to each station and discuss what they are seeing and observing. Their talk is much like the conversations that occur in museums as one travels from one object to the next (hence the name *gallery walk*).

3. These stations often include posted questions or multiple texts for students to ponder.

Seventh-grade teacher Simone Okeke uses gallery walks to explore shared knowledge about a topic under study. Her students are currently learning how to examine the different ways in which multiple authors write about the same topic. She places short excerpts from various texts on chart paper around the room. Her students are already familiar with the topic at hand—*What is art?*—which is an essential question her class has been considering. She reminds them that each excerpt they see in some way addresses this question. She also reminds them to look for the text structure as well as main idea and author's purpose, since these are the skills the class has been working on. She reviews the learning intention for the lesson (identifying main idea and text features that support the main idea) and success criteria for the lesson (to create a graphic organizer and accompanying notes in which the main idea is summarized and the text features are listed or noted for six out of eight texts), and explains the gallery walk. See Figure 5.4 for her lesson plan.

Figure 5.4   Lesson Plan for Seventh Grade Using a Gallery Walk

Assessed Need: I have noticed that my students need: To sharpen their ability to link author's main idea/purpose and central themes with text structure and evidence.

Standard(s) Addressed: TEKS ELA Grade 7 10.D

(10) Reading/Comprehension of Informational Text/Expository Text. Students analyze, make inferences and draw conclusions about expository text and provide evidence from text to support their understanding. Students are expected to:

(D) synthesize and make logical connections between ideas within a text and across two or three texts representing similar or different genres, and support those findings with textual evidence.

Text(s) I Will Use: Articles and critiques from various publications on graffiti, performance art, and publicly funded art.

Learning Intention for This Lesson: Identifying main idea, central themes, and text features that support the main idea

Success Criteria for This Lesson: Create notes and a graphic organizer in which the main idea is summarized and the text features are listed or noted for six out of eight texts

Direct Instruction:

Model: Strategies/skills/concepts to emphasize

Set the purpose: Review the learning intention and success criteria, and explain how partners will record their notes.

Model how to ask questions of one another ("How did you know that was the author's main idea?") and probe for evidence ("What text features do you notice? How do these support the main idea?").

Guide and Scaffold: Questions to ask

I will circulate among groups and work as needed with partners that appear to be having difficulty.

Assess: These are the students who will need further support

Pair Tommy with Elvira, who will be able to record notes for him.

Dialogic Instruction:

Teacher-Directed Tools

N/A

Student-Enacted Tools

Gallery walk: Students will visit eight stations with enlarged excerpts from texts about art, and make notes about each.

Assess: These are the students who will need further support

Check for understanding: Monitor groups as they work through each station, and assist as needed.

Feedback Opportunities: Partners will compare their written notes with those of their table mates at the end of the gallery walk. They can pose questions to each other about the items they examined. Partners will then choose a single text to read more closely. (Full articles are posted on class website.)

Independent Learning and Closure: Summarize the learning intentions and success criteria. Ask pairs to choose one article to read in its entirety and to write an exit slip about it.

"You and your classmate will use your notes to capture the main idea of each text, as well as list the text features you notice," Ms. Okeke explained. *"There are eight stations altogether. Look for central themes and check in with your partner. Be sure to ask each other to justify your answers. When someone has found a central theme, ask, 'Where did you find that?' When you've visited at least six stations, come back to your tables so you can compare your answers with those of the other pairs at your table."*

The students travel as partners through each station. Tomás and Adelle begin with an excerpt from an editorial about the street artist Banksy. *"Okay, so I can already tell this is from a newspaper,"* says Tomás, *"because it's got 'New York Times' written on it. What can you tell about the topic, though?"*

Adelle studies the excerpt, touching her pencil to the title. *"Well, it's called 'When does graffiti become art?' So I'm thinking it is probably an opinion piece. I wonder what this person's opinion is, though,"* she says.

"Well, let's read a little bit and see," says Tomás. He traces his eraser across the line, *'The art world has already acknowledged the value of it [graffiti]'* so that makes me think this writer considers it art."*

"Okay," says Adelle, *"I also can tell from the picture with the article that this author's central theme is that it is art, because graffiti it shows looks a lot like something you'd see in a museum."*

"You think that's a text feature, too?" asks Tomás. *"I mean, when I think of graffiti I think of letters, not really drawings. This makes me reconsider it being just scribbling."* Adelle agrees, and says, *"At first I just thought the picture was there because that's what newspapers do, but now I see why the author included it to support her point."*

After the gallery walk is completed and table mates have had a chance to compare notes, Ms. Okeke briefly goes through each text and notes the text features and main ideas of each, while students check their notes and graphic organizers for accuracy. Tomás and Adelle were happy to share their ideas about the picture in the editorial about graffiti. Ms. Okeke closes this part of the lesson by reviewing the learning intention, and invites the pairs to continue their collaborative work.

"Please select one of the excerpts and find the full text on our class web page. Read the entire piece with your partner and complete today's exit slip on it," she says. *"Please summarize the author's main idea and explain how at least three text features support the author's purpose for writing."*

Adelle and Tomás choose to read the entire piece on graffiti as art. *"Let's do this one,"* says Adelle. *"I'm really interested in this guy Banksy and want to see what else there is to know about him."*

Book Clubs

Perhaps the most popular way to organize student-led dialogic learning in literacy is through book clubs. These are organized around a theme, with each group of students in a classroom choosing a book within a set of texts that express this theme. Small groups of students form based on their interest in a particular book, and remain together until the book is finished. This also allows the teacher to differentiate reading levels while building a common set of understandings. Students function within their book club somewhat autonomously. They make agreements about what will be read in advance of each meeting, and fulfill roles for the collective good of the group.

These skills are especially important for the tenth graders in Antonio Michael's class. The skills they are working on include arriving at discussions already prepared and making decisions about deadlines. For a unit on experiences in young adulthood, Mr. Michaels organized his class into book clubs, each consisting of four or five members, and each reading one of four books:

- *Persepolis,* by Marjane Satrapi

- *The Absolutely True Diary of a Part-Time Indian,* by Sherman Alexie

- *The Kite Runner,* by Khaled Hosseini

- *I Know Why the Caged Bird Sings,* by Maya Angelou

The books are *bildungsromans* (coming of age stories) about people from various backgrounds, which provides the teacher with common ground for building background knowledge with his students. Mr. Michaels previewed the titles for students and shared an excerpt from each of the books with them so they could sample the author's writing style. Students rank-ordered the titles, and the teacher constructed groups based on student preferences.

"I'm more inclined to support student choice over a reading level," explained Mr. Michaels. "I'm just not going to tell students they can't read a book they've chosen because I think it's too hard." He went on to state that he gives them a two-day trial period with the book club they have selected. "I give them the opportunity to change groups if they need to. It actually doesn't end up being too much of a hassle. A few kids will realize the book they chose is not for them, but most of them stay because they like their group."

The book clubs meet twice per week for discussion and planning. He doesn't assign specific roles for students, although he does review the major activities they need to complete, including examining unfamiliar or confusing words and phrases, discussing plot and character, and look-ing for symbolism. "I also remind them that they will write a response to a writing prompt on the discussion board, after their book clubs have met."

The students in the book clubs meet initially with Mr. Michaels to dis-cuss deadlines for the book to be read, as well as the tasks they will com-plete during the three weeks set aside for this unit. Mr. Michaels brings a calendar with him so that each group can plot out its pacing for the book they have selected, as well as the interim due dates for the response logs the students submit to him. By making students active decision makers in the planning, he increases the level of engagement and responsibility.

Once the planning has been completed, students are now free to read, meet, discuss, and write about their reading. Mr. Michaels designates times for formal book club meetings each week, and it is during these times that student-led dialogic learning takes place. Students meet to discuss the chapters they have read, first discussing the major events that took place in the story to make sure each member understood the plot. Since the growth and development of the protagonist is central to all four books, book clubs are charged with plotting the changes that happen to the main character over the course of the novel. In particular, they examine the moral and psychological evolution of the young per-son, and identify how the major conflicts shape these changes.

After each meeting has concluded, students return to their desks to com-pose responses to prompts that are posted in the discussion boards on the learning management system. "I have two separate book clubs read-ing each of the novels," said Mr. Michaels. "This is when they interact with another book club who is reading the same book."

Mr. Michaels spends time teaching about discussion, accountable talk, and the norms in digital environments. "The book clubs give them the face-to-face time to interact, but I also need to continue to build their online communication skills. They'll use this all through college, too."

Readers Theatre

Readers Theatre is a choral reading strategy that that uses scripts of poems, plays, and literature to create a performance piece. Unlike tra-ditional school plays, the performers do not utilize costumes, staging, lighting, or even gestures. Instead, they use their voices to convey the appropriate meaning of the text. As well, they do not memorize their parts, instead using the script to read, including at the performance. A useful analogy is to think of this kind of performance as a radio play or podcast, where visuals play no role whatsoever. Readers Theatre is an effective reading practice for older students because they engage in

The *VISIBLE LEARNER*

In a literature group discussing Nikolai Gogol's short story "The Nose," all of the students were stuck. The absurdist and satirical tone had left the group casting about for meaning in the protagonist's loss of his nose, which goes on to enjoy a life of its own. The group members have been talking about this for some time when Chris says, *"We should try something new. None of us knows, right?"*

In response, Charlene says, *"Let's just look it up online; I am sure we can find something there."* Staci counters, *"Well, why don't we try a little longer before we do that. What if we went back to the part where Major Kovalyov discovers his nose is missing from his face, and reread the section when he spots his nose dressed as a police officer. What do you all think?"*

Veronica said, *"That's a good idea. Plus if that doesn't work, we can call over Ms. Tallerico and ask for more advice. Or we could look on the Internet to see if we are right."*

Visible learners know what to do when they don't know what to do.

repeated readings while perfecting their parts, thus building their fluency while deepening their comprehension. Struggling readers in particular may resist reading anything more than once, but the accountability of performance in front of peers can eliminate such hesitancies (Tyler & Chard, 2000). Readers Theatre in middle and high school is especially useful for spoken word texts. Speeches, poems, plays, and Shakespearean dialogue can be difficult to understand when read on the page, but can come to life when performed aloud.

> EFFECT SIZE FOR
> REPEATED READING
> PROGRAMS = **0.67**

Beyond fluency and comprehension building, Readers Theatre can be an excellent platform for student-enacted discussion. Martinez, Roser, and Strecker (1998) propose a five-day instructional plan for managing multiple Readers Theatre groups. Here's how it works:

1. Day 1. The teacher introduces the entire class to the text that will be performed, discussing meaning, building background knowledge, and teaching vocabulary. Students are grouped and assigned a passage to perform later in the week.

2. Days 2, 3, and 4. On each of the subsequent days, the groups reread their script, discuss roles, and rehearse. It is within this space that students must figure out how they will resolve problems.

3. Day 5. Each group performs for the class.

A summary of the five-day instructional plan appears in Figure 5.5.

Figure 5.5   Five-Day Instructional Plan for Readers Theatre

Day 1	Teacher
	• Models fluency by reading aloud the stories on which the week's scripts are based
	• Provides direct instruction that presents explicit explanation of some aspect of fluency
	• Discusses each of the stories
	• Distributes scripts for students to read independently
Day 2	Students
	• Gather in collaborative groups using scripts with parts highlighted
	• Read the script several times, taking a different part with each reading
	Teacher
	• Circulates and coaches, providing feedback
Day 3	Procedures are the same as on Day 2.
	During final 5 minutes, students within each group negotiate and assign roles.
	Students are encouraged to practice their part at home.
Day 4	Students read and reread their parts with their collaborative group.
	During final 10 minutes, each group makes character labels and decides where each member will stand during the performance.
Day 5	Collaborative groups perform, reading before the audience.

Source: Adapted from Martinez, M., Roser, N. L., & Strecker, S. (1998). "I never thought I could be a star": A Readers Theatre ticket to fluency. *The Reading Teacher, 52,* 326–334.

 Available for download at **https://resources.corwin.com/vl-literacy6-12**

Reciprocal Teaching

Developed by Palincsar and Brown (1986) as a reading comprehension strategy, reciprocal teaching involves student-directed groups of four working together with a piece of informational text that has been segmented into smaller chunks. These stopping points (chunks) allow students to discuss the text more deeply throughout the reading. This is accomplished through a discussion format and is repeated several times until the reading is complete. The teacher may create stopping points in advance, although more experienced groups can decide on their own how best to break up the text. At each stopping point, students apply four kinds of reading comprehension strategies to understand the text:

- **Questioning the text passage** by asking text-explicit (literal) and text-implicit (inferential) questions of one another

- **Clarifying understandings** through discussion of any confusion that might need to be cleared up (for example, using the glossary, consulting another source, asking the teacher)

- **Summarizing** the main points contained in the passage

- **Predicting** what the writer will discuss next, based on what is known thus far

A strength of reciprocal teaching is that it fosters consolidation of knowledge and comprehension. Once learned, the four strategies do not need to be performed in a strict order, and all members are encouraged to use these freely in their discussions.

Charles Peck's Year 10 students are seated at tables of four to engage in the familiar practice of reciprocal teaching. They have been reading and discussing *Interpreter of Maladies* by Jhumpa Lahiri as part of a larger unit on living within two cultures. This book, written by an Indian-American author, resonates with Mr. Peck's students as well, since many of them share Lahiri's heritage and struggle to manage conflicting cultural values.

Discussion of the book has raised many questions about cultural clashes. In response to their queries, Mr. Peck has selected an informational reading excerpted from a longer academic paper (Nandi & Platt, 2013). This informational text discusses aspects of acculturation among immigrants in Great Britain. The students read and discussed the portion of the paper devoted to four potential outcomes: integration, assimilation, separation, and marginalization. The larger purpose was to equip the students with a deeper understanding of acculturation so that they could better analyze how the characters in the nine short stories in Lahiri's book responded to cross-cultural struggles.

Zahra, Ted, Alison, and Faizal have used reciprocal teaching a number of times and quickly begin to chunk the text into manageable sections. They also utilize a discussion notes guide to capture their ideas, and it further serves to remind them about the comprehension strategies they will employ during their discussion (see Figure 5.6).

The excerpt featured a matrix illustrating the relationship between cultural maintenance (asking the question, "Is it considered to be of value to maintain one's identity and characteristics?") and contact participation (posing the question, "Is it considered to be of value to maintain relationships with larger society?") (Nandi & Platt, 2013, p. 26). The students examined the diagram and read each of the four definitions provided in the text.

Figure 5.6   Reciprocal Teaching Note-Taking Guide

Members: Date: Text:	Learning Intention:
During Reading	**After Reading**
Your Predictions: Section 1: Section 2: Section 3:	Were your predictions accurate? Why or why not?
Your Questions: Section 1: Section 2: Section 3:	Do you have unanswered questions?
Your Clarifications: Section 1: Section 2: Section 3:	What tools did you use to clarify your understanding?
Summary Statement of Complete Reading:	

Zahra began, *"The diagram has a lot of information in it. I'm going to try to interpret it, but help me if I get it wrong. It says that people who experience marginalization don't maintain their cultural identity and also don't have relationships with the larger society. But immigrants who maintain their cultural identity and at the same time have lots of relationships with the new society they live in experience integration. Do I have that right?"*

Ted added, *"Yes, that's the way I'm reading it, too. But I wasn't clear on the difference between assimilation and integration. I thought they were the same thing. Did anyone else think that? I had to check the definitions again to see that in both cases, individuals have lots of relationships with the new society. But with assimilation, the individuals are really just giving up their cultural identity to blend in to the new culture."*

Faisal then responded, *"But a question I have is in the first sentence of the paragraph. The authors say that in this study the individuals responded to a 'Britishness question.' I can guess that it is going to have something to do with a national identity, but I'd like to find out more about how they worded this."*

Allison reacted to Faisal's observation, saying, *"Exactly. It seems like a pretty obvious question, so I would predict that the writers are going to explain this in more detail in the next section."*

Fifteen minutes later, they have cocreated some summary sentences that their group will use when Mr. Peck leads the entire class in a discussion of the article and its connections to *Interpreter of Maladies*. Using the information gleaned from this informational passage, they will conduct a character analysis of Mrs. Sens, Mr. and Mrs. Das, Sanjeev, and Twinkle, protagonists in the short stories they have read so far, who have experienced marginalization, assimilation, integration, or separation. His lesson can be found in Figure 5.7.

Peer Tutoring

A final example of student-led dialogic learning is peer tutoring. These partnerships can be same-age peers, or cross-age, with an older student tutoring a younger one. Peer tutoring is best accomplished in pairs, as it can be difficult for students to manage the learning of a group of peers. Tutors and tutees can be of similar ability, or may be partnered because one is more skilled than the other. As with other forms of peer-assisted learning discussed in this chapter, peer tutoring works because it leverages the social dynamics present in relationships. There are intrinsic rewards, including friendship, and motivation to perform well academically and behaviorally (Bowman-Perrott, et al., 2014).

EFFECT SIZE FOR SUMMARIZING = 0.63

EFFECT SIZE FOR RECIPROCAL TEACHING = 0.74

EFFECT SIZE FOR QUESTIONING = 0.48

EFFECT SIZE FOR PEER TUTORING = 0.55

Figure 5.7   Lesson Plan for Year 10 Using Reciprocal Teaching

Assessed Need: I have noticed that my students need: *To analyze informational text systematically.*
Standard(s) Addressed: *Key Stage 4 Literacy: Listening and Speaking interactions: working effectively in groups of different sizes and taking on required roles, including leading and managing discussions, involving others productively, reviewing and summarizing, and contributing to meeting goals/deadlines.* *Key Stage 4 Reading: Understand and critically evaluate texts through reading in different ways for different purposes, summarizing and synthesizing ideas and information, and evaluating their usefulness for particular purposes.*
Text(s) I Will Use: *Interpreter of Maladies, and excerpt from "Understanding Society"* *(pp. 26–27)*
Learning Intention for This Lesson: *Utilize the information on acculturation to analyze characters in* *Interpreter of Maladies (Mrs. Sen, Mr. & Mrs. Das, Sanjeev, and Twinkle)*
Success Criteria for This Lesson: *I will compose notes about the informational reading, using the note-taking guide, to support our analysis.*

Direct Instruction: Model: Strategies/skills/concepts to emphasize *Review reciprocal teaching protocol with class. Since they are familiar with it, spend more time on errors to avoid (e.g., no one takes notes, leaving the group unprepared for the discussion; forgetting to invite others into the conversation when they have not yet participated).* Guide and Scaffold: Questions to ask *As groups are working through the reciprocal teaching task, ask students about their processes. Are they using all four methods (summarize, question, predict, and clarify)?* Assess: These are the students who will need further support *Prisha has been struggling with this process. I will sit in with her group first and then check in with her later to make sure she understood the process.*

Dialogic Instruction: Teacher-Directed Tools *After students read the informational article, we will revisit the experiences of the named characters. I will use a close reading of the chapter "Mrs. Sens" to launch the groups' analyses of the remaining characters.* Student-Enacted Tools *Reciprocal teaching groups of four will read and discuss the acculturation excerpt to prepare for a class discussion about our understanding of the characters in Interpreter of Maladies.* *Learning circle discussion on the effects of acculturation on the lives of immigrants, both historically as well as today. Ashley and Priyanka will lead the discussion. Opening question to begin discussion: "What happens when belief systems of different societies collide?" Closing question: "Can understanding another's experience change how we view our own?"*

Assess: These are the students who will need further support

Join Stefan's reciprocal teaching group, because he has only used RT once before since moving here recently.

Feedback Opportunities: *Use guided instruction as needed with Stefan; debrief with Prisha's group after RT to see what they have concluded.*

Independent Learning and Closure: *Students will write character analyses of Sanjeev and Twinkle ("The Blessed House") using acculturation as the lens.*

Available for download at **https://resources.corwin.com/vl-literacy6-12**

It is important to support both tutors and tutees in this endeavor. Irma Chen presents peer tutoring arrangements to the entire class together, in order to provide directions to all of her sixth graders at the same time.

"Students are paired, usually a stronger reader and one who is struggling a bit more," she said. Ilian and Billy are two students who have been paired together today. Ilian is the stronger of the two readers, so he will assume the initial role as the first reader. The boys have copies of the same text, which is about space junk, and Ilian begins by reading the entire passage aloud, while Billy follows silently in his text. Billy's role is to correct any errors Ilian makes. Of course, what's really occurring is that the stronger reader is modeling prosody, accuracy, and fluency. After the initial reading is completed, the boys switch roles, and now Billy is the second reader. He reads the same passage to Ilian, who is now serving as a coach, and who makes similar corrections as needed.

After the passage has been read a second time, the students discuss the content of the text and write a joint summary of the piece. "I try to do this once or twice a week, especially when the article we're reading is a more challenging one. It gives me a different way of having them engage in some repeated reading," said Ms. Chen. Importantly, the passages have another life beyond paired reading. "Sometimes I'll use paired reading at the beginning of a close reading lesson. That way they can read it through a few times with a peer tutor, write an initial summary, and begin to get a grasp of the literal level of meaning of the text."

CONCLUSION

There is a role for the teacher in much of the learning that students do. Having said that, this chapter focuses on learning that students do in the presence of their peers. Of course, the teacher has a hand in organizing the learning environment and monitoring the impact on students' learning, but the differences in the lessons contained within this chapter related to the role of peer-mediated learning. Some of what we all know was mediated by our peers. In the world of work, most of us engage with others, trying to get our point across and recognizing that other people have good ideas. The same processes can be used in the classroom to create learners who make their own learning visible.

INDEPENDENT LEARNING

© Bob Daemmrich/PhotoEdit

Sixth-grade English teacher Patricia Dinh meets regularly with her students to discuss their reading lives. "This is a turning point in young people's lives," she said. "They'll either turn toward books, or away from them. I'm here as a guide to point them down the right path. I want them to become lifelong readers, so these conversations are really important to me."

Ms. Dinh uses independent reading in her classroom to build students' reading habits. She knows that exposure to reading, from her read-alouds to students independent reading, is important practice. Students are encouraged to select books to read from a collection she has assembled. Each of the books on her shelf has been carefully selected to appeal to young adolescents, and many focus on the social studies or science themes they are studying in their other classes. Independent reading builds students' background knowledge and their vocabulary, and develops their reading habits.

But she also knows that simply making reading materials and time available is insufficient. "I've got to build a sense of urgency with them," she said. As part of each conference, she and the student examine their current progress toward reading goals, as measured by an independent reading software program. At the beginning of the school year, students completed a diagnostic test to determine their Lexile level at that time.

> Independent reading builds students' background knowledge and their vocabulary, and develops their reading habits.

But it didn't stop there. During the first two weeks of school, they learned about reading expectations for their grade level, across middle school, in high school, and as graduates. "It was a real eye-opener for some students, who weren't necessarily aware that they were well behind," Ms. Dinh remarked.

Of course, we don't leave students in despair. Ms. Dinh then leveraged this information about her students in a unit on aspirations. "It gave me a chance to talk about growth mindset and the role of deliberate practice in learning," she explained. "We even listened to a podcast interview of Anders Ericsson, the psychologist who has done so much research on expertise and human performance!" (The podcast Ms. Dinh is referring to can be accessed at http://freakonomics.com/podcast/peak/.) They examined the research on the relationship between reading volume and achievement (Anderson, Wilson, & Fielding, 1988; Donahue, Voelkl, Campbell, & Mazzeo, 1999). The chart in Figure 6.1 is one of the items she shared with them. She then steered her students toward goal setting. "They learned about the difference between mastery goals ['I will read more complex literature'] versus performance goals ['I will get an A in English']. We keep the focus on mastery in this classroom." Using the reading diagnostic information and grade expectations, students, under the guidance of Ms. Dinh, write quarterly reading goals. She's there to advise them if the goal is unrealistic but is careful not to discourage them. "That's why we confer. Many of them need opportunities to adjust goals based on present progress." She also discusses what they are doing to meet their goals. "We talk about deliberate practice in reading, like volume, as well as the aesthetic aspects, like enjoyment, interest, and so on. I want them to appreciate that as they become increasingly proficient readers, they are also improving the quality of their lives. Reading can open up the world to them. It would be terrible if I let them see this only as making quantitative gains, without taking the time to appreciate what reading does for the human spirit."

The goal of a reading conference has always been to engage a student in a conversation about the book he or she is reading. But in light of technology advancements in adaptive independent reading software, there has been an upswing in the number of schools using these tools. Unfortunately, there is a gap between what students are doing on the computer and what more they can achieve in conversations with a teacher. Many secondary students don't know the purpose of such programs, let alone why their English teacher is requiring them to use one. Instead, using the software becomes one more compliance issue, one more hoop to jump through. Is there any wonder there is a proliferation

> EFFECT SIZE
> FOR GOALS
> = 0.50

There are instructional times when independent learning is valuable. And there are also ways to bore students to tears with independent tasks.

Figure 6.1   Relationship Between Achievement and Outside Reading

Percentile Rank	Minutes of Reading per Day (Books)	Words Read per Year
98	65.0	4,358,000
90	21.1	1,823,000
80	14.2	1,146,000
70	9.6	622,000
60	6.5	432,000
50	4.6	282,000
40	3.2	200,000
30	1.8	106,000
20	0.7	21,000
10	0.1	8,000
2	0.0	0

Source: Adapted from Anderson, R. C., Wilson, P. T., & Fielding, L. G. (1988). Growth in reading and how children spend their time outside of school. *Reading Research Quarterly, 23,* 285–303. Used with permission.

 Available for download at **https://resources.corwin.com/vl-literacy6-12**

of cheat codes and hacks all over the Internet to avoid having to put eyes on print?

What those adaptive reading software programs are really good at is providing informative feedback, which is necessary for deliberative practice. But what they can't do so well is provide motivation, a second necessity. Teachers like Ms. Dinh are leveraging the promise of such tools by taking the best of what we know about the importance of independent reading and conferring and using these as opportunities to provide motivation, set goals with students, and foster a growth mindset. In doing so, students become visible learners as they use self-regulatory skills and personal goals to actively teach themselves (Hattie, 2012). In fact, she calls these events "visible learner conferences," because she knows how important it is to provide motivation and feedback, examine goals, and monitor progress. The content of the conference is jointly determined by the teacher and student together, because the conversation should be a give and take of questions and ideas.

Video 18

Conferring With Students During Independent Learning

https://resources.corwin.com/ vl-literacy6-12

EFFECT SIZE
FOR WIDE READING
= 0.42

EFFECT SIZE
FOR WIDE READING
= 0.42

EFFECT SIZE
FOR TEACHER
CLARITY = 0.75

Teaching Takeaway

Communicate the purpose or goal of independent work to students, so students see its relevance.

In the meantime, the rest of Ms. Dinh's students are reading widely, building their background knowledge and vocabulary. During the class period, students read and write every day and spend time working with their teacher, collaborating with peers, and working independently. As we have noted, some of this time is used for direct instruction, and other time is used for dialogic instruction. But teaching is not a simple dichotomy between these two. There are instructional times when independent learning is valuable. And there are also ways to bore students to tears with independent tasks.

As we noted in Chapter 2, teacher clarity includes relevance. As it is applied to independent learning, relevance means that students understand why they are asked to complete certain tasks, or that they have a goal that directs their own independent learning. That's why Ms. Dinh emphasizes the purpose of independent reading, whether using adaptive software or print books, and individual goal setting. Relevance matters throughout the instructional period, but it is even more crucial during independent learning, because otherwise students perceive these tasks as busy work that they are required to complete. That perception is understandable if the teacher has not communicated the ways in which these tasks contribute to their learning. And in some cases, students see independent learning for the busy work that it sometimes is. Far too many students are required to complete worksheet page after worksheet page to practice skills and concepts they have already mastered. We call these "shut-up sheets" because they keep students quiet and busy, despite the fact that they are not learning much.

FINDING FLOW

Mihaly Csikszentmihalyi (1990) believes that the optimal state for humans is a balance between skill and challenge. When we have sufficient skills (especially at the surface level) and the challenge is appropriate, we fall into a state of flow in which we are cognitively engaged, often losing track of time. When our skills exceed the challenge, we are bored. This is too often the case in school. Students expect school to be challenging and appreciate when it is. They know we're not wasting their time. Having said that, when the challenge far exceeds our skill level, we become frustrated or anxious. Who hasn't seen students become so frustrated that they act out? Flow is the careful balance between skills and challenge, as noted in Figure 6.2.

When the teacher is present, the challenge level can increase. That's what happens during direct and dialogic approaches to instruction. But

Figure 6.2   Flow

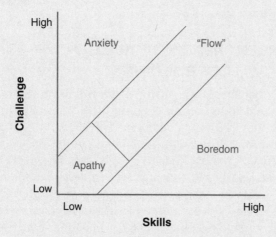

when students work independently, the challenge has to be reduced a bit to ensure that they enter the state of flow. If the demand is reduced too much, boredom ensues.

Yes, it's challenging. If creating flow with and for students was easy, everyone would be a teacher. Expert teachers know their students well, know their content well, have formative evaluation data that identify learning gaps, and then plan assignments and tasks to close the gap between students' current performance and their expected performance. And it bears repeating, independent learning is not the only tool that teachers have to close the gap! Students move from surface to deep to transfer when teachers use a combination of direct, dialogic, and independent tasks. The remainder of this chapter focuses on independent learning tasks that are not boring or repetitive. Rather, they allow students to engage in deliberative practice and apply what they have learned, and to gain new knowledge that they can use later. Unlike direct and dialogic instruction, independent learning tasks require that students develop habits of learning. They need to remain focused on the task at hand. They need to persevere in the face of challenge. And they need to recognize their successes and celebrate them. Ideally, students enter a state of flow when they are engaged in independent learning, as many of

Video 19
Independent Learning

https://resources.corwin.com/ vl-literacy6-12

Ms. Dinh's students did during their reading. In the English classroom, independent learning focuses on three major elements: reading, writing, and vocabulary.

INDEPENDENT READING FOR FLUENCY AND KNOWLEDGE BUILDING

Fluency—to be fluent—has many connotations in education. One focuses on the skills in learning language, as in "she is a fluent speaker." Another focuses on learning additional languages, as in "she is newly fluent in Spanish." However, the one we use in this book concerns the rate and accuracy at which students process text. "Reading fluency is the ability to read quickly and accurately, with appropriate and meaningful expression" (Rasinski, 2003, p. 16). In other words, reading fast is not the true goal of fluency. Readers must understand what they are reading and add expressiveness to their oral reading. Comparing fluency with music, Worthy and Broaddus (2001/2002) note that fluency "consists not only of rate, accuracy, and automaticity, but also of phrasing, smoothness, and expressiveness. Fluency gives language its musical quality, its rhythm and flow, and makes reading sound effortless" (p. 334).

Reading fast is not the true goal of fluency.

Let's define some of those terms that were just mentioned. Rate is the speed at which the learner reads. If the reader's rate is too slow (less than 50 words per minute), it will interfere with comprehension, because the reading becomes choppy: Some ideas will be disconnected from other ideas in the sentences and paragraphs. If the reading is too fast, especially in oral reading, this may also interfere with comprehension, as the reader rushes too quickly past the details that make the passage meaningful. Reading too fast may also indicate that the learner lacks prosody, the ability to adjust tone, pitch, and rate to read with expression appropriate to the meaning of the words. After all, a reader can only use expression when the meaning of the message is understood. Finally, accuracy refers to the ability to read the words correctly. Remember that the relative accuracy of a reader reflects text difficulty. Automaticity is the ability to recognize words with a minimum of attention, allowing readers to direct most of their attention to matters of comprehension.

In addition to being fluent in oral reading, students must also be fluent in silent reading. While less attention has been given to this area, the goal of reading is that students read independently for both enjoyment and information. Again, they must read fast enough to make sense of the information and accurately enough to gain information. Independent reading is a way to build fluency through deliberative practice. As Rasinski (2010) notes, slow, inefficient, and disfluent reading should be taken seriously. Readers with these problems will likely have reading difficulties for their entire school experience if nothing is done. Therefore, it is useful to attend to both silent and oral fluency rates throughout the academic year to monitor progress. Figure 6.3 offers a chart of silent and oral fluency rates by grade level. You'll notice that the chart only goes to Grade 8, because fluency rates top out at that level. High school students should be reading at the silent and oral fluency levels indicated for eighth grade.

As we noted in the direct and dialogic instruction chapters, there are many things that teachers can do to build students' fluency. Readers Theatre, for example, provides students with opportunities to practice their oral fluency, both rate and prosody. But if they don't know what is expected of them and where they are performing relative to these expectations, students may fail to understand why they continue to struggle with reading. Students equipped with self-assessment data become assessment-capable learners who can visibly teach themselves. However, it is up to us to make sure they are aware of their current status and where they need to be so that they can set goals and monitor their progress. This requires that students have data to analyze, which is very easy to do with digital recording devices available on most tablets and smartphones.

The following oral fluency exercise is predicated on the value of repeated readings. Many students can benefit from hearing the sound of their voice on a digital recording, and reading into an electronic device capitalizes on this motivation. The student selects a brief reading (50–100 words) and records his voice while reading aloud. After stopping the recorder, the student reads the same passage three more times aloud. For the fifth reading, the student records himself again and then plays the entire tape back. Students are often astounded at how the quality of their oral reading has improved.

> EFFECT SIZE FOR REPEATED READING PROGRAMS = 0.67

Although it may seem like an oversimplification, fluency in any skill, whether it is reading or writing or making free throws, requires time to practice. There is an oft-repeated story about basketball player Michael Jordan, the third-highest scorer in the NBA (32,292 points over his entire career) and his penchant for daily practice. Like Jordan, even good readers benefit from daily practice through the act of reading. Wide, independent reading increases reading volume, the overall amount of reading a student does. In turn, reading volume is correlated to reading achievement (Stanovich, 1986). Thus, teachers should provide students time to engage in wide, independent reading not only to build their background knowledge and vocabulary but also to provide spaced practice for developing fluency.

> EFFECT SIZE FOR SPACED VERSUS MASS PRACTICE = 0.71

Figure 6.3   Norms for Reading Fluency (in words correct per minute)

Oral Reading Fluency Norms, Grades 1–8

WCPM: Words correct per minute

SD: Standard deviation

Count: Number of student scores

Grade	Percentile	Fall WCPM	Winter WCPM	Spring WCPM
1	90		81	111
	75		47	82
	50		23	53
	25		12	28
	10		6	15
	SD		32	39
	Count		16,950	19,434
2	90	106	125	142
	75	79	100	117
	50	51	72	89
	25	25	42	61
	10	11	18	31
	SD	37	41	42
	Count	15,896	18,229	20,128
3	90	128	146	162
	75	99	120	137
	50	71	92	107
	25	44	62	78
	10	21	36	48
	SD	40	43	44
	Count	16,988	17,383	18,372
4	90	145	166	180
	75	119	139	152
	50	94	112	123
	25	68	87	98
	10	45	61	72
	SD	40	41	43
	Count	16,523	14,572	16,269
5	90	166	182	194
	75	139	156	168
	50	110	127	139
	25	85	99	109
	10	61	74	83
	SD	45	44	45
	Count	16,212	13,331	15,292

6	90	177	195	204
	75	153	167	177
	50	127	140	150
	25	98	111	122
	10	68	82	93
	SD	42	45	44
	Count	10,520	9,218	11,920
7	90	180	192	202
	75	156	165	177
	50	128	136	150
	25	102	109	123
	10	79	88	98
	SD	40	43	41
	Count	6,482	4,058	5,998
8	90	185	199	199
	75	161	173	177
	50	133	146	151
	25	106	115	124
	10	77	84	97
	SD	43	45	41
	Count	5,546	3,496	5,335

Source: Hasbrouck, J., & Tindal, G. A. (2006). Oral reading fluency norms: A valuable assessment tool for reading teachers. *Reading Teacher, 59*(7), 636–644. Used with permission.

Available for download at **https://resources.corwin.com/vl-literacy6-12**

It is essential to state that we believe reading is more than a skill to be taught. It is how knowledge is built. Independent reading is rightly viewed as an activity to build the knowledge needed to be successful in the English classroom and across the school day. In fact, knowledge of a topic can serve as a counterweight for an otherwise struggling reader. In an iconic study of the effects of prior knowledge and reading skills (Recht & Leslie, 1988), middle school students were identified as members of one of four groups:

- Group 1: High topical knowledge/high reading skills

- Group 2: Low topical knowledge/high reading skills

- Group 3: High topical knowledge/low reading skills

- Group 4: Low topical knowledge/low reading skills

They were given a reading about the game of baseball. It comes as no surprise to learn that the Group 1 students performed best on a series of comprehension and memory tasks, while those in Group 4 were the least proficient. But it took the researchers by surprise to see the performance of those Group 3 students. Not only did they outperform their Group 2 peers, but their performance approached that of Group 1. In other words, the fact that they knew a lot about baseball elevated their reading comprehension to a level that was nearly as strong as that of those who possessed both high topical knowledge and high reading ability.

The implications for this are profound. Getting better at reading isn't solely about acquiring skills (although they are important); it's also about acquiring knowledge. When we identify struggling readers based solely on their skills, we capture only half the picture. "Struggle" is situational, and all students at some stage struggle (and should struggle)—it is not an identity. Therefore, we need to examine the prior knowledge a student possesses, not only the reading skill. All three of us are strong readers, but John's deep knowledge of the game of cricket means that he will understand any cricket-related text at a deeper level than either Doug or Nancy could approach. One of the very best ways to build reading ability is to ensure that some of the independent reading students do is building the background knowledge they need.

Sandra Lopez is well aware of this. She is getting ready to teach William Shakespeare's *Hamlet* but knows her students have spotty background knowledge about the author, the Elizabethan era, and the role of theatre in 16th-century England. In advance of the unit, planned for the following month, Ms. Lopez administered a preassessment to gauge their background knowledge and then built a content block on her learning management system for students to complete independently. "I used to try to teach all of this content at the same time I was teaching the play," she said. "Now I build their background knowledge in advance, so that by the time we turn our attention to the play, they're more prepared."

In the two weeks leading up to the Shakespeare unit, Ms. Lopez developed or curated resources to build their knowledge. She included several short introductory readings about Shakespeare and his contributions to the English language, including a web link to a page of Shakespearean insults. She created Quizlet flashcards of vocabulary in the play, such as *wax*, *pernicious*, and *pith* (more on Quizlet later in this chapter). "I don't need them to learn the characters and the plot structure right now," she explained. "We'll get to that in the unit. But I do want to frontload a bit of the vocabulary in advance of their reading."

Ms. Lopez collaborated with the teacher who had taught world history to her students the previous year to repurpose familiar readings students had completed then on Elizabethan England. She selected specific informational articles related to the time period, drama in theatre, and Shakespeare's life, and loaded them into an adaptive reading software program her school uses to augment students' independent reading. Finally, she loaded several videos into the learning management system, including "Shakespeare on the Silver Screen" and several from TED-Ed, including "The Development of English Drama," "Why Tragedies Are Alluring," and "Did Shakespeare Write His Plays?" Ms. Lopez said, "I especially like the TED-Ed lessons because they have short quizzes built in, and if a student answers incorrectly, the lesson takes them back to the point in the video when the answer is discussed."

"Let's face it, Shakespeare is a difficult read for even the strongest readers. But it gets a lot more comprehensible when students possess a fair amount of background knowledge," she said. Throughout the two weeks leading up to the unit, students could earn virtual badges to mark their progress in developing this knowledge. "I try to have some fun with it," Ms. Lopez said. "They can earn a 'Something's Rotten' badge for completing the Shakespearean insults content, a 'Groundlings' badge for the theatre readings, and a 'QE1' badge for mastering the historical context," she said. "Those badges are the success criteria," she added. Her lesson plan for the online independent assignments for students in advance of the *Hamlet* unit appears in Figure 6.4.

INDEPENDENT WRITING

EFFECT SIZE
FOR WRITING
PROGRAMS = 0.44

Students should write every day in class. Some of the writing they do will be brief, and sometimes they will write longer pieces, extended over several days. Writing requires thinking, and often students clarify their thinking as they write. Writing provides teachers with glimpses into students' thinking and allows for additional instruction based on that thinking. Writing requires that students put pen to paper or fingers to keyboard and flow their ideas. As is the case with many other things, you don't get good at something you don't do. Students need regular writing practice if they are going to get better. But writing independently, in and of itself, does not necessarily result in improvement. Students need robust instruction in writing that includes both direct and dialogic approaches, and time to practice. Practice alone does not make perfect, but it does make permanent.

Power Writing

To increase writing fluency, students should be provided opportunities to engage in timed writings on a regular, nearly daily, basis. Fearn and Farnan (2001) called this process *power writing* and recommended that

Figure 6.4   Eleventh-Grade Lesson Plan for Building Knowledge for *Hamlet* Unit

Assessed Need: I have noticed that my students need: Background knowledge in advance of the Hamlet unit, especially on Elizabethan theatre, 16th-century English history, and Shakespeare's biography and contributions to the English language.
Standard(s) Addressed: RL.11–12.4. Determine the meaning of words and phrases as they are used in the text, including figurative and connotative meanings; analyze the impact of specific word choices on meaning and tone, including words with multiple meanings or language that is particularly fresh, engaging, or beautiful. (Include Shakespeare as well as other authors.)   RI.11–12.7. Integrate and evaluate multiple sources of information presented in different media or formats (e.g., visually, quantitatively) as well as in words in order to address a question or solve a problem.   L.11–12.5. Demonstrate understanding of figurative language, word relationships, and nuances in word meanings.   a. Interpret figures of speech (e.g., hyperbole, paradox) in context and analyze their role in the text   b. Analyze nuances in the meaning of words with similar denotations.
Text(s) I Will Use: World history readings from last year on 16th-century English history, TED-Ed online materials on theatre and Shakespeare, "Shakespeare and the Silver Screen" video, Quizlet vocabulary cards for Hamlet, and informational readings from adaptive reading program
Learning Intention for This Lesson: We will acquire background knowledge needed for the upcoming unit on Hamlet by William Shakespeare.
Success Criteria for This Lesson: Virtual badges will be awarded for each of the four content blocks: Something's Rotten badge for Shakespearean Insults   Groundlings badge for knowledge of the 16th-century English theatre   QE1 badge for knowledge of 16th-century English history   Words, words, words badge for language contributions
Direct Instruction: Model: Strategies/skills/concepts to emphasize   Monday only   **Name the strategy, state its purpose, explain its use:** Explain to students that the Hamlet unit will begin in two weeks, and that the background knowledge needed to understand it is substantial. Share graphed class results of preassessment administered last week to show current knowledge gaps. Tell them I have developed four content blocks for them to complete on the learning management system during independent learning. These can be completed in or out of class, but should be done before the Hamlet unit begins.   **Demonstration:** Show students where the content blocks are located and remind them that the blocks can be completed in any order.   **Errors to avoid:** Don't wait until the night before this is due! The purpose is to build background knowledge, which is not effectively accomplished in a cram session. Remind them of the article we read earlier this year on the difference between mass and distributed practice.   **Assess the skill:** Virtual badges are awarded on successful completion of the short quizzes and constructed responses for each of the four content blocks. Quizzes are timed.   Guide and Scaffold: Questions to ask   N/A   Assess: These are the students who will need further support   Check in with Stephany, who is new and has had limited experience with using the learning management system. Coordinate with Mr. Hendricks, the special education teacher, to meet with students with disabilities who are accessing a modified version of the content blocks.

Dialogic Instruction:
Teacher-Directed Tools
N/A
Student-Enacted Tools
N/A
Assess: These are the students who will need further support
N/A
Feedback Opportunities: Check in every other day to monitor progress; include checking for dates and times when content blocks were last accessed. Meet individually as needed with students who have not started or who are falling behind the expected pace, providing additional support as needed.
Independent Learning and Closure:
Closure: The learning intentions and success criteria are posted on the content block. On Friday (halfway through), have students check their status. They should have earned two badges by this point.
Independent Learning: After students have successfully completed all four content blocks, readminister the preassessment to gauge student learning and measure impact of instruction.

Available for download at **https://resources.corwin.com/vl-literacy6-12**

students write for one minute as fast as they can and as much as they can, and then repeat this two more times per day. The topic changes for each round. Following each timed minute, students are asked to count the number of words they have written, circling any errors they notice as they reread. The goal is to increase volume while decreasing errors. When any of us write fast enough, we make errors. But if we notice our own errors, we don't need instruction. When writers don't notice their own errors, they likely need additional instruction.

For example, students in Tanya Oswald's eighth-grade class were learning about Greek and Roman myths. On a given day, Ms. Oswald used single words to get students writing about what they knew. The first minute, students wrote about *nemesis*. The second minute, they wrote about *zenith*. And during the third minute, they wrote about *allegory*. In his writing, Stephan did not use the correct version of *their* but had accurate information about what a nemesis was, and he used examples from a myth they had read. Trisha incorrectly used *zenith* and did not notice that her answer was inaccurate. Ricardo noticed several errors that he made, including some sentence fragments and comma splices. These errors, missed by the student or not, provided Ms. Oswald a glimpse into students' thinking and provided her with information about their writing and content

Teaching Takeaway

Provide students with opportunities to engage in timed writings on a regular, nearly daily, basis to increase writing fluency.

knowledge development. As an added benefit, power writing topics or prompts can activate students' background knowledge on a given topic. Ms. Oswald's students' were primed for their next lesson on myths, a Readers Theatre production about Hades and Persephone, because of the writing and thinking that they did early in the class period.

As part of the power writing process, about every three weeks students set goals for themselves. These goals tend to focus on increasing fluency or decreasing errors. Ms. Oswald has her students individually graph the highest number of words they write each day on a histogram that students keep in their writer's notebooks. On the first page of their notebooks is a list of the goals they have set for themselves and an indication of their progress toward each.

Importantly, power writing builds fluency but is not a comprehensive writing activity. Students need examples, modeling, mentor texts, time to talk with others about their writing, and feedback from readers to become strong writers who can influence the world with their words. Having said that, it's important to note that it's hard to edit and revise when you don't have anything written. Fluency in writing is just as important as fluency in reading; it's fodder for understanding.

Error Analysis

Grammar, punctuation, and syntax errors . . . these are the bane of every English teacher. Shouldn't they have learned this already? We sigh, circle, correct, hand back papers . . . and nothing changes. In desperation, we turn to grammar worksheets and hope for the best. And still nothing changes. Middle and high school students need direct instruction on mechanics and conventions, and they benefit greatly when we point out how a writer has utilized or broken these rules for effect. But one learns editing by engaging in authentic tasks. Rather than rely on contrived and artificial editing items, use examples from their own writing. Repeated performance of a task is another key component of deliberative practice. Your analysis of student writing errors should be more than simply cataloging the mistakes they make. When you detect error patterns, cull examples from their own writing to reteach and to provide practice items.

EFFECT SIZE FOR GOALS = 0.50

Simone Okeke's seventh-grade students focused on comma splices and run-on sentences, since this was a common error she saw in their recent writing. She has worked with other error patterns in the past in small groups, but these two seemed to be more widely problematic. Therefore, Ms. Okeke chose to address the whole class in preparation for their revisions. In other words, she didn't simply tell students to go home and practice grammar drills in isolation, and then hope for the best.

She began by modeling and providing some direct instruction about comma splices. She then displayed sentences with comma splice or run-on errors gathered from her students' writing. ("Hey, I think that's my sentence!" one student laughed when she first saw it.) She projected the sentences on the smartboard, and students worked in pairs to circle where they thought the errors were. Then they worked together to revise the sentences so they were correct. Ms. Okeke watched as partners worked through the corrections, providing her own corrective feedback as needed. "This is immediate feedback for them," she said. "Noticing where they have made errors as a class helps focus their revisions of their own writing." After this activity, as part of their independent learning, each student took the same short timed quiz on comma splices each day until the student scored 100%. These quizzes were posted on the learning management system, so Ms. Okeke could get a report of the results each day. Students who still were not successful after three attempts met with her for further personalized instruction. Ms. Okeke's weekly grammar lesson plan can be found in Figure 6.5.

> EFFECT SIZE
> FOR FEEDBACK
> = 0.75

In addition to self-corrected grammar exercises, students learn to correct grammar and sentence structure during direct and dialogic instructional time. Teachers can focus students' attention on errors as they find them in class writing assignments and as they work on successive revisions of their work. A short small group or individualized session focused on specific grammar errors in which the student is really paying attention can pay big dividends in learning. It is important to remember, however, that these times should be used to focus on errors that are from a larger writing assignment; they should not be isolated grammar lessons.

Extended Writing Prompts

In addition to high-quality instruction and time to develop their writing fluency, students need to practice writing longer pieces. To facilitate their writing, teachers (and test makers) design writing prompts. A good writing prompt has the following components:

- **Topic.** What the writing is to be about

- **Audience.** Who is reading this piece of writing

- **Format.** Rhetorical structure, text type, or genre to be produced

- **Texts.** Source from which ideas are used

- **Demands.** Additional writing and cognitive challenges that increase complexity

Figure 6.5   Seventh-Grade Weekly Lesson Plan for Self-Corrected Grammar

Assessed Need: I have noticed that my students need: Spaced practice to strengthen sentence structure and use of semicolons.
Standard(s) Addressed: TEKS Grade 7 Writing and Writing Processes (C) revise drafts to ensure precise word choice and vivid images; consistent point of view; use of simple, compound, and complex sentences; internal and external coherence; and the use of effective transitions after rethinking how well questions of purpose, audience, and genre have been addressed; (D) edit drafts for grammar, mechanics, and spelling.
Text(s) I Will Use: Errors in their own writing
Learning Intention for This Lesson: We will use what we know about run-on sentences and comma splices to make our writing clearer.
Success Criteria for This Lesson: 100% accuracy by the end of the week!
Direct Instruction: Model: Strategies/skills/concepts to emphasize Monday only <u>Name the strategy, state its purpose, explain its use:</u> The sentences we will focus on this week are fused sentences with more than one main idea. I know that a sentence should have one controlling idea, so when I look through my writing and find sentences that are really long, I want to check them and make sure they don't contain comma splices. A comma splice occurs when I separate two independent clauses, which are essentially complete sentences, with a comma instead of a period or semicolon. We are going to find comma splices and practice fixing them. <u>Analogy:</u> Have you ever had a set of sticky notes you've written things on, but they keep sticking together? Since they are one on top of another, you can't see each idea clearly. We need to separate them, which is what a semicolon will do. <u>Demonstration:</u> I am going to scan this very long sentence to see if each part of either side of the comma is a complete sentence. If it is, I have a comma splice on my hands. If they are, like this one [read an example] I have a few options. I can add a period or I can add a semicolon, which indicates that the second sentence is related to or will clarify the sentence before it. <u>Errors to avoid:</u> If there is proper punctuation, a sentence may not be a run-on, so be sure to read carefully. <u>Assess the skill:</u> I will grade myself against the answers I provide at the end of class. Guide and Scaffold: Questions to ask N/A Assess: These are the students who will need further support Monday: Use error analysis sheet from essay scores to see who made the most mistakes and check in with them while students work individually.
Dialogic Instruction: Teacher-Directed Tools Selected students will work in pairs at the smartboard to identify where the errors are, and to correct them. Student-Enacted Tools N/A Assess: These are the students who will need further support N/A
Feedback Opportunities: I will observe their corrections and support partners as needed.

Independent Learning and Closure:

Closure: The learning intentions and success criteria are posted on the quiz section of the learning management system.

Independent Learning: Students will take a seven-item quiz on comma splices and run-on sentences each day until they pass with 100% accuracy. I will run a quiz report each day to monitor student progress. Those that have not passed after three attempts will meet with me for small-group guided instruction.

Available for download at **https://resources.corwin.com/vl-literacy6-12**

Students should not have to guess what their teacher wants them to write. The prompt should be clear enough to actually guide students in thinking about their response. Here's an example of an all-too-common prompt:

> What dreams do you have for yourself? Who or what influences your dream?

This prompt is certainly motivating for some students, but how will they know what the teacher is looking for? Are they supposed to include only their experiences, or should they make connections with the text they are reading? Consider a better prompt on a similar topic. Eleventh-grade English teacher Sandra Lopez used this timed in-class writing prompt with her unit of study on *A Raisin in the Sun*. (An earlier lesson from this unit of study appears in Chapter 4.)

> What happens to dreams? In a well-developed literary essay of at least 350 words, discuss how one of the main characters in *A Raisin in the Sun* contributes to the development of a major theme of the play—that of dreams pursued, deferred, and attained. In each body paragraph, provide textual support (at least two quotes per paragraph) to illustrate the character's personality traits, and explain how these traits affect the character's dreams (or the dreams of others around the character). In the conclusion, discuss what one can learn about pursuing or deferring dreams from your character's experiences in the play.

In analyzing this prompt, we notice the following:

- **Topic.** Character analysis based on the theme of dreams

- **Audience.** Knowledgeable others

- **Format**. Well-developed literary essay of at least 350 words

Teaching Takeaway

The prompt makes a difference! A good place to get help developing writing prompts for students is the Literacy Design Collaborative. They provide templates for creating writing prompts (they call them *task templates*) and they can be found at www.ldc.org.

- **Texts.** *A Raisin in the Sun*

- **Demands.** Compare the character's personality traits and actions, discuss the character's contribution to the theme of dreams, provide specific evidence of the character's actions, and note the impact on you.

As an example, an excerpt from Maxwell's essay can be found in Figure 6.6.

LEARNING WORDS INDEPENDENTLY

An important element of literacy learning is instilling a love for words. English teachers are known for it, and sometimes we're mocked just a bit for being logophiles (from the Latin, meaning *a friend of words*). We can't

---

Figure 6.6   Excerpt From Maxwell's A *Raisin in the Sun* Essay

The major dramatic question in this play is whether or not will Walter achieve his dream. At first we thought this question would be if Walter would get his money or not but by the end of the play Walter realizes that his dream is to take care of his family and he does that by standing up and moving into the new house. The main characters in this play are Walter, Mama, Beneatha and Ruth. Walter is the protagonist of this play and he serves the role of pushing this story forward. He is affected by the conflict because he is constantly feeling that his dreams are being ripped away from him. Mama serves the purpose of preventing both Walter and Beneatha from achieving their dreams at first because she is trying to be controlling. Ruth is Walter's wife and she is just trying to keep the family together and happy. She becomes affected by the conflict because she is pregnant and has to decide if she wants to bring up another child in an already cramped living space. Beneatha is Mama's daughter and her purpose in the conflict is to show the Younger family a different way of thinking. She is affected by the conflict because she wants to be a doctor and find ways to express herself but that kind of lifestyle is extremely hard to support in poverty and especially so after Walter lost the money.

The inciting incident is when Big Walter dies because this caused the life insurance check to come in which is the reason for all of the conflict of this play. The climax of this play occurs when Walter is telling Karl Lindner, who is the man that tells the Younger family that the neighborhood does not want them, that he is still moving in. This moment finally answered the question if the Younger family would move in

and if Walter would get his dream in a very dramatic way. This scene ends in the denouement which shows Mama leaving the tenement with her plant for her new life in a nice house.

This play is host to many different themes and messages. The first message of this play is that just because a dream has been pushed off for many years or even dried up it can still be sweet and worth the wait. This can be seen with Mama who has dreamed of getting a new house for many years and when she finally got it it was amazing. This also relates to Walter because his dream of owning a liquor store may have dried up but he still achieved his dream of finding a better life for his family. A theme in this play is about self expression. This theme mostly affects Mama and Beneatha. Beneatha is going through college and uses many different activities to express herself. This is met by much resistance from Mama especially but slowly Mama realizes that self expression is important. Another message in this play is that just because there is an easy way out you should not take it if it means giving up your dignity. This is shown when Walter is emotionally broken and is about to take the money from Lindner to not move in.

This play shows how even though some dreams may die they can form into other dreams that can be satisfying. It also shows that just because there might be an easy way out of a situation you still must stand up for yourself and your family. In closing this play shows that the answer to, "What happens to a dream deferred?" is not always negative and can be an extremely satisfying thing.

help ourselves, right? We're guilt of *epeolatry* (first uttered by polymath Oliver Wendell Holmes Sr.—it means *the worship of words. A polymath* is someone who is expert at a broad range of disciplines . . . we could go on). One way to do this is for teachers to model their interest in words and their word-solving strategies. This direct instruction approach was discussed in Chapter 3. Another way to instill a love of words is to engage students in collaborative conversations, which were discussed in Chapters 4 and 5 as dialogic approaches to learning. Having said that, we recognize that the majority of words that students learn come from their reading. As such, teachers must ensure that their students engage in significant amounts of wide reading. As noted by sixth-grade teacher Patricia Dinh at the beginning of the chapter, there is a correlation between students' achievement and their reading volume (Anderson et al., 1988). In a large part, this is because of the vocabulary knowledge that develops through reading.

Of course there are other ways that teachers can develop students' independent word learning. We will highlight a few approaches here, but it's important to consider what they have in common:

- First, they directly involve students, who notice that they need to learn a word.

- Second, students keep records of the words they want to learn.

- Third, students share their ideas with others so that their peers can choose to add new words to their learning goals. Here are three effective approaches:

  ○ **Vocabulary Self-Awareness.** Teaching vocabulary is complicated by the varying word knowledge levels of individual students. Even when the text is held in common, students bring a range of word knowledge to the reading. Rather than apply a one-size-fits-all approach to vocabulary instruction, it is wise to assess students before the reading. The assessment is valuable for students as well, because it highlights their understanding of what they know as well as what they still need to learn in order to comprehend the reading. One method for accomplishing this is through Vocabulary Self-Awareness (Goodman, 2001). Words are introduced at the beginning of the reading or unit, and students complete a self-assessment of their knowledge of the words, resulting in a personalized vocabulary chart. An excerpt of a tenth-grade student's vocabulary chart for Isaac Asimov's novella *The Bicentennial Man* can be found in Figure 6.7. Notice that this student identified his understanding of key words with

EFFECT SIZE FOR VOCABULARY PROGRAMS = 0.67

Figure 6.7   Vocabulary Self-Awareness Chart

Directions:					
Put the date in the "+" column when you can can write an example and definition of the word.					
Put the date in the "✓" column when you can either write a definition or an example, but not both.					
Put the date in the "–" column for words that are new to you.					
Word	**–**	**✓**	**+**	**Example**	**Definition**
intransigence		9/15		Stubborn child who refuses to go to bed	Unwilling to compromise
colloquial			9/15	Slang	Informal speech, like when you're talking to a friend
diffident	9/15				Shy, without confidence
shirk		9/15		Skipping chores even though the family needs your help to run the house	Refuse to take responsibility for your duties
inanimate			9/16	Any nonliving thing	Without life

dates to match the codes. As the unit of study progresses, and he reads other Asimov novellas in the *Robot* series, he will update his self-awareness chart, adding new dates when he masters a new level of understanding.

○ **Vocabulary Self-Selection (VSS).** Students identify words they believe are important for themselves and the class to learn. These words can occur in their readings, their independent research, or their interactions with others. Students independently record how they located the word (for example, heard on television or read it on the Internet) and why they believe it is important. When developing VSS with her ninth graders, Mikaila Salmon read excerpts from Stephen King's book *On Writing* (2000). The class favorite was, "If you want to be a successful writer, you *must* be able to describe it, and in a way that will cause your reader to prickle with recognition" (p. 171). They also drew advice from King's declaration that "the adverb is not your friend. With adverbs, the writer usually tells us he or she is afraid he/she isn't expressing himself/herself clearly, that he or she is not getting the point or the picture across" (p. 117). These lines sparked a discussion about the need for an increasingly descriptive and varied vocabulary. Based on this discussion, the class located online resources to assist them with word choice when writing. Salmon's students know that one of the best ways to increase one's lexicon is by reading widely, defining unfamiliar words, and using them in one's own writing.

○ **Scavenger Hunts and Realia.** Like VSS, scavenger hunts challenge students to locate representations of new vocabulary. Students are given a list of words, both new and familiar, that are related conceptually. They have one week to find either visual examples (e.g., digital images), realia (the object itself), or evidence of the use of the word in something other than their textbooks. For instance, sixth graders can be given a list of vocabulary words like the ones in Figure 6.8.

> EFFECT SIZE FOR
> VOCABULARY
> PROGRAMS = 0.67

INDEPENDENTLY WORKING WITH WORDS

If students are to deepen their understanding of vocabulary, they need to engage with words both collaboratively and independently. Dialogic approaches to instruction provide students with opportunities to use words and clarify meanings. If we want students to develop their academic language, they have to use that language. We don't get good at things we don't do. Having said that, it's important to recognize that students also have to engage with the words (and the concepts behind those words) individually. One way to do so is to have students create vocabulary cards to use as study aids.

> If we want students to develop their academic language, they have to use that language. We don't get good at things we don't do.

Students are given a set of 4″ × 6″ index cards and instructed to divide each into quadrants (see Figure 6.9). For example, eighth-grade teacher

Figure 6.8 Vocabulary Scavenger Hunt for Sixth Graders

Literary Terms	
Anthropomorphism	Hyperbole
Metaphor	Imagery
Dialogue	Protagonist
Flashback	Antagonist
Foreshadowing	Conflict

Figure 6.9   Student-Created Vocabulary Cards in Eighth Grade

Template	
Vocabulary word	Definition in student's own words
Graphic or picture	Antonym or reminder of what the word does not mean

Example	
autocracy	a government system where one person with all the power rules
	In an autocracy, individuality is not valued.

Image source: © iStockphoto.com/Bolkins

Ben Gage selected terms related to the Latin root word *auto-* meaning "to make." Students created their vocabulary word cards for *autonomy*, *automaton*, and *autocracy*. The target word is written in the top left quadrant, and the definition, after class instruction, is recorded using the student's own words in the upper right quadrant of the card. An antonym is written in the lower right quadrant, and an illustration or graphic symbol representing the term is drawn in the lower left quadrant.

Student-constructed digital flashcards are appealing for secondary students and can be incorporated into most learning management systems. A favorite is Quizlet (www.quizlet.com), a free flashcard generator invented by high school freshman Andrew Sutherland in 2005 when he had to study terms for his French class. Although many existing sets already exist due to a programming interface that allows users to access and modify each others' flashcards, we encourage students to construct their own, because the act of conceptualizing the definitions and images is in itself a study aid.

Constructing vocabulary cards serves several uses. First, when placed on a binder ring or digitally on a learning management system, the flashcards become an easily accessible reference for the student. The time involved in creating each card also provides an opportunity for the student to spend an extended period of time concentrating on the meaning, use, and representation of the term, thereby increasing the likelihood that the term will become a part of permanent vocabulary.

The *VISIBLE LEARNER*

Mohamed and Zinnia had finished their independent learning tasks in preparation for persuasive speeches each would be delivering the following week in their eighth-grade English class. Mohamed had created a short screencast to use in his speech on whether plastic shopping bags should be banned, and Zinnia was researching the topic of whether to pay college athletes. Noticing that she was finished, Mohamed approached Zinnia and asked if she had time to review his screencast. *"Do you think you could check out my screencast and make sure it's good? I think I have all the information I need in there, but I want to make sure my audience isn't left with any questions. Could you watch it and write down any areas I need to include more information on?"*

Zinnia agreed and said, *"I wrote an outline for my speech but I'm not sure about my last transition statement. Can you read it? I'm not sure if it's in a logical order."*

Visible learners actively seek feedback.

Use Games to Foster Retention

Once students have learned a set of terms in a given lesson, there is a risk that the words will be forgotten due to disuse. One way that teachers can provide students some practice with retention is to cycle previously taught terms in with new ones. This provides students an opportunity to draw words from memory. Teachers can also use word activities and games that provide students with an opportunity to use the words they have learned. Finally, teachers can ensure that students have multiple opportunities to write during the day. Games are an excellent method for creating opportunities for rehearsal and practice, which facilitates retention. Because games are engaging, they also are chosen frequently by students during collaborative learning time. These include board games like Scrabble, Concentration, and Boggle. Our middle school colleague Amy Miles has attached a Scrabble board to a wall in her classroom and added Velcro to letter tiles. She has an ongoing game of students and adults (including visitors to the classroom), complete with an arrow indicating who's turn is next.

Online word games can also facilitate rehearsal and retention. Quizlet provides several games, including one called Gravity, a timed game that requires the user to correctly identify terms being hurled as asteroids before they hit a planet. Another favorite of ours is Free Rice, sponsored by the World Food Programme (freerice.com). For every correct answer, ten grains of rice are donated to feed people around the world. Players select the subject, including humanities, English, and SAT test preparation, as well as world languages and discipline-specific subjects such as chemistry symbols. Games such as these can be linked to the class learning management system for use during independent learning time.

BIG IDEAS ABOUT INDEPENDENT LEARNING

Across the examples we have provided, there are three indicators of quality opportunities to deepen learning in the independent phase of instruction: thinking metacognitively, setting goals, and developing self-regulatory skills.

To ensure that students continue learning as they engage in tasks, assignments, or activities on their own, teachers should consider the following questions:

- Does it promote metacognition?

- Does it promote goal setting?

- Does it promote self-regulation?

The *VISIBLE LEARNER*

Soraya uses the questions her Year 10 English teacher, Mr. Peck, introduced several weeks ago as she studies for an upcoming English literature exam in her flat in the East End of London. When asked to explain her thinking about her thinking, Soraya responded,

- What are you trying to accomplish? *"I'm reviewing my notes on the units of study about Dickens. We read* Great Expectations *and* Silas Marner, *so I need to refresh my memory about the two books."*

- What strategies are you using? *"I've been going through my notes. I've highlighted the ones I think are going to be important, and I'm rewriting them on another page."*

- How well are you using the strategies? *"Rewriting seems to help me with remembering details. I know it's slower when I write them out, but it helps my memory. Sometimes I can almost see my notes in my mind when I'm taking an exam."*

- What else could I do? *"I noticed that I don't have much down about the author. I guess I thought I knew it at the time, but it's been a few weeks. I should probably look him up online and read up a bit. And I'll have to take notes this time."*

Visible learners have metacognitive skills and can talk about them (systematic planning, memory, abstract thinking, critical thinking, problem solving, etc.).

Does It Promote Metacognition?

The first question to pose when analyzing the rigor of an independent task is whether or not it promotes metacognition. Awareness of one's own learning evolves over a lifetime, and this habit is developed through opportunities to think about one's own thinking. Metacognitive questions embedded in the task provide these opportunities. It is common to ask reflective questions at the end of a complex task, and to be sure their regular use encourages the habit of post hoc analysis. But metacognition should also occur *during* a task. Year 10 English teacher Charles Peck uses four questions designed by Anderson (2002). His students are preparing for the General Certificate of Secondary Education exams (GCSE) they'll be taking next year; this time of preparation is highly stressful in the lives of British adolescents. His intention is to introduce a metacognitive framework for reflecting on their learning. Before his students begin an independent task, he reminds them to think through the tasks as they work.

EFFECT SIZE FOR METACOGNITIVE STRATEGIES = 0.69

Figure 6.10   Lesson Plan for Year 10 Using Metacognitive Strategies

Assessed Need: I have noticed that my students need: *To make their learning visible to themselves through the use of self-questioning.*
Standard(s) Addressed: *N/A*
Text(s) I Will Use: *Classroom poster of metacognitive questions for independent learning.*
Learning Intention for This Lesson: *To acquire tools for reflecting on learning and making a plan of action.*
Success Criteria for This Lesson: *I use these questions before I begin a task, and to check in with myself to monitor my own progress toward goals.*
Direct Instruction: Model: Strategies/skills/concepts to emphasize *Introduce and model the use of four questions for checking in with myself. Explain to students that I use these same questions when I've got a complicated job in front of me.* *"What am I trying to accomplish?" This first question reminds me to check in with the purpose. The learning intention is a good place to start, as it can orient my thinking as I focus on the outcomes.* *"What strategies am I using?" I like to build furniture, and I've done it enough that I know I need to make sure I've got the tools I need at the ready. It takes me off my game when I have to stop to go searching for some tool I suddenly realize I need. It's no different with an academic task. Part of my preparation is making sure I've got the tools I need. If I'm diving in to a dense reading, I expect that I'm going to need to take notes, maybe annotate right in the margins. Before I go on to a new section, I take the time to review my notes and summarize. My notes, the annotations, the time I take to summarize—these are all tools, or strategies, that I'm putting into play.* *"How well am I using the strategies?" From time to time when I'm building furniture, I stop and take a few steps back to look at my progress. Sometimes I make adjustments because I don't like what I see. It's no different when I'm taking on an academic task. I pause and take a few metaphorical steps back to ask myself how I'm doing. These questions give me a frame for analyzing my progress.* *"What else could I do?" Sometimes I don't like what I see. But I can't just scrap the whole thing and walk away. I have to push forward and ask myself if there are alternatives. If I'm really stuck, I check in with someone else for advice or guidance.* Guide and Scaffold: Questions to ask *How might these questions help you to resolve a problem?* *Are there other parts of your life where you could apply these same questions to resolve a dilemma?* Assess: These are the students who will need further support *Talk individually with Eugene, because he gives up on himself quickly. Check with Fatima, because she rushes and in her hurry makes needless errors. I'd like her to use these questions to slow down a bit.*
Dialogic Instruction: Teacher-Directed Tools *N/A* Student-Enacted Tools *After students have applied these metacognitive strategies to an independent reading task for GCSE preparation they'll be completing today, meet as a fishbowl group (inside/outside circles). The first group in the inside circle will discuss what worked and why. The second group will discuss difficulties, and how students can get better at using these strategies to solve problems.* Assess: These are the students who will need further support *Have Eugene and Fatima in the second inside group, so they can listen to the comments of others first.*

1. **"What am I trying to accomplish?"** This first question encourages students to locate the purpose. In Mr. Peck's case, it causes his learners to think about what the task or assignment is asking of them.

2. **"What strategies am I using?"** The second question requires students to determine what will be required of them to support their learning, such as making a decision about whether to keep notes in a journal or annotate directly on the text.

3. **"How well am I using the strategies?"** Students need to monitor a complex task in order to see if it is working, which means they must pause to see if they are headed in the right direction. The ability to make a midcourse correction is an important factor when deepening knowledge. Mr. Peck promotes this by setting a two-minute timer to remind students to stop and evaluate their progress.

4. **"What else could I do?"** We expect students to get stuck; if that doesn't occur from time to time, then the work is too easy. But we also need to promote resilience and flexible thinking. This last question reminds Mr. Peck's students that thinking critically involves reasoning, synthesizing information, and exploring alternative solutions and perspectives. Mr. Peck's lesson plan can be found in Figure 6.10.

Does It Promote Goal Setting?

A second indicator of quality concerns goal setting by the student. Students should understand how a task advances their goals, as this is the basis of intrinsic motivation. Students' motivators vary, but they are likely to include some mix of performance (grades and recognition),

EFFECT SIZE
FOR GOALS
= 0.50

mastery (acquiring knowledge), and work-avoidant (conserving effort) goals. While "work-avoidant" may not sound like something positive, it is something that all of us consider in our own decisions. For example, we may weigh an opportunity by thinking about the possible reward and the chance to advance our learning, but these are always considered within the context of the amount of effort it will require.

Our students are no different. Written essays and research projects require quite a bit of effort, but there are performance and mastery elements at stake as well. Seventh-grade teacher Irma Rodriguez builds goal setting into such assignments. After discussing the research project at hand, she asks students to set a performance goal (the grade they want to achieve) and a mastery goal (what they propose to learn during the a process), and to determine their planned effort (how many hours they will invest). They submit their goals to her in advance, and she uses these during conferences. At the time of submission of the project, they also rate themselves on attainment of their goals: the expected grade, evidence of achievement of the learning goal, and the amount of time actually spent on the assignment.

"I'm careful about the performance goals," she said. "I don't want them to detach learning from achievement, which is why there's always a mastery goal, too." She continued, "However, I do want them to see the link between achievement, effort, and attainment. These are not unrelated, and understanding that empowers them." She adds that she asks students to assess their final projects based on the grading criteria as well as their responses to two questions: (1) How much time did you devote to this project? and (2) If you had two more hours, what would you do next on this project? "It's amazing how accurate and forthcoming they are," said Ms. Rodriguez. "Sometimes I think the self-assessment is the most valuable part of the project, because it prompts self-reflection."

> EFFECT SIZE FOR
> SELF-REPORTED
> GRADES/STUDENT
> EXPECTATIONS
> = 1.44

Does It Promote Self-Regulation?

A third indicator for independent learning concerns the ability to assume autonomy and develop a sense of efficacy. Self-regulation doesn't stand apart from the first two quality indicators; in fact, metacognition and goal setting are necessary in order to self-regulate one's learning. Choice is critical for developing a sense of autonomy. We don't mean that an independent learning task should be an "anything goes," freewheeling assignment. However, students should have the freedom to explore and customize their learning.

Independent reading is one example of how the principles of self-regulation can be developed. Teachers often assign texts to be read independently. For example, eighth graders are told to read Chapter 3 of *The Adventures of Huckleberry Finn* at home—which they may or may not do—for a discussion the next day. But when learners are presented with themes or essential questions and then choose books that will help them address the theme or answer the question, they get the opportunity to formulate a reading plan. This is far superior to the usual "read this for tomorrow" assignments that are usually given.

A final aspect of self-regulation is providing students with opportunities to explore and expand their own learning. This can be accomplished by allowing time for students to research and write about a topic of their choosing. Called "genius hour" by many, it is inspired by Google's practice of releasing engineers for 20% of their work time to explore their own learning. Genius hour at school encourages students to ask questions, find out answers, and share what they have learned with others.

For example, in their sixth-grade English class, Patricia Dinh's students had time each week to work on an investigative project of their own choosing. Each student had to identify a topic and write a proposed course of study, including timelines and deliverables. Imagine how much surface and deep learning was required for students to do this. Angel chose to learn about the Great Pacific Garbage Patch. As he said, he would like to either find a way to reduce additions to the patch or figure out how to use it for something. He read widely, both print and digital texts; interviewed people, including an oceanographer from the local university; and visited the aquarium on a free admission day after school one afternoon with his family. In other words, his investigation extended beyond the genius hour. A few weeks later, Angel and his classmates were ready for the world café that his teacher organized. On this day, the classroom was transformed into a café, and students were each assigned a time to host a table discussion about their learning. During their unassigned times, they were free to visit other tables and learn about topics of interest to their peers.

And isn't that what we want every student to be able to do? We can't possibly teach them everything they need to know. We need them to join us in this fight. That means that we must create the conditions necessary for them to visibly teach themselves.

CONCLUSION

Learning shouldn't stop when independent work begins. This seems obvious, but in too many cases the tasks and the thinking required to complete independent tasks are limited to regurgitation of knowledge.

> **Teaching Takeaway**
>
> To ensure student learning, when thinking about the tasks, assignments, and activities you plan, ask yourself these three questions: Does it promote metacognition? Does it promote goal setting? Does it promote self-regulation?

> EFFECT SIZE FOR STUDENT-CENTERED TEACHING = 0.54

The work itself doesn't forward students' learning; it is simply assigned to determine how closely their factual knowledge pairs with what the teacher has taught. We use the phrase *independent learning* intentionally, as it is more than *independent practice*. Practice is a necessary intermediate step in the knowledge-building process, but it must be deliberative, which is to say, goal driven. *Independent learning* conveys an expectation that knowledge acquisition continues; it doesn't cease in order for the brain dump to begin. It is driven by goals, metacognition, and self-regulation. Importantly, independent learning should be combined with direct and dialogic approaches to instruction. Teachers have to identify the level of learning students need to accomplish (surface, deep, or transfer) and then design experiences for them that work. These practices are likely a combination of direct, dialogic, and independent approaches. Knowing what level students need for their learning requires assessment. And understanding whether the direct, dialogic, or independent approach worked requires using assessment information to determine impact.

TOOLS TO USE
IN DETERMINING
LITERACY IMPACT

"Well, you're going to like these results!" Sonya Brown said, looking up from her laptop.

These encouraging words were shared at a professional learning community meeting of the eighth-grade teaching team following the administration of a series of vocabulary matching assessments. The team had been monitoring the impact that they had on students' literacy development for several months, using term acquisition as a proxy for overall learning and knowledge. The evidence for using vocabulary matching of terms and definitions as a curriculum-based measure of progress at the secondary level is strong (Espin, Shin, & Busch, 2005).

© iStockphoto.com/Mauro Grigollo

The teachers on this team, representing the disciplines of English, science, social studies, and mathematics, understood the value of monitoring students' growing lexicons. They had implemented a number of classroom routines, not directly related to vocabulary, to improve student learning. They were not simply drilling students to learn words in isolation, but rather using content vocabulary matching assessments to determine if students were advancing in content knowledge. The teachers met weekly and included vocabulary test data in their conversations once a month. For the first month of the year, vocabulary achievement data were flat. Although students might have been progressing in other areas, they were not developing content knowledge of the subjects.

Starting in late November and running through December, the teachers had refocused their energy on argumentation in writing. The English teachers engaged students in lessons about rhetorical stances, use of evidence, and organization. They taught students how to give effective feedback to their peers, and they organized small group, needs-based instruction that aligned with the patterns of errors they noticed in students' writing. In partnership with their English colleagues, the social studies, science, and math teachers also taught about discipline-specific argumentation writing in their classes. And their January data suggested that students' performance had improved.

In response to Ms. Brown's comment, science teacher Tad Santillan said, "That's awesome! I want to see that what we're doing is making a difference. This shared focus is paying off for our students."

DO YOU KNOW YOUR IMPACT?

A foundational assumption in education is that what we do has a positive impact on the learning lives of our students. But how do we know what our impact truly is? We can't rely solely on grades and state test scores, which serve as decontextualized data points, because often there is nothing to compare them to. And waiting until high-stakes test results are returned and students have moved to a new teacher seems unwise and unproductive. These end-of-unit exams and state test scores are mere snapshots; without preassessment measures of where students actually began, there's no real way to understand how your teaching influenced their learning. And here's why that's important: How can you make wise adjustments to your teaching when you don't know what worked and what didn't work?

> A foundational assumption in education is that what we do has a positive impact on the learning lives of our students. But how do we know what our impact truly is?

Assessment is assessment. Any assessment can be used formatively or summatively. In other words, there's nothing magical in the tool itself; it's what you do with it (or don't do with it) that matters. Using assessments for the purpose of formative evaluation casts a light on our teaching practices. It has the potential to be eye opening—to help us consider what worked and what didn't as we carefully examine the evidence of student progress. Unfortunately, it has more often been used as an isolated measure of a given student's achievement at one point in time than it has as a nuanced consideration of the overall trajectory of the student's learning experience.

As you have read throughout this book, John's work has focused on calculating the effect size of instructional and curricular approaches to identify those that have a high impact—at least a year's worth of growth for a year in school. But what if you could determine your own effect sizes about your own practice? John maintains that teachers should be able to determine their impact. The same statistical tool used to examine the results of 300 million learners—effect size—can be used to determine the impact that a given influence has on your students' learning. To calculate an effect size, first determine your students' average score for the posttest and the average for the pretest. It's easy to do this in an Excel spreadsheet. Here's how:

Video 20

Measuring Impact

https://resources.corwin.com/ vl-literacy6-12

1. Type the students' names in one column.

2. Type their scores for the pre- and postassessments in other columns.

3. Highlight the column with the preassessment scores, select the "average" tool, and place the average at the bottom of that column.

4. Do the same for the postassessment column.

However, this portion of the calculation only gets you so far. Let's say you are using a writing rubric as your assessment instrument, and after a semester of writing instruction, your class has made an average gain of one point on a seven-point rubric. Is that a worthy impact? It's hard to judge, because one point average growth isn't a meaningful metric; you need to calculate the effect size. The next step in determining the effect size is to calculate standard deviation. Excel will do this as well:[1]

1. Type =STDEV.P and then select the student scores in the pre-assessment column, putting them in parentheses. For example, your entry might look like =STDEV.P(A1:A15). The standard deviation will be in the cell where you typed the formula.

2. Do the same in the postassessment column.

3. Subtract the preassessment average from the postassessment average, and then divide by the standard deviation average for the two groups.

---

[1] You can quickly calculate standard deviation on a number of websites, such as graphpad.com/ quickcalcs/CImean1.cfm.

Here's the formula:

$$\text{Effect size} = \frac{\text{Average (postassessment)} - \text{Average (preassessment)}}{\text{Average standard deviation or SD}}$$

As a note of caution, effect sizes do not establish causation. No teacher can say with confidence that her specific actions caused her students' writing to be better, but she should be encouraged to share this approach with others so that they can determine the impact her teaching strategies might have on their students. You may have noticed that the value she calculated for effect size is an average value for the group, so really the teacher should say that the efforts to improve writing worked on average. That's why we suggest that teachers also calculate effect sizes for individual students. It's pretty simple to do: Subtract an individual student's preassessment score from his or her postassessment score and divide by the average standard deviation. The formula looks like this:

$$\text{Effect size} = \frac{\text{Individual score (postassessment)} - \text{Individual score (preassessment)}}{\text{Average standard deviation or SD for the class}}$$

By drilling down to the individual level, you gain a clearer picture of what worked or didn't work for a targeted student. Although you may not choose to calculate the effect size of your instruction for every student in your class, it should be a priority for those working above or below expected levels, as well as for students who are new to your class.

DO YOU KNOW YOUR COLLECTIVE IMPACT?

Now let's take another step forward. You will recall that of the 195 effect sizes John has calculated, one of the top influences on student learning is collective teacher efficacy. Collective teacher efficacy describes a constellation of attitudes and beliefs about the efforts of a school to affect student learning (Goddard, Hoy, & Hoy, 2000). But the day-to-day demands make it difficult for most teachers to know what their colleagues are doing, and this lack of knowledge about each other's work undermines perceptions. Instead, we begin to think, "Am I the only one doing this?" Schools must take deliberate actions to ensure that teachers have regular opportunities to collaborate with one another. We're not calling for more department meetings to discuss the next field trip, but we hold firm in the belief that without meaningful teacher collaboration, learning is harmed.

One common structure for fostering teacher collaboration to improve the quality of learning has been the formation of professional learning communities (PLCs). PLCs usually involve small groups of educators who have come together to support each other's learning for the purpose

Teaching Takeaway

Teachers can calculate effect sizes for their classes and individual students to determine the impact their instruction and intervention have had.

of improving student achievement. These are not book clubs or professional development sessions. The use of these four PLC questions keeps the focus relentlessly on the student learning, and explains why the impact of PLCs is powerful (DuFour, DuFour, & Eaker, 2008):

- What is it we expect our students to learn?

- How will we know when they have learned it?

- How will we respond when some students do not learn?

- How will we respond when some students already know it?

These discussions have resulted in improved instruction as well as better outcomes for students, particularly when there is "a climate of openness among the teachers, as well as a willingness to open up their practice . . . [for] deep level collaboration, going beyond sharing ideas, concepts, and particular lessons, but also discussing preferred outcomes and student results" (Vangrieken, Meredith, Packer, & Kyndt, 2017, p. 54).

In other words, PLCs who regularly employ impact data get results. A large-scale study illustrates the usefulness of PLCs who use impact data. Lai, Wilson, McNaughton, and Hsiao (2014) examined the effects on literacy growth at seven secondary schools in New Zealand, serving students between the ages of 13 and 18. For three years, PLCs at these schools focused on impact data, with an emphasis on collaborative analysis. In collaborative teams, teachers identified learning targets and discussed ideas for instruction. They met to review student work and figure out when their efforts had been fruitful, and made changes when they were not. The study yielded effect sizes ranging from 0.50 to 0.62 in reading comprehension achievement, well above the hinge point of 0.40. This is particularly heartening knowing that middle and high schools can be particularly complex places for engaging in cross-disciplinary PLCs.

As educators, we have to continually ask ourselves, how will I know if students have learned what they were supposed to learn? Obviously, the answer is "through assessment," which implies that teachers need to know how to assess students and then work collaboratively with their peers to respond when students do, or do not, learn. But what if students already knew the information before the lesson? What if teachers used the effect size method to proactively address the fourth PLC question? In doing so, teachers could understand their impact on students' learning, and separate this from knowledge students already possessed in advance of our teaching. That understanding, in turn, would guide improvements to instruction and intervention, especially for those students who either already knew the content, or who continue to struggle.

EFFECT SIZE
FOR COLLECTIVE
TEACHER EFFICACY
= 1.57

The *VISIBLE LEARNER*

Video 21

Visible Learners: "How do you know when you're successful?"

https://resources.corwin.com/ vl-literacy6-12

Cesar reviewed his writing and compared it with the descriptions of writing development that were posted on a four-point rubric on his ninth-grade class's website. When asked about his progress, he said, "*When I started the school year, I was mostly scoring 1's and 2's [not yet apparent or emerging] for use of evidence and elaboration. One thing that was dragging me down was I didn't always introduce my quotations with my own words and explain them fully. But now I'm scoring a 4. Look, I used a lead-in [points to a poster in the room with common lead-ins to quotations] for this quotation, which is good. But, see, I also explained how it links to my thesis after I summed it up. That's a lot better than I was doing. I'm working on tying the controlling idea to the evidence that I cite. I have to get better at using transitions that link it back to the thesis.*"

Visible learners are assessment capable—they understand the assessment tools being used and what their results mean, and they can self-assess to answer the key questions: Where am I in my learning? Where am I going? and What do I need to do to get there?

Lots of books have a chapter on assessment, and in this regard we are no different. But we hope that you will see the added value in two essential elements:

- The first, which we have already discussed, is how to calculate your impact on your class and on individual students, and how to then use that information to leverage professional learning with your colleagues to build efficacy.

- The second is to know the wide range of tools available to help you engage in formative evaluation. In addition to your own teacher-created assessments, we believe you will find these to be of value. Best of all, most of these tools are in the compendium at the end of this book.

ASSESSING READING

ASSESSING BACKGROUND KNOWLEDGE

Thus far in this chapter, we have focused on specific ways for teachers to determine impact. As we noted, this is dependent on having appropriate assessment tools that teachers can use at the outset of a unit and then again as the unit ends, and even at various points during the lesson.

Here, we provide a list of tools that teachers can use to determine students' prior knowledge about the topic of study.

Cloze Procedure

One of our favorite ways to glean what our students know about a topic is the cloze procedure. We use a reading passage that captures the essential understandings of an upcoming unit of study, either one that is written by the teacher or one extracted from another source. We omit every fifth word from a reading passage, leaving the entire first sentence and last sentence of the passage preserved in their entirety to assist the reader in gaining context. The reader fills in the missing words using context clues and syntactic strategies to complete the passage accurately. The words the student supplies must match those of the original text exactly to be considered accurate. Although some will argue that synonyms should be counted as an accurate response, research on this scoring procedure has found that too many variables are introduced when synonyms are allowed (Henk & Selders, 1984). Cloze procedure passages are easily constructed using online tools, and can be administered either individually or to an entire class.

Sandra Lopez constructed her own cloze passage (see Compendiums 1 and 2) as a preassessment of background knowledge for her next unit, a comparison of the play *Death of a Salesman* to the film of the same name. "I had taught these elements of drama last semester when we read *A Raisin in the Sun,*" she explained. "I need to know how much they've retained," she said, "and I want to build on this knowledge as we go more deeply into looking at filmed and live productions. Their responses let me know what I still need to review and reteach, versus concepts that I can now refer to and build on." She said the first time she administered a cloze assessment with her eleventh graders, they were a bit intimidated and confused. She explained to them that the results help her figure out what she doesn't need to reteach, instead allowing her to devote time to what they still need to learn.

Ms. Lopez asks her students to do their best in filling in the blanks, reminding them once again that this is so she can better plan on their behalf. "I'm not giving you word boxes, and in some cases the word that's missing is an article. Write the word you believe makes sense in the sentence." Although she constructs the cloze using conventional methods (first and last sentence intact, and deleting every fifth word), she collaborates with the special education support teacher to create a modified one for 18 students across her class periods with special education needs. "I deleted every seventh word, rather than every fifth, so they can use some additional contextual and grammatical clues." She uses the conventional scoring system to evaluate the results. These figures indicate the percentage of missing words that her students were able to fill in correctly:

- 60% and above indicates an independent level

- 40–59% indicates an instructional level

- 39% or below indicates this is at the frustration level

"Given that this is previously learned material from earlier in the year, I expect them to do well. I also ran this through a Lexile text analyzer and the passage came out at 930L, well below their expected reading levels. I want to make sure the passage doesn't accidentally turn into an assessment of their ability to read complex text. I'm focused on the content." After she wrote the passage, "a good intellectual exercise for me to summarize what had been previously learned," Ms. Lopez used an online cloze generator to delete every fifth word. "I then checked it to see if the deleted words included enough content," she said, "and in some cases I restored a deleted article in favor of a technical term." She noted that she doesn't remove all of them. "Many of my students are English learners, so it gives me additional information about how well a student is using grammatical and syntactic clues, as well as content knowledge."

Ms. Lopez stated that her colleagues use cloze assessments for different purposes. "My history and science colleagues will sometimes take the summary passage at the end of a unit in the textbook as the cloze," she said. "They administer it as a preassessment, and then again at the end of the unit so they can measure their impact," she said. "I'm glad I was able to share this approach with them, even though I like writing my own sometimes, too."

Vocabulary Matching Assessment

The teachers in the opening scenario of this chapter tracked the learning progress of a group of students for several months using a vocabulary matching task they administered periodically to gauge their impact. This is a well-known curriculum-based measure for use in secondary schools. A vocabulary matching assessment can also be used for learning within a single class, which is just what seventh-grade English teacher Simone Okeke did with her students. In the first weeks of school, Ms. Okeke administered a vocabulary matching assessment for literary devices (see Compendium 3) to determine what her students knew and did not know about common structures used by authors to convey meaning. "The results of the first administration gave me a better sense of what each period collectively knew, so I could adjust my teaching across sections. I saw that third period was quite a bit less knowledgeable than the other classes," she said.

As she taught each unit of study during the first semester, Ms. Okeke would periodically readminister the assessment to track progress. "Some units lend themselves to particular literary devices," said the teacher. "The short story unit featured works like 'Thank you, Ma'am' by Langston Hughes and 'An Occurrence at Owl Creek Bridge' by Ambrose Bierce, so we really got to untangle mood from tone. That was a common error I found they were making." Her impact on learning grew as well. "After the first unit, I calculated an effect size of 0.38. I had to go back and look at what I was doing. Not bad, but I wanted to improve it." After the second unit, her effect size had increased to 0.46 overall. "One improvement I made in the second unit was that I got better at targeting those students who needed additional small group instruction. A few of them were just not on my radar at first, because they seemed engaged and completed all their work. But that's not the same as learning." By tracking student learning over a longer period of time, she was able to fine-tune her teaching and offer student-specific intervention. "Something new I'm doing this year is sharing my impact data with my students in real time. If I want them to be assessment capable learners, I have to walk the talk. So I tell them that I want to be above the 0.40 hinge point, I set my goals, and I monitor my own progress. That way they know I'm not asking them to do anything I'm not willing to do myself," she said.

ASSESSING READING COMPREHENSION

Reading comprehension is influenced by knowledge, vocabulary, and experiences—what Thorndike described a century ago as a "cooperation of forces" (1916). Therefore, reading comprehension is a measure of a student's ability to consolidate of all these elements. Arrasmith and Dwyer (2001) described six traits of effective readers, which were further developed by the Northwest Regional Laboratory (NWREL) as a means of assessment. NWREL (now called Education Northwest) is one of ten federally funded information networks across the nation that serve as clearinghouses for resources and research for teachers, parents, administrators, and policy makers. They describe efficient and effective readers as being able to use

- Decoding conventions to read new or unfamiliar words

- Comprehension strategies to determine meaning

- Context to determine setting or time period

- Synthesis of information to make connections

- Interpretations to formulate opinions

- Evaluation to support those opinions

The assessments used by teachers of adolescents focus on the above named aspects of reading. This is accomplished through informal reading inventories, metacomprehension assessments, attitude surveys, and self-assessments.

Informal Reading Inventories

One of the most useful ways of assessing reading comprehension with older readers is with a criterion-referenced assessment called an informal reading inventory, or IRI. An informal reading inventory uses a series of passages written at various grade levels. These are used to measure students' accuracy, as well as their ability to answer literal and inferential questions about a text at a specific level of complexity. The most popular ones are commercially prepared narrative and expository passages of 100–150 words. The student first reads the passage silently, then aloud. During the oral reading, miscues are coded using the system specified in the IRI directions. Postreading questions probe the student's understanding of the text. Each IRI comes with an extensive set of directions for administering and scoring the reading. Figure 7.1 features a list of some of the most widely available IRIs in schools.

The middle school where Lamont Kennedy works tracks the reading comprehension progress of targeted students using a commercially prepared informal reading inventory. This is administered three times a year across the district and is used as a metric for the benchmarks reported to schools. "We have a number of English learners at our school, primarily speaking Tagalog and Aramaic," he explained. "Other kids are reading well below grade level because they have disabilities, and sometimes we just don't know why. But they all bear watching. We have several interventions in place to support them, but IRIs are a major way to figure out if those interventions are resulting in gains," said Mr. Kennedy.

He went on to explain how the data are used in his PLC. "I administer a lot of them, because I'm the English teacher. Mr. Genovese [the reading specialist] helps out, and so does the special educator. So I get to interpret what the data mean. That always sparks lots of discussion," he said. "My PLC is a grade-level one, so it's all the sixth-grade teachers. We each add what we're noticing in our own classes, and how we can better support each other's efforts, both in core instruction and in intervention." The decision by his district to begin using IRIs as benchmarks for students

Figure 7.1   Informal Reading Inventories

IRI	Grades	Special Features
Adolescent Reading Inventory (Brozo & Afflerbach, 2015)	6–12	• Graded word lists • Uses authentic passages from science, history, mathematics, and literature textbooks
Burns/Roe Informal Reading Inventory (Burns & Roe, 2010)	PreK–12	• Graded word lists • Silent and oral reading measures • Expository and narrative passages
Critical Reading Inventory (Applegate, Quinn, & Applegate, 2007)	K–12	• Evaluates critical literacy skills • Expository and narrative passages • Includes case study examples
Flynt-Cooter Comprehensive Reading Inventory-2 (Cooter, Flynt, & Cooter 2013)	K–12	• Uses sentences for passage selection • Includes Spanish passages • Expository and narrative passages
Qualitative Reading Inventory (Leslie & Caldwell, 2016)	K–12	• Questions for prior knowledge • Graded word lists • Expository and narrative passages • Enhanced e-package includes online audio samples

Available for download at **https://resources.corwin.com/vl-literacy6-12**

not yet making expected progress has been a boon for him. "I've been teaching for 16 years, and the usual thinking was that it was up to the English teacher to teach reading," said Mr. Kennedy. "But the IRI we use has passages from science, math, and social studies textbooks, not just literature," he said. "That makes it a lot more relevant to the content area teachers. They've got a vested interest in the results," he said.

Reading Fluency

Fluency is a measure of the rate and accuracy a student is able to achieve during silent or oral reading. You will recall that Chapter 6 features normed grade-level expectations (Grades 1–8+) for assessing oral and silent reading fluency. A more fluent reader is able to free up cognitive space for comprehending text through increasing automaticity in recognizing words in running text. But equally important is the student's ability to read fluently, that is, with the correct prosody, emphasis, and expression. These are important qualitative indicators of readers' comprehension, as they are unlikely to exhibit these reading behaviors without understanding the content of the text. Hudson, Lane, and Pullen (2005, p. 707) provide a detailed checklist of a student's prosody:

- Student placed vocal emphasis on appropriate words.

- Student's voice tone rose and fell at appropriate points in the text.

- Student's inflection reflected the punctuation in the text (e.g., voice tone rose near the end of a question).

- In narrative text with dialogue, student used appropriate vocal tone to represent characters' mental states, such as excitement, sadness, fear, or confidence.

- Student used punctuation to pause appropriately at phrase boundaries.

- Student used prepositional phrases to pause appropriately at phrase boundaries.

- Student used subject–verb divisions to pause appropriately at phrase boundaries.

- Student used conjunctions to pause appropriately at phrase boundaries.

Eighth-grade teachers Matthew Stewart and Briana Taylor use the normed grade-level expectations found in Chapter 6 as a means for their students to formulate goals for themselves. "We include these norms as part of our presentation of expectations for our students. Those expectations include Lexile levels for independent reading, correlation tables showing the relationship between minutes of reading and school achievement, and content about goal setting," explained Ms. Taylor. "We also show them how to assess one another for fluency measures. It saves us time, and they have a stake in it." Mr. Stewart added, "I appreciate when I confer with a student who says, 'My current rate of WCPM is 130, but I want to get it up to 150 by the winter break.' Once I know the goal, I've got the opening I need to talk about the plan to get there." The teachers themselves complete the prosody checklist. "The easiest and most natural time to do this is during Readers Theatre," said Mr. Stewart. "They're already focused

A more fluent reader is able to free up cognitive space for comprehending text through increasing automaticity in recognizing words in running text. But equally important is the student's ability to read fluently, that is, with the correct prosody, emphasis, and expression.

on prosody, so I'm getting good results," he said. "That means I have to hold myself accountable for getting Readers Theatre in on a regular basis. I make sure we do it at least once per quarter. They want to see their data, and if I'm not holding up my end of the bargain, they let me know it."

Metacomprehension Strategies Index (MSI)

Comprehension is linked to the strategic use of cognitive tools to make predictions, determine the importance of information, and restore meaning when it is lost. Skilled readers are those who can consciously employ such tools when they are needed (Afflerbach, Pearson, & Paris, 2008). But although we frequently teach students to use comprehension strategies, it is more rare that we actually measure their usage. The MSI is a 25-item questionnaire that asks students about their use of comprehension strategies during the reading of narrative texts (Schmitt, 1990). This tool can be administered either individually to students in an interview format, or to the entire group as an independent task. Many teachers like to preview this assessment by first telling students about the purpose (to find out about the way they use strategies in their reading), and then giving them a short independent reading. Students are invited to pay attention to how they read and understand. After the reading, they complete the MSI. Compendiums 4 and 5 include the entire MSI, including administration and analysis of results.

Scoring of the MSI is straightforward, with an answer key and categorization chart included in Compendium 5. Responses are regrouped into six categories:

- **Predicting and Verifying**. Good readers make predictions about a reading, and then check and adjust their predictions as they read.

- **Previewing.** Good readers scan the text to foster predictions.

- **Purpose Setting.** Good readers understand the purpose for reading (to gain knowledge, etc.).

- **Self-Questioning.** Good readers generate questions as they read and search for answers to these questions.

- **Drawing From Background Knowledge.** Good readers use prior experiences and knowledge to understand the text.

- **Summarizing and Applying Fix-Up Strategies.** Good readers summarize as they read and know what to do when they are having difficulty understanding what they are reading.

Ninth-grade teacher Sadie Pinto uses the MSI as a way to guide her own planning and instruction. "The MSI gives me a good sense of what they're conscious of doing," she said. "When I see low levels of implementation, I know that's something to model as I do think-alouds." Ms. Pinto explains that she administers the MSI twice a year—at the beginning of the school year, and then at the midpoint. "I saw some good gains for everyone except first period," she said. "I'm actually doing a few interviews with some students to explore this a little more closely. I don't know if they're still not metacognitively aware, or if it's the strategy itself that is what's giving them trouble."

After analyzing the results of the second administration, Ms. Pinto discovered that many of her students in first period were having trouble with self-questioning. "There just doesn't seem to be a lot going on. When I did some follow-up interviews, I discovered that many of them don't routinely write questions to themselves when they annotate." Her second semester lessons for first period place a greater emphasis on this. "I'm pausing when we're annotating and asking them to share questions they've written in the margins," she said. "It's not writing the questions that's so important. It's the habit of pausing and questioning the text. Using strategies is really just forming habits. I'm building this into our routine a bit more overtly so they can get in the habit of posing questions to themselves," said Ms. Pinto. "It's fit in perfectly with my Unreliable Narrators unit," she said. "We're learning to question Poe. He can't be trusted!"

ASSESSING ATTITUDES TOWARD READING

Motivation to read and interest in reading are important factors in reading proficiency. After all, if a student is not interested in reading, this is likely to inhibit his exposure to texts and thereby limit time spent practicing the strategies needed to comprehend text. A decline in attitudes toward reading occurs throughout the elementary years, precisely at the time when the use of reading as a vehicle for learning content begins to rise (Kush & Watkins, 1996). The impact of negative reading attitude persists for many into adulthood, where those who perceive reading negatively continue to engage in less reading that their peers who enjoy reading (Pew Research Center, 2013).

Motivation and interest in reading are important factors in reading proficiency.

By middle school, the decline in interest toward reading becomes more complicated for some students, whose beliefs are bound up in issues of efficacy ("Am I good at this?") and agency ("Can I get better at this?"). There are too many young adolescents who gave up on reading long before they reach our classrooms. And it's understandable, when you think about it. We all avoid doing the things we're not good at. (There's a reason Nancy doesn't ski. . . .) But it's harder to dodge reading when you're in school. The Reader Self-Perception Scale 2 (Henk, Marinak, & Melnick, 2012) is a normed instrument to gauge how adolescent readers feel about themselves relative to reading. Designed for use with students in Grades 7–10, it casts a light on a student's beliefs, and can provide further meaning when taken in tandem with the results of her IRI results. The questionnaire consists of 47 items the student rates on a five-point Likert scale (from *Strongly Agree* to *Strongly Disagree*). Statements include items such as "My classmates think I read pretty well" and "I have improved on tests and assignments that involve reading." The student form appears in Compendium 6, along with directions for administering, scoring, and interpreting the instrument, and a scoring sheet can be found in Compendium 7.

Of course, simply measuring self-perceptions and then doing nothing about them is unacceptable. Middle school English teacher Clayton Lewiston just happens to be the soccer coach as well, and he uses his coaching position to change attitudes and beliefs about reading. "Every season, we read a sports-themed book as a team and talk about how it speaks to us as athletes," he said. "They know Mr. Lewiston is the English teacher, but here I'm just Coach. And I want them to see that you can be a reader and a jock at the same time." Coach Lewiston read *Booked* by Kwame Alexander this season with the boys' team and the girls' team. It's about soccer, of course, but "told as poetry, mostly free verse," he laughed. "They get so caught up in the story that they don't even notice the genre at first." His department has seen reader self-perceptions rise among Coach Lewiston's athletes. "I've got some kids requesting more books by Kwame Alexander, which is great. I'm not sure some of them could have named a favorite author before the season started."

Every practice includes some academic time, with students helping teammates maintain the required grade point average needed to play. They end with a 15–20 minute discussion of the book before going home. His approach is catching on with other coaches at the school, too. The girls' basketball coach, Melinda Weiss, a science teacher, is going to read *Boost* by Kathy MacKel, a novel about a female athlete who begins using performance-enhancing drugs. "I don't know why we didn't think of it before," remarked Ms. Weiss. "We're teachers all day long. That doesn't stop when we step onto the court or the field."

ASSESSING WRITING

Like the reading assessments used by teachers, writing assessments are used to make instructional decisions about the class and about individual learners. These decisions may include grouping, introduction of new skills, or reteaching. Effective writing assessment requires examination of multiple aspects of writing. Some assessments target particular sub-skills of writing like spelling and fluency. Other assessments look at the overall quality of the writing using a holistic rubric to articulate how well the student is progressing in becoming a more competent writer. In this section, we will look at useful tools for assessing fluency and spelling, and then examine holistic scoring of writing. Finally, we will return to the notion of attitude and motivation in writing.

ASSESSING WRITING FLUENCY

Writers need to write smoothly and quickly in order to compose meaningful text. This aspect of writing is referred to as *fluency,* and it is assessed through timed writing sessions. There are no set grade-level benchmarks for writing fluency expectations, and of course a writer's fluency is impacted by a number of factors, including topic, background knowledge, and motivation. However, timed writing samples should be collected each grading period to track students' progress as they become more proficient and fluent writers. This can be easily accomplished by administering a five-minute timed writing prompt. These writing prompts should be general in nature so that background knowledge does not confound performance. Useful topics for collected timed writing samples include the following:

- Describe a time when you were surprised.

- Tell about a time when you tasted a new food.

- If you could travel to any place in the world, where would it be and why?

Students are encouraged to write as much as they can and as well as they can and to write continuously for the entire period. At the end of five minutes, the papers are collected and analyzed to yield several measures of student success. First, the overall number of words is counted, whether they are spelled correctly or not. Numbers, regardless of digits, count as one word. Next, the piece is read and each error in spelling, punctuation, syntax, or grammar is underlined, yielding a total number of errors. Finally, the overall number of sentences is counted. Based on these numbers, the average number of errors per sentence, mean sentence length, and total number of words can be recorded. This quantitative measure can serve as a way of reporting the overall fluency of each student. A classroom log of writing fluency can be found in Compendium 8.

A ninth-grade teacher, Ms. Nugent, tracks the writing fluency of her students throughout the year. Several times a week, she leads her students through three rounds of power writing, in which she encourages them to "write as much as you can, as well as you can." They keep track of their best effort each time on graphs inside their writer's notebooks.

"I have been doing power writing in my classes for a couple of years now," she said. "But I never connected it with goals students can set. With the emphasis on short constructed responses on state exams, fluent writing has taken on a new relevance for me. I do the five-minute timed writing samples every quarter. When they confer with me, they've got the data from their power writing graphs, as well as the quarterly timed writing scores. Writing fluency isn't all there is to writing, but if you can't get your ideas down on the document in a smooth fashion, it's difficult to show what you know."

ASSESSING SPELLING

So what's up with spelling? We know we said a few chapters ago that poor grammar is the bane of an English teacher's existence, but poor spelling runs a close second. And while spelling instruction is not featured in secondary English curriculum, the expectation to use conventional spelling is in the standards. There is a misconception that the path to correct spelling is memorization, but the truth is that spelling is a developmental process, and at the secondary level is reflective of a student's knowledge of syllables and word derivations. These developmental stages have been described by Henderson (1990) and illustrated by Ganske (2000), whose stages are shown in Figure 7.2:

- **Emergent.** Uses few or no sound–letter associations.

- **Letter Name.** Spells by sound.

- **Within Word Pattern.** Uses familiar patterns to spell one-syllable words.

- **Syllable Juncture.** Uses syllables and double consonants to arrive at spellings.

- **Derivational Constancy.** Uses word origins to spell new words.

Even with autocorrect tools, writers need to be able to spell. While most secondary students spell with reasonable levels of accuracy, a smaller

Figure 7.2   Stages of Spelling Development

	Emergent Prephonetic Ages: 1–7 Grades: PreK to Mid-1	Emergent Semiphonetic 1–7 PreK to Mid-1	Letter Name 4–9 1–2	Within Word Pattern 6–12 2–4	Syllable Juncture 8–12 3–8	Derivational Constancy 10+ 5–8+
pan	b∃igt	n	pan	pan	pan	pan
stem	132tb	cm	sam	stem	stem	stem
bike	erl88i	k	bik	biek	bike	bike
chart	abge	ht	crt	chrat	chart	chart
dotted	∃a23	dd	didt	dotid	doted	dotted
drizzle	iabtt	z	jrezl	drizul	drizzel	drizzle
criticize	bbegba	k	cretsiz	critusize	critasize	critisize
majority	8bgre	m	mgrt	mujortea	mejoraty	mejority

Source: Ganske, K. (1999). The developmental spelling analysis: A measure of orthographic knowledge. *Educational Assessment*, 6(1), 41–70.

Available for download at **https://resources.corwin.com/vl-literacy6-12**

number misspell to the point where it interferes with their ability to convey their message. You'll know who those students are the first few times you ask them to submit something in writing. (This should be every day, even in the form of exit slips and other short constructed responses.) It is useful to assess these targeted students at the beginning of the year to determine what developmental spelling stage they are currently working in. This can be accomplished through the use of the Developmental Spelling Analysis Screening Inventory featured in Compendium 9 (Ganske, 2000).

Administration and scoring of the screening inventory can be completed quickly. The inventory is divided into four sets of five words. The first set is administered, and subsequent sets are used only if the student gets at least two correct answers in a set. When a student gets only one or none of the words correct, the assessment ends. Each correct spelling earns one point, and the total number of correct answers is compared to the chart in Compendium 10 to determine the student's developmental spelling level.

Tenth-grade English teacher Tina O'Neill grew concerned about several students during the first week of school after examining writing samples they had submitted. "Their spelling was atrocious," she said with a sigh. After checking to see if they were English learners, had disabilities, or were receiving supplemental intervention services, she still had seven students who were falling between the cracks. "I used to teach elementary school," she said. "So I got my developmental spelling inventory out." After administering and scoring it, she shared the results with each student individually. "It was a good starting point, even though they were embarrassed about the results. All of them said they avoided writing because they knew they weren't good spellers."

Several were still in the syllable juncture stage, while the rest were at the early derivational constancy phase. "I gave them spelling words aimed at their developmental stage, which they practiced on the learning management system. It was easy enough to link a few online games to the LMS," she said. While spelling remains a struggle for these students, most have expressed relief at getting some extra help in becoming more accurate. "No one talks about spelling in high school, but when there are kids who struggle with spelling, or avoid using words they can't spell, it interferes with their fluency and their message," she said. "I'm happy to give them some extra support as part of their writing instruction."

ASSESSING WRITING HOLISTICALLY

In addition to assessing the mechanics of writing related to spelling and fluency, there are also times when teachers want to evaluate the writing as a whole. This requires that they use an instrument that addresses both the content of the piece and the extent to which the writer conveyed the message with clarity and accuracy. This type of writing evaluation is referred to as a *holistic assessment.* The term *holistic* comes from the study of holism, a theory utilized in biology, anthropology, and physics that the universe can be correctly viewed only as systems of whole organisms, not as the sum of its parts. In the same fashion, holistic writing assessments measure the merits of a piece across several indicators. Most commonly, this is accomplished through the use of a rubric. Holistic writing rubrics are not confined to informal classroom assessments; indeed, they are widely used for large-scale state writing assessments at all school levels. Be sure to check your state, territorial, or provincial Department of Education website to view the holistic writing rubric used. These rubrics can be useful in gauging your students' progress on state accountability measures.

"I use the National Curriculum and Assessment for GCSE in my class-room so students can assess their own writing," said Year 10 teacher Charles Peck. Students are assessed periodically throughout their school careers in English literature, writing, and language conventions. "I share a modified version of the criteria the assessors use," he said, "and teach them how to look for these in their own writing." Mr. Peck posts anchor samples from previous classes for students to critique. "It's helpful to have exemplars and nonexamples to work with," he said. "We've actually made good progress analyzing these papers."

Throughout the year, Mr. Peck's writing instruction includes elements of writing, from use of conventions to structuring paragraphs to organize arguments. "Extended formal writing assignments always include an element of self-assessment," he said. "They need to be able to review their own work and self-edit."

Literacy Design Collaborative Student Work Rubrics

Among all the rubrics we have utilized, many of our favorites come from the Literacy Design Collaborative. These rubrics have been designed and revised by a consortium of public educators and private business partners to develop instructional modules, curricula, and rubrics for addressing literacy standards. We have found the student work rubrics to be of value because they are developmentally aligned by grade bands, are individualized for argumentation and explanatory purposes, and can be applied to either written or oral work. They are organized according to seven scoring elements:

- **Focus,** in that the work addressed the prompt accurately and completely.
- **Controlling idea,** such that a claim or concept is maintained throughout.
- **Reading research (when applicable)** is used and the student makes direct links to it.
- **Development** of details that link to the focus and controlling idea.
- **Organizational structure** is apparent and suited to the task and purpose.
- **Conventions** of Standard English are evidenced.
- **Content understanding** is such that the student uses and understands the sources of information used.

These rubrics are vetted through a juried process and are frequently updated and improved. The rubrics are free and available at https://ldc .org/resources#Grades-K-12-Student-Work-Rubrics-3.0.

WHY ASSESS? KNOW YOUR IMPACT

Let's not forget why this chapter exists. Our purpose was not to simply catalog all the wonderful tools teachers can use to assess students. Assessment alone doesn't yield anything. A farmer can tell you that you can't fatten sheep by weighing them. It's what you *do* with the assessment data you have that determines whether students will continue to grow or not. Some will grow no matter what, and their accidental growth is not a gauge of your teaching prowess. Using assessment for the purpose of formative evaluation, in order to figure out what works, moves your teaching from the realm of chance to one of intentional design.

Key to student growth is time—time for teachers to talk and evaluate their own practice and its impact on student learning. First off, teachers need time to talk about what they want students to learn. This involves analyzing standards and addressing both academic and nonacademic expectations. And it involves sharing ideas for high-impact instruction. We teachers also need time to talk about assessment results with our colleagues, to get the support we need to make changes to our lessons, and, in turn, to strengthen our impact. In so doing, we all stand to learn a lot about effective approaches and to grow as professionals. These opportunities for collaboration are based on student data, and we have found that impact analysis facilitates the conversations that teachers have with one another.

CONCLUSION

There are any number of ways to assess students' literacy learning. This chapter has provided a few of them. Again, what's more important is what teachers do with the assessment information. All of the teachers profiled in this chapter, and in this book, used assessment information to determine their impact. They noted when their instruction worked and when it did not. And when the impact was less than desired, these teachers took action. They talked with their colleagues, reviewed their data, and made changes.

In addition to profiling teachers in this book, we described a number of strategies, actions, and routines that teachers can use to impact students' literacy learning. We hope readers do not simply adhere to these approaches, but rather use the data they collect to determine if students have learned. In many cases, hopefully more often than not, the approaches outlined in this book, for which there are sufficiently large effect sizes, will work to improve students' learning. But when they don't work for your students, in your grade, change it up and try something else. Never hold a strategy in higher esteem that students' learning. It's all, and always, about impacting students' literacy learning.

When this happens, students become their own teachers. They understand what they need and want to learn, seek feedback, understand that errors are opportunities to learn, engage in challenging tasks, and think about their thinking and their understanding. This will serve them well as they enter middle and high school classrooms, not to mention college and the workforce. As educators, we have chosen to be our own teachers for a long time. We seek out opportunities to learn, and we should share that experience with our students.

COMPENDIUM
OF ASSESSMENTS

COMPENDIUM 1. CLOZE ASSESSMENT OF A PASSAGE ABOUT DRAMATIC ELEMENTS OF A PLAY

Cloze Passage: Teacher Version

Directions: Approximately every fifth word has been deleted from this passage. Read the passage and write the words on a separate sheet of paper that best fit both the meaning and the structure of the sentence. You may read the passage more than once.

> **Note to teachers:** We have left the passage intact so you can view it in its entirety. In the student version, a blank line is substituted for the underlined words.

Most plays in Western literature can be analyzed by identifying specific elements related to their plot, character development, and dramatic arc. The first elements of <u>dramatic</u> analysis lie in understanding <u>how</u> the plot develops. <u>Every</u> play begins with an <u>inciting</u> incident that occurred just <u>before</u> the story begins. It <u>is</u> the trigger for everything <u>else</u> to come. For example, the <u>inciting</u> incident in <u>a</u> play that begins with <u>a</u> funeral scene is the <u>death</u> of the deceased person. <u>We</u> didn't see him or <u>her</u> die, but it sets the rest of <u>the</u> play <u>in</u> motion.

Characters <u>are</u> then introduced, including the <u>protagonist</u> and antagonist. The <u>protagonist</u> is the character who propels <u>the</u> play forward. He or <u>she</u> has the major dramatic <u>question</u>, which will not be <u>answered</u> until the end of <u>the</u> play. The moment of <u>engagement</u> happens early in <u>the</u> play, when the protagonist <u>commits</u> to his or her <u>goal</u>. The <u>antagonist</u> is the obstacle, as she or <u>he</u> prevents the protagonist from <u>achieving</u> goals. The <u>protagonist</u> is not necessarily the <u>hero</u>, and the antagonist is not always the <u>villain</u>. They <u>are</u> in opposition to one <u>another</u>. Characters are developed using <u>direct</u> characterization, such as when <u>the</u> playwright tells the audience <u>about</u> the character's personality. <u>Indirect</u> characterization shows a character's <u>personality</u> through dialogue, actions, thoughts, and the <u>reaction</u> of others.

The dramatic arc <u>of</u> the play includes the <u>rising</u> action, as each event <u>builds</u> background, interest, and suspense. The <u>majority</u> of the play <u>consists</u> of rising action. The <u>climax</u> of the play is <u>when</u> the major dramatic <u>question</u> is answered. Did the <u>protagonist</u> achieve his goals? In a <u>tragedy</u>, it may <u>be</u> an explosive confrontation between <u>characters</u>. In a comedy, the <u>climax</u> may happen when the <u>two</u> main characters are reunited <u>in</u> love. The play <u>ends</u> with the denouement. This <u>is</u> the final scene, when <u>any</u> remaining questions are now <u>resolved</u>. These elements are present in all plays, and knowledge of them can aid you in understanding the play.

Cloze Passage: Student Version

Directions: Approximately every fifth word has been deleted from this passage. Read the passage and write the words on a separate sheet of paper that best fit both the meaning and the structure of the sentence. You may read the passage more than once.

Most plays in Western literature can be analyzed by identifying specific elements related to their plot, character development, and dramatic arc. The first elements of _____ analysis lie in understanding _____ the plot develops. _____ play begins with an _____ incident that occurred just _____ the story begins. It _____ the trigger for everything _____ to come. For example, the _____ incident in _____ play that begins with _____ funeral scene is the _____ of the deceased person. _____ didn't see him or _____ die, but it sets the rest of _____ play _____ motion.

Characters _____ then introduced, including the _____ and antagonist. The _____ is the character who propels _____ play forward. He or _____ has the major dramatic _____, which will not be _____ until the end of _____ play. The moment of _____ happens early in _____ play, when the protagonist _____ to his or her _____. The _____ is the obstacle, as she or _____ prevents the protagonist from _____ goals. The _____ is not necessarily the _____, and the antagonist is not always the _____. They _____ in opposition to one _____. Characters are developed using _____ characterization, such as when _____ playwright tells the audience _____ the charac-ter's personality. _____ characterization shows a character's _____ through dialogue, actions, thoughts, and the _____ of others.

The dramatic arc _____ the play includes the _____ action, as each event _____ background, interest, and suspense. The _____ of the play _____ of rising action. The _____ of the play is _____ the major dramatic _____ is answered. Did the _____ achieve his goals? In a _____, it may _____ an explosive confrontation between _____. In a comedy, the _____ may happen when the _____ main characters are reunited _____ love. The play _____ with the denouement. This _____ the final scene, when _____ remaining questions are now _____. These elements are present in all plays, and knowledge of them can aid you in understanding the play.

COMPENDIUM 2. SAMPLE CLOZE PROCEDURE ANSWER KEY

1. dramatic	16. are	31. protagonist	46. consists
2. how	17. protagonist	32. hero	47. climax
3. Every	18. protagonist	33. villain	48. when
4. inciting	19. the	34. are	49. question
5. before	20. she	35. another	50. protagonist
6. is	21. question	36. direct	51. tragedy
7. else	22. answered	37. the	52. be
8. inciting	23. the	38. about	53. characters
9. a	24. engagement	39. Indirect	54. climax
10. a	25. the	40. personality	55. two
11. death	26. commits	41. reaction	56. in
12. We	27. goal	42. of	57. ends
13. her	28. antagonist	43. rising	58. is
14. the	29. he	44. builds	59. any
15. in	30. achieving	45. majority	60. resolved

Available for download at **https://resources.corwin.com/vl-literacy6-12**

COMPENDIUM 3. SAMPLE VOCABULARY MATCHING ASSESSMENT FOR LITERARY DEVICES

Directions: Match the following terms to their definitions, using the number.

_____ Allegory	1. When an object or action means something more than its literal meaning
_____ Alliteration	2. Language that evokes one or more of the senses
_____ Allusion	3. A story used to teach an important lesson
_____ Flashback	4. A direct comparison in which one thing is said to be like another
_____ Foreshadowing	5. A pause in the action to portray an incident that happened earlier
_____ Hyperbole	6. The atmosphere of the story (scary, exciting, etc.)
_____ Imagery	7. An exaggerated comment used for effect and not meant to be taken literally
_____ Irony	8. Use of the same letter or sound to start each word in a string of words
_____ Metaphor	9. Something said when the opposite or reverse is true
_____ Mood	10. A reference to a well-known person, myth, historical event, or religious story
_____ Personification	11. Animals, ideas, or actions with human qualities
_____ Point of view	12. The writer's attitude about the subject
_____ Simile	13. A statement in which two things are compared using _like_ or _as_
_____ Symbolism	14. A hint of things to come in the plot
_____ Tone	15. The perspective of the narrator

COMPENDIUM 4. METACOMPREHENSION STRATEGIES INDEX: STUDENT FORM

Name: _____   Date: _____

Metacomprehension Strategies Index

Directions: Think about what kinds of things you can do to help you understand a story better before you read it, while you're reading, and after you read it. Read each of the lists of four statements and decide which one of them would help you the most. Circle the letter of the statement you choose.

I.   From each set of four, choose the one statement that describes a good thing to do to help you understand a story better *before* you read it.

1. Before I begin reading, it's a good idea to
    A. See how many pages are in the story.
    B. Look up all of the big words in the dictionary.
    C. Make some guesses about what I think will happen in the story.
    D. Think about what has happened so far in the story.

2. Before I begin reading, it's a good idea to
    A. Look at the pictures to see what the story is about.
    B. Decide how long it will take me to read the story.
    C. Sound out the words I don't know.
    D. Check to see if the story is making sense.

3. Before I begin reading, it's a good idea to
    A. Ask someone to read the story to me.
    B. Read the title to see what the story is about.
    C. Check to see if most of the words have long or short vowels in them.
    D. Check to see if the pictures are in order and make sense.

4. Before I begin reading, it's a good idea to
    A. Check to see that no pages are missing.
    B. Make a list of words I'm not sure about.
    C. Use the title and pictures to help me make guesses about what will happen in the story.
    D. Read the last sentence so I will know how the story ends.

5. Before I begin reading, it's a good idea to:
    A. Decide on why I am going to read the story.
    B. Use the difficult words to help me make guesses about what will happen in the story.
    C. Reread some parts to see if I can figure out what is happening if things aren't making sense.
    D. Ask for help with the difficult words.

6. Before I begin reading, it's a good idea to
    A. Retell all of the main points that have happened so far.
    B. Ask myself questions that I would like to have answered in the story.

C. Think about the meaning of the words that have more than one meaning.

D. Look through the story to find all of the words with three or more syllables.

7. Before I begin reading, it's a good idea to
A. Check to see if I have read this story before.

B. Use my questions and guesses as a reason for reading the story.

C. Make sure I can pronounce all of the words before I start.

D. Think of a better title for the story.

8. Before I begin reading, it's a good idea to
A. Think of what I already know about the things I see in the pictures.

B. See how many pages are in the story.

C. Choose the best part of the story to read again.

D. Read the story aloud to someone.

9. Before I begin reading, it's a good idea to
A. Practice reading the story out loud.

B. Retell all of the main points to make sure I can remember the story.

C. Think of what the people in the story might be like.

D. Decide if I have enough time to read the story.

10. Before I begin reading, it's a good idea to
A. Check to see if I am understanding the story so far.

B. Check to see if the words have more than one meaning.

C. Think about where the story might be taking place.

D. List all of the important details.

II. From each set of four, choose the one statement that describes a good thing to do to help you understand a story better *while* you are reading it.

11. While I am reading, it's a good idea to
A. Read the story very slowly so that I will not miss any important parts.

B. Read the title to see what the story is about.

C. Check to see if the pictures have anything missing.

D. Check to see if the story is making sense by seeing if I can tell what's happened so far.

12. While I am reading, it's a good idea to
A. Stop to retell the main points to see if I am understanding what has happened so far.

B. Read the story quickly so that I can find out what happened.

C. Read only the beginning and the end of the story to find out what it is about.

D. Skip the parts that are too difficult for me.

13. While I am reading, it's a good idea to
A. Look all of the big words up in the dictionary.

B. Put the book away and find another one if things aren't making sense.

C. Keep thinking about the title and the pictures to help me decide what is going to happen next.

D. Keep track of how many pages I have left to read.

14. While I am reading, it's a good idea to
   A. Keep track of how long it is taking me to read the story.
   B. Check to see if I can answer any of the questions I asked before I started reading.
   C. Read the title to see what the story is going to be about.
   D. Add the missing details to the pictures.

15. While I am reading, it's a good idea to
   A. Have someone read the story aloud to me.
   B. Keep track of how many pages I have read.
   C. List the story's main characters.
   D. Check to see if my guesses are right or wrong.

16. While I am reading, it's a good idea to
   A. Check to see that the characters are real.
   B. Make a lot of guesses about what is going to happen next.
   C. Not look at the pictures because they might confuse me.
   D. Read the story aloud to someone.

17. While I am reading, it's a good idea to
   A. Try to answer the questions I asked myself.
   B. Try not to confuse what I already know with what I am reading about.
   C. Read the story silently.
   D. Check to see if I am saying the new vocabulary words correctly.

18. While I am reading, it is a good idea to
   A. Try to see if my guesses are going to be right or wrong.
   B. Reread to be sure I haven't missed any of the words.
   C. Decide on why I am reading the story.
   D. List what happened first, second, third, and so on.

19. While I am reading, it is a good idea to
   A. See if I can recognize the new vocabulary words.
   B. Be careful not to skip any parts of the story.
   C. Check to see how many of the words I already know.
   D. Keep thinking of what I already know about the things and ideas in the story to help me decide what is going to happen.

20. While I am reading, it's a good idea to
   A. Reread some parts or read ahead to see if I can figure out what is happening if things aren't making sense.
   B. Take my time reading so that I can be sure I understand what is happening.
   C. Change the ending so that it makes sense.
   D. Check to see if there are enough pictures to help make the story ideas clear.

III. From each set of four, choose the one statement that describes a good thing to do to help you understand a story better *after* you have read it.

21. After I've read a story it's a good idea to
   A. Count how many pages I read with no mistakes.
   B. Check to see if there were enough pictures to go with the story to make it interesting.
   C. Check to see if I met my purpose for reading the story.
   D. Underline the causes and effects.

22. After I've read a story it's a good idea to
    A. Underline the main idea.
    B. Retell the main points of the whole story so that I can check to see if I understood it.
    C. Read the story again to be sure I said all of the words right.
    D. Practice reading the story aloud.

23. After I've read a story it's a good idea to
    A. Read the title and look over the story to see what it is about.
    B. Check to see if I skipped any of the vocabulary words.
    C. Think about what made me make good or bad predictions.
    D. Make a guess about what will happen next in the story.

24. After I've read a story it's a good idea to
    A. Look up all of the big words in the dictionary.
    B. Read the best parts aloud.

C. Have someone read the story aloud to me.
D. Think about how the story was like things I already knew about before I started reading.

25. After I've read a story it's a good idea to
    A. Think about how I would have acted if I were the main character in the story.
    B. Practice reading the story silently for practice of good reading.
    C. Look over the story title and pictures to see what will happen.
    D. Make a list of the things I understood the most.

Source: Adapted from Schmitt, M. C. (March 1990). A questionnaire to measure children's awareness of strategic reading processes. *The Reading Teacher, 43,* 454–461.

 Available for download at **https://resources.corwin.com/vl-literacy6-12**

COMPENDIUM 5. METACOMPREHENSION STRATEGIES INDEX: ADMINISTRATION AND SCORING DIRECTIONS

Interpreting Results of the Metacomprehension Strategies Index

The MSI (Schmitt, 1990) is a measure of a student's use of strategies with narrative text. It may be read to the student or administered silently. The wording of the items can be changed for use with expository text. For example, you can replace the wording of #2 to read,

Before I begin reading, it's a good idea to

    A. Look at the illustrations to see what the chapter will be about.

    B. Decide how long it will take for me to read the chapter.

    C. Sound out the words I don't know.

    D. Check to see if the information is making sense.

Answer Key: These answers represent the best answers; choices may also include strategies that are somewhat useful but not as efficient for the situation described.

1. C	6. B	11. D	16. B	21. C
2. A	7. B	12. A	17. A	22. B
3. B	8. A	13. C	18. A	23. C
4. C	9. C	14. B	19. D	24. D
5. A	10. C	15. D	20. A	25. A

Interpreting: The following item analysis is organized to more fully describe the types of metacomprehension strategies tested.

Strategies	Items
Predicting and Verifying Predicting and verifying the content of a story promotes active comprehension by giving readers a purpose to read (i.e., to verify predictions). Evaluating predictions and generating new ones as necessary enhances the constructive nature of the reading process.	1, 4, 13, 15, 16, 18, 23
Previewing Previewing the text facilitates comprehension by activating background knowledge and providing information for making predictions.	2, 3

Purpose Setting Reading with a purpose promotes active, strategic reading.	5, 7, 21
Self-Questioning Generating questions to be answered promotes active comprehension by giving readers a purpose for reading (i.e., to answer the questions).	6, 14, 17
Drawing From Background Knowledge Activating and incorporating information from background knowledge contributes to comprehension by helping readers make inferences and generate predictions.	8, 9, 10, 19, 24, 25
Summarizing and Applying Fix-Up Strategies Summarizing the content at various points in the story serves as a form of comprehension monitoring. Rereading or suspending judgment and reading on when comprehension breaks down represents strategic reading.	11, 12, 20, 22

Source: Adapted from Schmitt, M. C. (1990, March). A questionnaire to measure children's awareness of strategic reading processes. *The Reading Teacher, 43,* 454–461.

Available for download at **https://resources.corwin.com/vl-literacy6-12**

COMPENDIUM 6. READER SELF-PERCEPTION SCALE 2

Directions for Use

The Reader Self-Perception Scale 2 (RSPS2) enables educators and researchers to gauge how students in Grades 7 through 10 feel about themselves as readers. The scale consists of 47 items that address reader self-perceptions according to four dimensions of self-efficacy (Progress, Observational Comparison, Social Feedback, and Physiological States). Students are instructed to indicate how strongly they agree or disagree with each statement using a five-point scale ranging from Strongly Agree (5) to Strongly Disagree (1). Information derived from the RSPS2 can assist in devising ways to enhance students' self-confidence in reading and to increase their motivation to read. The following directions explain what should be done to administer, score, and interpret the instrument.

Administration

For the results to be useful, students must (1) understand exactly what they are to do, (2) have ample time to complete all items, and (3) respond honestly and thoughtfully. Briefly explain to them that they are being asked to complete a questionnaire to find out more about how students in their grade feel about themselves as readers. Tell them that they will be reading a series of statements and indicating how strongly they feel about each statement. Note that the task should take 15 to 20 minutes to complete, but that they can take as long as necessary. Emphasize that this is not a test, and that there are no right answers. Tell them that their responses will be kept confidential.

To begin, ask the students to fill in their names, grade levels, and classrooms as appropriate. Read the directions aloud, and work through the example with the students as a group. Discuss the response options, and make sure that all students understand the rating scale before continuing. It is important that students know they may raise their hands to ask quietly about any words or ideas they do not understand. The student should then begin to read each item silently and to circle their responses. When all items are completed, the students should stop and await further instructions. Students who work more slowly should not be disturbed by others who have completed the task.

Scoring

To score the RSPS2, enter a point value for each item number under the appropriate scale on the scoring sheet (Strongly Agree = 5, Agree = 4,

Undecided = 3, Disagree = 2, Strongly Disagree = 1). Sum each column to obtain a raw score for each of the four scales.

Interpretation

The total score for each scale varies because the number of items differs in each scale. Because the Progress scale consists of 16 items, the maximum score is 80 (i.e., 16 × 5). Observational Comparison and Social Feedback each have 9 items, so their top scores will be the same (45), but the 12-item Physiological States scale top score will be 60 (12 × 5). Each scale score can be interpreted by comparing it with the criteria on the scoring sheet. For example, a Progress score between 49 and 73 would be in the average range, whereas scores of 48 or below would be low, and scores of 74 and above would be in the high range. Evaluators should be sensitive to the fact that scores at the extremes of the average range could represent very different results.

Reader Self-Perception Scale

Listed below are statements about reading. Please read each statement carefully. Then circle the letters that show how much you agree or disagree with the statement. Use the following scale:

SA = Strongly Agree   A = Agree   U = Undecided   D = Disagree   SD = Strongly Disagree

Example:

I think pizza with pepperoni is the best.	SA	A	U	D	SD

If you are *really positive* that pepperoni is the best, circle SA (Strongly Agree).

If you *think* that it is good but maybe not great, circle A (Agree).

If you *can't decide* whether or not it is best, circle U (Undecided).

If you *think* that pepperoni pizza is not all that good, circle D (Disagree).

If you are *really positive* that pepperoni pizza is not very good, circle SD (Strongly Disagree).

1. Reading is a pleasant activity for me. (PS)	SA	A	U	D	SD
2. I read better now than I could before. (PR)	SA	A	U	D	SD
3. I can handle more challenging reading materials than I could before. (PR)	SA	A	U	D	SD
4. Other students think I'm a good reader. (SF)	SA	A	U	D	SD
5. I need less help than other students when I read. (OC)	SA	A	U	D	SD
6. I feel comfortable when I read. (PS)	SA	A	U	D	SD
7. When I read, I don't have to try as hard to understand as I used to. (PR)	SA	A	U	D	SD
8. My classmates like to listen to the way that I read. (SF)	SA	A	U	D	SD
9. I am getting better at reading. (PR)	SA	A	U	D	SD
10. When I read, I can figure out words better than other students. (OC)	SA	A	U	D	SD
11. My teachers think I am a good reader. (SF)	SA	A	U	D	SD
12. I read better than other students in my class. (OC)	SA	A	U	D	SD
13. My reading comprehension level is higher than other students. (OC)	SA	A	U	D	SD
14. I feel calm when I read. (PS)	SA	A	U	D	SD
15. I read faster than other students. (OC)	SA	A	U	D	SD
16. My teachers think that I try my best when I read. (SF)	SA	A	U	D	SD
17. Reading tends to make me feel calm. (PS)	SA	A	U	D	SD
18. I understand what I read better than I could before. (PR)	SA	A	U	D	SD
19. I can understand difficult reading materials better than before. (PR)	SA	A	U	D	SD
20. When I read, I can handle difficult ideas better than my classmates. (OC)	SA	A	U	D	SD
21. When I read, I recognize more words than before. (PR)	SA	A	U	D	SD
22. I enjoy how I feel when I read. (PS)	SA	A	U	D	SD

23. I feel proud inside when I think about how well I read. (PS)	SA	A	U	D	SD
24. I have improved on assignments and tests that involve reading. (PR)	SA	A	U	D	SD
25. I feel good inside when I read. (PS)	SA	A	U	D	SD
26. When I read, my understanding of important vocabulary words is better than other students. (OC)	SA	A	U	D	SD
27. People in my family like to listen to me read. (SF)	SA	A	U	D	SD
28. My classmates think that I read pretty well. (SF)	SA	A	U	D	SD
29. Reading makes me feel good. (PS)	SA	A	U	D	SD
30. I can figure out hard words better than I could before. (PR)	SA	A	U	D	SD
31. I think reading can be relaxing. (PS)	SA	A	U	D	SD
32. I can concentrate more when I read than I could before. (PR)	SA	A	U	D	SD
33. Reading makes me feel happy inside. (PS)	SA	A	U	D	SD
34. When I read, I need less help than I used to. (PR)	SA	A	U	D	SD
35. I can tell that my teachers like to listen to me read. (SF)	SA	A	U	D	SD
36. I know the meaning of more words than other students when I read. (OC)	SA	A	U	D	SD
37. I read faster than I could before. (PR)	SA	A	U	D	SD
38. Reading is easier for me than it used to be. (PR)	SA	A	U	D	SD
39. My teachers think that I do a good job of interpreting what I read. (SF)	SA	A	U	D	SD
40. My understanding of difficult reading materials has improved. (PR)	SA	A	U	D	SD
41. I feel good about my ability to read. (PS)	SA	A	U	D	SD
42. I am more confident in my reading than other students. (OC)	SA	A	U	D	SD
43. Deep down, I like to read. (PS)	SA	A	U	D	SD
44. I can analyze what I read better than before. (PR)	SA	A	U	D	SD
45. My teachers think that my reading is fine. (SF)	SA	A	U	D	SD
46. Vocabulary words are easier for me to understand when I read now. (PR)	SA	A	U	D	SD

Source: Henk, W. A., Marinak, B. A., & Melnick, S. A. (2012). Measuring the reader self-perceptions of adolescents: Introducing the RSPS2. *Journal of Adolescent & Adult Literacy, 56*(4), 311–320, figure on p. 315.

 Available for download at **https://resources.corwin.com/vl-literacy6-12**

COMPENDIUM 7. READER SELF-PERCEPTION SCALE 2: SCORING SHEET

Student Name: _____   Grade: _____

Teacher: _____   Date: _____

Scoring Key
5 = Strongly Agree (SA)   4 = Agree (A)   3 = Undecided (U)   2 = Disagree (D)   1 = Strongly Disagree (SD)

Progress (PR)	Observational Comparison (OC)	Social Feedback (SF)	Physiological States (PS)
2. _____	5. _____	4. _____	1. _____
3. _____	10. _____	8. _____	6. _____
7. _____	12. _____	11. _____	14. _____
9. _____	13. _____	16. _____	17. _____
18. _____	15. _____	27. _____	22. _____
19. _____	20. _____	28. _____	23. _____
21. _____	26. _____	35. _____	25. _____
24. _____	36. _____	39. _____	29. _____
30. _____	42. _____	45. _____	31. _____
32. _____			33. _____
34. _____			41. _____
37. _____			43. _____
38. _____			
40. _____			
44. _____			
46. _____			

	Progress (PR)	Observational Comparison (OC)	Social Feedback (SF)	Physiological States (PS)
Raw Score	_____ of 80	_____ of 45	_____ of 45	_____ of 60
Percentile	_____	_____	_____	_____
High	74+	39+	35+	50+
Above Average	66–73	34–38	31–34	44–49
Average	60–65	28–33	28–30	35–43
Low	48–	28–	27–	34

Source: Henk, W. A., Marinak, B. A., & Melnick, S. A. (2012). Measuring the reader self-perceptions of adolescents: Introducing the RSPS2. *Journal of Adolescent & Adult Literacy, 56*(4), 311–320, figure on p. 314.

Available for download at **https://resources.corwin.com/vl-literacy6-12**

COMPENDIUM 8. CLASS RECORD OF WRITING FLUENCY

Teacher Name: _____   Grade: _____

Name	Date				Date				Date				Date			
	TW	TS	EPS	MSL	TW	TS	EPS	MSL	TW	TS	EPS	MSL	TW	TS	EPS	MSL

TW = Total words written

TS = Total sentences written

EPS = Average number of errors per sentence (TS ÷ # of errors)

MSL = Mean sentence length (TW ÷ TS)

COMPENDIUM 9. DEVELOPMENTAL SPELLING ANALYSIS SCREENING INVENTORY

Directions: I am going to say some words that I want you to spell for me. Some of the words will be easy to spell, and some will be more difficult. When you don't know how to spell a word, just do the best you can. Each time, I will say the word, then use it in a sentence, and then I will say the word again.

1.	hen	The hen sat on her eggs.
2.	wish	The boy made a wish and blew out the candles.
3.	trap	A spider web is a trap for flies.
4.	jump	A kangaroo can jump high.
5.	brave	A brave dog scared the robbers.
6.	smile	A smile shows that you're happy.
7.	grain	One kind of grain is called wheat.
8.	crawl	The baby can crawl but not walk.
9.	clerk	The clerk sold some shoes to me.
10.	clutch	The clutch in the car needs fixing.
11.	palace	The king and queen live in a palace.
12.	observe	I like to observe birds at the feeder.
13.	shuffle	Please shuffle the cards before you deal.
14.	exciting	The adventure story I'm reading is very exciting.
15.	treason	The man was found guilty of treason.
16.	column	His picture was in the first column of the newspaper.
17.	variety	A grocery store has a wide variety of foods.
18.	extension	The workers need an extension ladder to reach the roof.
19.	competition	There was much competition between the two businesses.
20.	illiterate	An illiterate person is one who cannot read.

Stop when a child has spelled no words or 1 word correctly out of any set of five.

Source: Ganske, K. (2000). *Word journeys: Assessment-guided phonics, spelling, and vocabulary instruction.* New York: Guilford. Reprinted with permission of Guilford Press.

Available for download at **https://resources.corwin.com/vl-literacy6-12**

COMPENDIUM 10. DEVELOPMENTAL SPELLING ANALYSIS SCREENING INVENTORY PREDICTION CHART

> **Letter Name (LN)**—Students learn about beginning sounds, blends (bl, sl, etc.), word families, and short-vowel sounds. This is the stage in which students are usually taught to read.
>
> **Within Word (WW)**—Students spell most short-vowel sounds correctly, and they learn about long-vowel sounds and patterns in one-syllable words. In this stage, students can read and spell many words correctly because of their automatic knowledge of letter sounds and short-vowel patterns.
>
> **Syllable Juncture (SJ)**—Students learn about the conventions of joining syllables in words with two or more syllables. Students are expected to spell many words of more than one syllable. Students consider spelling patterns where syllables meet and at meaning units such as affixes (prefixes and suffixes).
>
> **Derivational Constancy (DC)**—Students learn that meaning as well as sound and pattern are important in the spelling of the English language. This last stage in the developmental model continues through adulthood.

Inventory Score	Predicted Stage(s)	Inventory Score	Predicted Stage(s)
20	DC	10	WW/SJ
19	DC	9	WW
18	DC	8	WW
17	DC	7	WW
16	SJ/DC	6	LN/WW
15	SJ/DC	5	LN/WW
14	SJ	4	LN
13	SJ	3	LN
12	SJ	2	LN
11	WW/SJ	1	LN*
		0	LN*
			* Children who achieve a score of 0 or 1 may or may not be letter name spellers.

Source: Ganske, K. (2000). *Word journeys: Assessment-guided phonics, spelling, and vocabulary instruction.* New York: Guilford. Reprinted with permission of Guilford Press.

Available for download at **https://resources.corwin.com/vl-literacy6-12**

Rank	Influence	ES
1	Self-reported grades/student expectations	1.44
2	Piagetian programs	1.28
*3	Response to intervention	1.07
*4	Teacher credibility	0.90
5	Providing formative evaluation	0.90
6	Micro-teaching	0.88
*7	Classroom discussion	0.82
8	Comprehensive interventions for students who are learning disabled	0.77
9	Teacher clarity	0.75
10	Feedback	0.75
11	Reciprocal teaching	0.74
12	Teacher–student relationships	0.72
13	Spaced versus mass practice	0.71
14	Metacognitive strategies	0.69
15	Acceleration	0.68
16	Classroom behavioral	0.68
17	Vocabulary programs	0.67
18	Repeated reading programs	0.67
19	Creativity programs on achievement	0.65
20	Prior achievement	0.65
21	Self-verbalization and self-questioning	0.64
22	Study skills	0.63
23	Teaching strategies	0.62
24	Problem-solving teaching	0.61
25	Not labeling students	0.61
26	Comprehension programs	0.60
27	Concept mapping	0.60
28	Cooperative versus individualistic learning	0.59
29	Direct instruction	0.59
30	Tactile stimulation programs	0.58
31	Mastery learning	0.58
32	Worked examples	0.57

(Continued)

Rank	Influence	ES
33	Visual perception programs	0.55
34	Peer tutoring	0.55
35	Cooperative versus competitive learning	0.54
36	Phonics instruction	0.54
*37	Student-centered teaching	0.54
38	Classroom cohesion	0.53
39	Pre-term birth weight	0.53
40	Keller's Master Learning	0.53
41	Peer influences	0.53
42	Classroom management	0.52
43	Outdoor/adventure programs	0.52
44	Home environment	0.52
45	Socio-economic status	0.52
46	Interactive video methods	0.52
47	Professional development	0.51
48	Goals	0.50
49	Play programs	0.50
50	Second/third chance programs	0.50
51	Parental involvement	0.49
52	Small group learning	0.49
53	Questioning	0.48
54	Concentration/persistence/engagement	0.48
55	School effects	0.48
56	Motivation	0.48
57	Student ratings of quality of teaching	0.48
58	Early interventions	0.47
59	Self-concept	0.47
60	Preschool programs	0.45
61	Writing programs	0.44
62	Expectations	0.43
63	School size	0.43
64	Science programs	0.42
65	Cooperative learning	0.42

Rank	Influence	ES
66	Exposure to reading	0.42
67	Behavioral organizers/adjunct questions	0.41
68	Mathematics programs	0.40
69	Reducing anxiety	0.40
70	Social skills programs	0.39
71	Integrated curricula programs	0.39
72	Enrichment	0.39
73	Principals/school leaders	0.39
74	Career interventions	0.38
75	Time on task	0.38
*76	Psychotherapy programs	0.38
77	Computer-assisted instruction	0.37
78	Adjunct aids	0.37
79	Bilingual programs	0.37
80	Drama/arts programs	0.35
81	Creativity related to achievement	0.35
82	Attitude to mathematics/science	0.35
83	Frequent/effects of testing	0.34
84	Decreasing disruptive behavior	0.34
*85	Various teaching on creativity	0.34
86	Simulations	0.33
87	Inductive teaching	0.33
88	Ethnicity	0.32
89	Teacher effects	0.32
90	Drugs	0.32
91	Inquiry-based teaching	0.31
*92	Systems accountability	0.31
93	Ability grouping for gifted students	0.30
94	Homework	0.29
95	Home visiting	0.29
96	Exercise/relaxation	0.28
97	Desegregation	0.28

(Continued)

Rank	Influence	ES
98	Teaching test-taking	0.27
99	Use of calculators	0.27
*100	Volunteer tutors	0.26
101	Lack of illness	0.25
102	Mainstreaming	0.24
103	Values/moral education programs	0.24
104	Competitive versus individualistic learning	0.24
105	Programmed instruction	0.23
106	Summer school	0.23
107	Finances	0.23
108	Religious schools	0.23
109	Individualized instruction	0.22
110	Visual/audio-visual methods	0.22
111	Comprehensive teaching reforms	0.22
*112	Teacher verbal ability	0.22
113	Class size	0.21
114	Charter schools	0.20
115	Aptitude/treatment interactions	0.19
116	Extra-curricular programs	0.19
117	Learning hierarchies	0.19
118	Co-/team teaching	0.19
119	Personality	0.18
120	Within-class grouping	0.18
121	Special college programs	0.18
122	Family structure	0.18
*123	School counseling effects	0.18
124	Web-based learning	0.18
125	Matching learning styles	0.17
126	Teacher immediacy	0.16
127	Home-school programs	0.16
128	Problem-based learning	0.15
129	Sentence-combining programs	0.15

Rank	Influence	ES
130	Mentoring	0.15
131	Ability grouping	0.12
132	Diet	0.12
133	Gender	0.12
134	Teacher education	0.12
135	Distance education	0.11
136	Teacher subject matter knowledge	0.09
*137	Changing school calendar/timetable	0.09
138	Out-of-school curricular experiences	0.09
139	Perceptual motor programs	0.08
140	Whole language	0.06
*141	Diversity of students	0.05
142	College halls of residence	0.05
143	Multi-grade/age classes	0.04
144	Student control over learning	0.04
145	Open versus traditional learning spaces	0.01
146	Summer vacation	−0.02
147	Welfare policies	−0.12
148	Retention	−0.13
149	Television	−0.18
150	Mobility	−0.34

Source: Adapted from Hattie (2012). Reproduced with permission.

*Represents an effect that has been added to the original list since the publication of *Visible Learning: A Synthesis of Over 800 Meta-Analyses Relating to Achievement* (Hattie, 2009).

Note: Effect size for collective teacher efficacy published separately in Hattie (2015), The Applicability of Visible Learning to Higher Education, *Scholarship of Teaching and Learning in Psychology,* 1(1), 79–91. In-chapter references to effect sizes for identifying similarities and differences, note-taking, organizing and transforming notes, summarizing, transforming and organizing conceptual knowledge, and wide reading are not listed here and are based on the ongoing synthesis of learning strategies research.

REFERENCES

Adams, G. L., & Engelmann, S. (1996). *Research on direct instruction: 20 years beyond DISTAR*. Seattle, WA: Educational Achievement Systems.

Afflerbach, P., Pearson, P. D., & Paris, S. G. (2008). Clarifying differences between reading skills and reading strategies. *Reading Teacher, 61*(5), 364–373.

Ainsworth, L. (2014). *Unwrapping the standards: A simple process to make standards manageable*. New York: Houghton Mifflin Harcourt.

Alexander, A. (2008). *Towards dialogic teaching: Rethinking classroom talk* (4th ed.). York, England: Dialogos.

American Educational Research Association (AERA), Knowledge Forum. (2016). *Research fact sheet: Counter-intuitive findings from the science of learning*. Retrieved from http://www.aera.net/Portals/38/docs/Annual_Meeting/2016%20Annual%20 Meeting/2016%20Knowledge%20Forum/Chi.pdf

American Psychological Association, Coalition for Psychology in Schools and Education. (2015). *Top 20 principles from psychology for preK–12 teaching and learning*. Retrieved from http://www.apa.org/ed/schools/cpse/top-twenty-principles.pdf

Anderson, N. J. (2002). *The role of metacognition in second language teaching and learning*. Retrieved from http://www.cal.org/resources/digest/0110anderson .html

Anderson, R. C., Wilson, P. T., & Fielding, L. G. (1988). Growth in reading and how children spend their time outside of school. *Reading Research Quarterly, 23*, 285–303.

Applebee, A. N., Langer, J. A., Nystrand, M., & Gamoran, A. (2003). Discussion-based approaches to developing understanding: Classroom instruction and student performance in middle and high school English. *American Educational Research Journal, 40*, 685–730.

Applegate, M. D., Quinn, A. J., & Applegate, A. J. (2007). *Critical reading inventory: Assessing students' reading and thinking* (2nd ed.). Upper Saddle River, NJ: Prentice Hall.

Arrasmith, D., & Dwyer, K. (2001). The TRAITS of an effective reader. *Journal of School Improvement, 2*(1), 15–19.

Bandura, A. (1997). *Self-efficacy: The exercise of control*. New York: Freeman.

Betts, E. A. (1946). *Foundations of reading instruction*. New York: American Book Company.

Biggs, J., & Collis, K. (1982). *Evaluating the quality of learning: The SOLO taxonomy*. New York: Academic Press.

Bintz, W. P., & Williams, L. (2005). Questioning techniques of fifth and sixth grade reading teachers. *Middle School Journal, 37*(1), 45–52.

Blyth, C. (2009). *The art of conversation: A guided tour of a neglected pleasure*. New York: Gotham Books.

Bowman-Perrott, L. I., Burke, M. D., Nan, Z., & Zaini, S. (2014). Direct and collateral effects of peer tutoring on social and behavioral outcomes: A meta-analysis of single-case research. *School Psychology Review, 43*(3), 260–285.

Bransford, J. D., Brown, A. L., & Cocking, R. R. (Eds.). (2000). *How people learn: Brain, mind, experience, and school.* Washington, DC: National Academy Press.

Brozo, W., & Afflerbach, P. (2015). *Adolescent reading inventory.* Upper Saddle River, NJ: Pearson.

Burns, B., & Roe, P. C. (2010). *Burns/Roe informal reading inventory* (8th ed.). Independence, KY: Wadsworth.

Caughlan, S., Juzwik, M. M., Borsheim-Black, C., Kelly, S., & Fine, J. G. (2013). English teacher candidates developing dialogically organized instructional practices. *Research in the Teaching of English, 47*(3), 212–246.

Cazden, C. B. (1998). *Classroom discourse: The language of teaching and learning.* Portsmouth, NH: Heinemann.

Clarke, S., Timperley, H., & Hattie J. (2003). *Unlocking formative assessment: Practical strategies for enhancing students' learning in the primary and intermediate classroom* (NZ Ed.). Auckland: Hodder Moa Beckett.

Clay, M. M. (2003). Child development. In J. Flood, D. Lapp, J. R. Squire, & J. M. Jensen (Eds.), *Handbook of research in teaching the English language arts* (2nd ed., pp. 46–52). Mahwah, NJ: Erlbaum.

College Board. (2006). *The College Board English Language Arts framework.* Retrieved from https://www.collegeboard.org/sites/default/files/english-language-arts-framework-academic-advisory-committee.pdf

Connor, C., Phillips, B., Kaschak, M., Apel, K., Kim, Y., . . . & Lonigan, C. (2014). Comprehension tools for teachers: Reading for understanding from prekindergarten through fourth grade. *Educational Psychology Review, 26*(3), 379–401.

Cooter, R. B., Flynt, E. S., & Cooter, K. S. (2013). *Flynt-Cooter comprehensive reading inventory-2.* Upper Saddle River, NJ: Prentice Hall.

Csikszentmihalyi, M. (1990). *Flow: The psychology of optimal experience.* New York: Harper and Row.

Daiute, C., & Dalton, B. (1993). Collaboration between children learning to write: Can novices be masters? *Cognition and Instruction, 10,* 281–333.

Davey, B. (1983). Think aloud: Modeling the cognitive processes of reading comprehension. *Journal of Reading, 27*(1), 44–47.

Donahue, P. L., Voelkl, K. E., Campbell, J. R., & Mazzeo, J. (1999). *NAEP reading report card for the nation and states.* Washington, DC: US Department of Education, Office of Educational Research and Improvement.

DuFour, R., DuFour, R., & Eaker, R. (2008). *Professional learning communities at work: New insights for best practices.* Bloomington, IN: Solution Tree.

Durkin, D. (1978–79). What classroom observations reveal about reading comprehension instruction. *Reading Research Quarterly, 14,* 481–533.

Elliot, A., & Harackiewicz, J. (1994). Goal setting, achievement orientation, and intrinsic motivation: A meditational analysis. *Journal of Personality and Social Psychology, 66*(5), 968–980.

Espin, C. A., Shin, J., & Busch, T. W. (2005). Curriculum-based measurement in the content areas: Vocabulary matching as an indicator of progress in social studies learning. *Journal of Learning Disabilities, 38*(4), 353–363.

Fearn, L., & Farnan, N. (2001). *Interactions: Teaching writing and the language arts.* Boston: Houghton Mifflin.

Fendick, F. (1990). *The correlation between teacher clarity of communication and student achievement gain: A meta-analysis.* Unpublished doctoral dissertation, University of Florida, Gainesville.

Fisher, D., & Frey, N. (2008). Homework and the gradual release of responsibility: Making "responsibility" possible. *English Journal, 98*(2), 40–45.

Fisher, D., & Frey, N. (2012). Close reading in elementary school. *The Reading Teacher, 66*(3), 179–188.

Fisher, D., & Frey, N. (2014a). Closely reading informational texts in the primary grades. *The Reading Teacher, 68*, 222–227.

Fisher, D., & Frey, N. (2014b). *Text-dependent questions, grades K–5: Pathways to close and critical reading.* Thousand Oaks, CA: Corwin.

Fisher, D., Frey, N., Anderson, H., & Thayre, M. (2015). *Text-dependent questions: Pathways to close and critical reading, grades K–5.* Thousand Oaks, CA: Corwin.

Fisher, D., Frey, N., & Hattie, J. (2016). *Visible learning for literacy: Implementing the practices that work best to accelerate student learning.* Thousand Oaks, CA: Corwin.

Fisher, D., Frey, N., & Lapp, D. (2009). *In a reading state of mind: Brain research, teacher modeling, and comprehension instruction.* Newark, DE: International Reading Association.

Fisher, D., Frey, N., & Lapp, D. (2015). *Text complexity: Stretching readers with texts and tasks* (2nd ed.). Thousand Oaks, CA: Corwin.

Ganske, K. (1999). The developmental spelling analysis: A measure of orthographic knowledge. *Educational Assessment, 6*(1), 41–70.

Ganske, K. (2000). *Word journeys: Assessment-guided phonics, spelling, and vocabulary instruction.* New York: Guilford.

Goddard, R. D., Hoy, W. K., & Hoy, A. W. (2000). Collective teacher efficacy: Its meaning, measure, and impact on student achievement. *American Educational Research Journal, 37*, 479–507.

Goodman, L. (2001). A tool for learning: Vocabulary self-awareness. In C. Blanchfield (Ed.), *Creative vocabulary: Strategies for teaching vocabulary in grades K–12* (p. 46). Fresno, CA: San Joaquin Valley Writing Project.

Gray, W. S. (1925). Reading activities in school and society. In G. M. Whipple (Ed.), *The twenty-fourth yearbook of the National Society for the Study of Education, part I* (pp. 1–18). Bloomington, IL: Public School Publishing.

Halliday, M. A. K. (1975). *Learning how to mean: Explorations in the development of language.* London: Edward Arnold.

Hasbrouck, J., & Tindal, G. A. (2006). Oral reading fluency norms: A valuable assessment tool for reading teachers. *Reading Teacher, 59*(7), 636–644.

Hattie, J. (2009). *Visible learning: A synthesis of over 800 meta-analyses relating to achievement.* New York: Routledge.

Hattie, J. (2012). *Visible learning for teachers: Maximizing impact on learning.* New York: Routledge.

Hattie, J., & Donoghue, G. (2016). Learning strategies: A synthesis and conceptual model. *Nature: Science of Learning*, 1. doi:10.1038/npjscilearn.2016.13

Hattie, J., & Timperley, H. (2007). The power of feedback. *Review of Educational Research, 77*(1), 81–112.

Head, M. H., & Readence, J. E. (1986). Anticipation guides: Meaning through prediction. In E. K. Dishner, T. W. Bean, J. E. Readence, & D. W. Moore (Eds.), *Reading in the content areas* (2nd ed., pp. 229–234). Dubuque, IA: Kendall-Hunt.

Henderson, E. H. (1990). *Teaching spelling* (2nd ed.). Boston: Houghton Mifflin.

Henk, W. A., Marinak, B. A., & Melnick, S. A. (2012). Measuring the reader self-perceptions of adolescents: Introducing the RSPS2. *Journal of Adolescent & Adult Literacy, 56*(4), 311–320.

Henk, W. A., & Selders, M. L. (1984). Test of synonymic scoring of cloze passages. *The Reading Teacher, 38*, 282–287.

Herbel-Eisenmann, B. A., & Breyfogle, M. L. (2005). Questioning our patterns of questioning. *Mathematics Teaching in the Middle School, 10*(9), 484–489.

Hudson, R. F., Lane, H. B., & Pullen, P. C. (2005). Reading fluency assessment and instruction: What, why, and how? *Reading Teacher, 58*(8), 702–714.

Hunter, M. (1982). *Mastery teaching.* El Segundo, CA: TIP Publications.

Iacoboni, M., Molnar-Szakacs, I., Gallese, V., Buccino, G., Mazziotta, J. C., & Rizzolatti, G. (2005). Grasping the intentions of others with one's own mirror neuron system. *PLoS Biology, 3*(3), e79.

Joos, M. (1961). *The five clocks.* New York: Harcourt, Brace & World.

King, S. (2010). *On writing. 10th anniversary edition: A memoir of the craft.* New York: Scribner.

Knight, J. (2014). *Focus on teaching: Using video for high-impact instruction.* Thousand Oaks, CA: Corwin.

Kush, J. C., & Watkins, M. W. (1996). Long-term stability of children's attitudes toward reading. *Journal of Educational Research, 89,* 315–319.

Lai, M., Wilson, A., McNaughton, S., & Hsiao, S. (2014). Improving achievement in secondary schools: Impact of a literacy project on reading comprehension and secondary school qualifications. *Reading Research Quarterly, 49*(3), 305–334.

Leslie, L., & Caldwell, J. S. (2016). *Qualitative reading inventory* (6th ed.). Upper Saddle River, NJ: Prentice Hall.

Locke, E. A., & Latham, G. P. (1990) *A theory of goal setting and task performance.* Englewood Cliffs, NJ: Prentice-Hall.

Manning, M. L. (1994). Addressing young adolescents' cognitive development. *High School Journal, 78,* 98–104.

Marita, S. M. (1965). *A comparative study of beginning reading achievement under three classroom organizational patterns—modified individualized, three-to-five groups, and whole-class language-experience* (Report No. CRP-2659). Milwaukee, WI: Marquette University. (ERIC Document Reproduction Service No. ED003477)

Martinez, M., Roser, N. L., & Strecker, S. (1998). "I never thought I could be a star": A Readers Theatre ticket to fluency. *The Reading Teacher, 52,* 326–334.

McKenzie, J. (1997). A questioning toolkit. *Educational Technology Journal, 7*(3), 1–6.

Meece, J. L., Anderman, E. M., & Anderman L. H. (2006). Classroom goal structure, student motivation, and academic achievement. *Annual Review of Psychology, 57,* 487–503.

Moffett, J. (1992). *Detecting growth in language.* Portsmouth, NH: Heinemann.

Murphy, P. K., Wilkinson, I. A. G., Soter, A. O., Hennessey, M. N., & Alexander, J. F. (2009). Examining the effects of classroom discussion on students' high-level comprehension of text: A meta-analysis. *Journal of Educational Psychology, 101,* 740–764.

Nandi, A., & Platt, L. (2013). Britishness and identity assimilation among the UK's minority and majority ethnic groups. *Understanding Society Working Paper Series: No. 2013–08.* Retrieved from https://www.understandingsociety.ac.uk/research/publications/working-paper/understanding-society/2013–08.pdf

Palincsar, A. S., & Brown, A. L. (1986). Interactive teaching to promote independent learning from text. *The Reading Teacher, 39,* 771–777.

Parker, W. (2010). Listening to strangers: Classroom discussion in democratic education. *Teachers College Record, 112*(11), 2815–2832.

Pearson, P. D., & Johnson, D. D. (1972). *Teaching reading comprehension.* Boston: Cengage Learning.

Pearson, P. D., & Johnson, D. D. (1978). *Teaching reading comprehension.* New York: Holt, Rinehart, and Winston.

Pew Research Center. (2013). *E-reading rises as device ownership jumps*. Retrieved from http://www.pewinternet.org/files/old-media//Files/Reports/2014/PIP_E-reading_011614.pdf

Piaget, J. (1952). *The origins of intelligence in children*. New York: W. W. Norton.

Purkey, W. W. (1992). An introduction to invitational theory. *Journal of Invitational Theory and Practice, 1*(1), 5–15.

Rasinski, T. V. (2003). Fluency is fundamental. *Instructor, 113*(4), 16–20.

Rasinski, T. V. (2010). *The fluent reader: Oral reading strategies for building word recognition, fluency, and comprehension* (2nd ed.). New York: Scholastic.

Recht, D. R., & Leslie, L. (1988). Effect of prior knowledge on good and poor readers' memory of text. *Journal of Educational Psychology, 30*(1), 16–20.

Rizzolatti, G., & Craighero, L. (2004). The mirror-neuron system. *Annual Review of Neuroscience, 27*(1), 169–192.

Ross, P., & Gibson, S. A. (2010). Exploring a conceptual framework for expert noticing during literacy instruction. *Literacy Research & Instruction, 49*(2), 175–193.

Rowe, M. B. (1986). Wait time: Slowing down may be a way of speeding up! *Journal of Teacher Education, 37*, 43–50.

Schmitt, M. C. (1990). A questionnaire to measure children's awareness of strategic reading processes. *Reading Teacher, 43*, 454–461.

Schroth, M. L. (1992). The effects of delay of feedback on a delayed concept formation transfer task. *Contemporary Educational Psychology, 17*(1), 78–82.

Stanovich, K. E. (1986). Matthew effects in reading: Some consequences of individual differences in the acquisition of literacy. *Reading Research Quarterly, 21*, 360–406.

Thorndike, E. L. (1914). The measurement of ability in reading. *Teachers College Record, 15*, 1–70.

Vangrieken, K., Meredith, C., Packer, T., & Kyndt, E. (2017). Teacher communities as a context for professional development: A systematic review. *Teaching & Teacher Education, 61*, 47–59.

Vygotsky, L. S. (1962). *Thought and language*. Cambridge, MA: MIT Press.

Vygotsky, L. S. (1978). *Mind and society: The development of higher psychological processes*. Cambridge, MA: Harvard University Press.

Weatherford, C. B. (2015). *Voice of freedom: Fannie Lou Hamer, spirit of the civil rights movement*. Somerville, MA: Candlewick.

Wilkinson, I. A. G., & Nelson, K. (2013). Role of discussion in reading comprehension In J. Hattie & E. M. Anderson (Eds.), *International guide to student achievement* (pp. 299–302). New York: Routledge.

Worthy, J., & Broaddus, K. (2001/2002). Fluency beyond the primary grades: From group performance to silent, independent reading. *The Reading Teacher, 55*, 334–343.

Zohar, A., Schwartzer, N., & Tamir, P. (1998). Assessing the cognitive demands required of students in class discourse, homework assignments and tests. *International Journal of Science Education, 20*(7), 769–782.

INDEX

Notes

Notes

Notes

A SAGE Publishing Company

Helping educators make the greatest impact

CORWIN HAS ONE MISSION: to enhance education through intentional professional learning.

We build long-term relationships with our authors, educators, clients, and associations who partner with us to develop and continuously improve the best evidence-based practices that establish and support lifelong learning.

visible learning^{plus}

3 Ways to Get Started

1. Understand Your Baseline

School Capability Analysis

How does your school measure against the five strands of Visible Learning? Certified consultants will conduct a half-day site visit to collect and analyze baseline capability data to determine your school's readiness for Visible Learning^{plus}. A full written report is provided.

The Foundation Series

Begin your Visible Learning^{plus} journey by building your team's foundational knowledge of the Visible Learning research. Teachers and school leaders will receive tools for gathering evidence of effective practice and create a plan for making learning visible for all students.

2. Build Foundational Knowledge

3. Drive Whole-System Reform

Seminars
Training
Consulting

Collaborative Impact Program

The Collaborative Impact program is our gold standard for sustainable reform, as it aligns system leaders, school leaders, and teachers with a proven process to build capacity for change over 3-5 years, with measurable results.

**Contact your account manager at (800) 831-6640
or visit www.corwin.com/visiblelearning**

CORWIN
A SAGE Publishing Company

Use the Right Literacy Approach at the Right Time and Accelerate Student Learning

Discover the literacy practices that **ensure students demonstrate more than a year's worth of growth for every year spent in school.** Bring Douglas Fisher, Nancy Frey, or a member of their collaborative to your school or district for any of the following workshops.

INTRODUCTORY WORKSHOP

This workshop covers Visible Learning research; its connections to surface, deep, and transfer learning as it relates to literacy; the best literacy strategies to use in each stage of learning; and the tools for measuring your impact on student learning.

DETERMINING IMPACT

Participants will explore the importance of the effect sizes of different high-impact literacy approaches, and how to calculate your own effect size for classes and individual students. This workshop will also review effective components of successful response to intervention (RTI).

SURFACE LEARNING

Surface learning isn't superficial. A strong foundation of surface learning sets the stage for deeper learning. Participants will walk through different literacy approaches and participate in exercises that promote surface learning.

DEEP LEARNING

This workshop focuses on practical approaches for deep learning using Visible Learning research as a guide. Participants will walk through different approaches and participate in the exercises that promote deeper learning.

TRANSFER LEARNING

Participants will explore the importance of transfer learning, the paths that transfer learning can take, and the conditions needed for transfer. This workshop will also review strategies for teaching students to organize and transform conceptual knowledge.

RESPONSE TO INTERVENTION

With an effect size of 1.07, a successful RTI effort has great impact on students. Using examples and guides from *Visible Learning for Literacy*, participants will review successful approaches including screening, quality core instruction, progress monitoring, and supplemental and intensive intervention.

Who Should Attend:

- Principals
- Staff Development Directors
- Literacy/Reading Coaches
- English/Reading Department Chairs
- Reading Teacher/Specialists
- English Teachers
- Classroom Teachers

Learning Outcomes:

- Discover how to **build successful relationships with students,** critical to long-term student gains
- Understand **learning intentions and success criteria** and why they are so critical to student growth
- Explore the **three phases of learning— surface, deep, and transfer**
- Examine **key literacy strategies** that work best at each phase of learning and provide **built-in lessons and exercises**
- Discover how to use effect size and other assessment tools to **measure student learning**

To learn more about booking one or more of these workshops, please contact Corwin at 1-800-233-9936

DOUGLAS FISHER

NANCY FREY

M P A C T
Making Literacy Learning Visible